DECORUM OF THE MINUET, DELIRIUM OF THE WALTZ

MUSICAL MEANING & INTERPRETATION

Robert S. Hatten, editor

A Theory of Musical Narrative
BYRON ALMÉN

Approaches to Meaning in Music
BYRON ALMÉN & EDWARD PEARSALL

*Voicing Gender: Castrati, Travesti,
and the Second Woman in Early
Nineteenth-Century Italian Opera*
NAOMI ANDRÉ

The Italian Traditions and Puccini
NICHOLAS BARAGWANATH

Music and the Politics of Negation
JAMES R. CURRIE

Il Trittico, Turandot, and Puccini's Late Style
ANDREW DAVIS

Neil Young and the Poetics of Energy
WILLIAM ECHARD

*Interpreting Musical Gestures, Topics, and
Tropes: Mozart, Beethoven, Schubert*
ROBERT S. HATTEN

*Musical Meaning in Beethoven: Markedness,
Correlation, and Interpretation*
ROBERT S. HATTEN

Intertextuality in Western Art Music
MICHAEL L. KLEIN

*Musical Forces: Motion, Metaphor,
and Meaning in Music*
STEVE LARSON

*Is Language a Music? Writings on
Musical Form and Signification*
DAVID LIDOV

Pleasure and Meaning in the Classical Symphony
MELANIE LOWE

*From Decorum to Delirium: The Interaction of
Dance and Music from the Minuet to the Waltz*
ERIC MCKEE

The Musical Topic: Hunt, Military, Pastoral
RAYMOND MONELLE

*Musical Representations, Subjects, and Objects:
The Construction of Musical Thought in
Zarlino, Descartes, Rameau, and Weber*
JAIRO MORENO

*Deepening Musical Performance
through Movement: The Theory and
Practice of Embodied Interpretation*
ALEXANDRA PIERCE

*Expressive Forms in Brahms's
Instrumental Music: Structure and
Meaning in His Werther Quartet*
PETER H. SMITH

*Expressive Intersections in Brahms:
Essays in Analysis and Meaning*
PETER H. SMITH & HEATHER A. PLATT

*Music as Philosophy: Adorno
and Beethoven's Late Style*
MICHAEL SPITZER

*Music and Wonder at the Medici Court:
The 1589 Interludes for La pellegrina*
NINA TREADWELL

*Reflections on Musical Meaning
and Its Representations*
LEO TREITLER

*Debussy's Late Style: The
Compositions of the Great War*
MARIANNE WHEELDON

Decorum of the Minuet, Delirium of the Waltz

A STUDY OF DANCE•MUSIC
RELATIONS IN ¾ TIME

Eric McKee

INDIANA UNIVERSITY PRESS

Bloomington & Indianapolis

This book is a publication of

INDIANA UNIVERSITY PRESS
601 North Morton Street
Bloomington, IN 47404-3797 USA

iupress.indiana.edu

Telephone orders 800-842-6796
Fax orders 812-855-7931

◎ The paper used in this publication
meets the minimum requirements of the
American National Standard for Information Sciences – Permanence of Paper
for Printed Library Materials, ANSI
Z39.48–1992.

Manufactured in the
United States of America

Library of Congress
Cataloging-in-Publication Data

McKee, Eric, [date]-
    Decorum of the minuet, delirium
of the waltz : a study of dance-music
relations in $^3/_4$ time / Eric McKee.
    p. cm. – (Musical meaning and inter-
pretation)
    Includes bibliographical references
and index.
    ISBN 978-0-253-35692-5 (cloth : alk.
paper) 1. Waltzes – 18th century –
History and criticism. 2. Minuet – 18th
century. 3. Waltzes – 19th century –
History and criticism. 4. Minuet – 19th
century. I. Title.
    ML3465.M45 2012
    784.18'83509 – dc23

                                    2011021186

1 2 3 4 5 17 16 15 14 13 12

CONTENTS

· *Acknowledgments* vii

· Introduction *1*

1 Influences of the Early Eighteenth-Century
Ballroom Minuet on the Minuets from
J. S. Bach's French Suites, BWV 812–817 *15*

2 Mozart in the Ballroom: Minuet-Trio Contrast
and the Aristocracy in Self-Portrait *46*

3 The Musical Visions of Joseph Lanner
and Johann Strauss Sr. *90*

4 Dance and the Music of Chopin:
Historical Background *129*

5 The Musical Visions of Chopin *146*

6 Chopin's Approach to Waltz Form *172*

· *Notes* 221
· *Bibliography* 243
· *Index* 257

ACKNOWLEDGMENTS

This book would not have been possible without the kind and generous support of many people. To begin, I am grateful for the constant encouragement of Robert Hatten and for his close reading of my manuscript. His insightful suggestions and comments have improved the book on many levels. The expert team at Indiana University Press has guided me in the process of preparing my manuscript. I am particularly grateful to my copy editor, Mary M. Hill, whose careful reading of my prose saved me from some potentially embarrassing errors. Any mistakes that remain are, of course, entirely my own. The amazing Phil Torbert provided the musical examples, whose preparation was made possible by a grant from the Institute of Arts and Humanities at the Pennsylvania State University. Krzysztof Komarnicki provided many of the Polish translations.

I am grateful for my musicology and theory colleagues at the Pennsylvania State University School of Music for providing a friendly, supportive, and stimulating working environment. A faculty fellowship through Penn State's Institute of Arts and Humanities provided me a semester's release to complete much of chapter 3. A fellowship from the American Council of Learned Societies allowed a year's release to gather and develop material for chapter 4. I wish to acknowledge the journal *Music Analysis* for permission to rework two articles previously published in 2004 and 2008. Some of the material in chapters 4 and 5 originally appeared in an essay published in *The Age of Chopin*, edited by Halina Goldberg and published by Indiana University Press.

Above all, I am thankful for my family. The loving support of my parents has given me the confidence to pursue a career path that has led to this book, and my children's boundless energy and sense of wonderment have kept me grounded in a world where anything is possible. The greatest debt of gratitude I owe to my wife, Emily – she is my rock and inspiration.

DECORUM OF THE MINUET, DELIRIUM OF THE WALTZ

INTRODUCTION

M. JOURDAIN: Yet I never learnt music.
MUSIC MASTER: You should learn, Sir, the same as you do dancing. The two
arts are very closely allied.

...

DANCING MASTER: Music and dancing. Music and dancing. That is all that
is necessary.
MUSIC MASTER: There is nothing so useful to a State as music.
DANCING MASTER: There is nothing so indispensable to mankind as
dancing.
MUSIC MASTER: Without music the State would cease to function.
DANCING MASTER: Man can do nothing at all without dancing.

MOLIÈRE, *THE WOULD-BE GENTLEMAN*

This book investigates dance-music relations in two out of the three most influential social dances of the eighteenth and nineteenth centuries: the minuet
and the waltz (the contredanse being the other influential dance). I take the
position that if one wishes better to understand the musical structures and
expressive meanings contained in these dances, it is helpful to be aware of the
bodily rhythms of the dances upon which they are based and the social contexts in which they were performed. In doing so, I approach dance music as a
component within a multimedia art form, a form that involves the mutual interaction of physical motion, mental attitude, music, architecture, and dress.
Moreover, the activity of participating in a ball involves a dynamic network
of modalities (sight, sound, bodily awareness, touch, and smell), and these
modalities can be experienced from a variety of perspectives (as a dancer, as
a spectator, or as a musician). In reconstructing the social multimedia framework of the minuet and waltz, I hope to provide a critical vantage point that

yields fresh insight and meaning to the following questions: What did the dancers require of the music, and how did composers of the minuet and waltz respond to the practical needs of the dancers? In what ways did composers go beyond the practical requirements, incorporating into the music the aesthetics and cultural associations of the dance? What are the nature and function of minuet-trio contrast in the Viennese dance minuets of the second half of the eighteenth century? What was social dancing like in Warsaw during the 1820s, when Chopin was coming of age, and to what extent did Chopin participate in social dancing? In what ways did the visual experience of watching waltzers waltz influence the nature of the waltz's thematic material and its large-scale patterning? And to what extent was Chopin influenced by the ballroom waltzes of Lanner and Strauss Sr.?

The ubiquity and far-reaching influence of social dancing in the eighteenth and nineteenth centuries cannot be overestimated. The activity of dancing was a vital part of social life and was without question the most common form of social entertainment, especially during the winter months and carnival season. It pervaded all levels of society and served a broad range of social functions.[1] For the lower classes, dancing provided a diversion from the toils of the day; the upper classes used it as a way of defining themselves individually within their class and collectively apart from the lower classes; and for all levels, the activity of dancing was a vehicle for courtship, ceremonies, and celebrations. It seems that whenever and wherever people got together, there was bound to be dancing. Indeed, as the spoken lines from Molière's ballet suggest, "man could do nothing at all without dancing." Certainly this was proven true at the court of Louis XIV, for whom the ballet was first premiered in 1670. As a means of political and social control, the king required his large and lumbering retinue of lesser aristocrats to participate in an endless stream of royal balls. And a little over a century later, Molière's lines were famously proven true again by the foreign diplomats and dignitaries assembled at the Congress of Vienna of 1814–15, an affair that prompted the quip "le Congrès ne marche pas; il danse" (the Congress doesn't work; it dances).

The movements and bodily attitudes of dance were not restricted to the ballroom, though. In the eighteenth century, for example, dancing masters used the minuet as a model for genteel behavior – on and off the ballroom dance floor – in which all aspects of aristocratic comportment were carefully prescribed, including such basic activities as standing, walking, entering and leaving a room, taking off one's hat, stepping in and out of a carriage, and, most important, gestures of reverence. As a means of attaining a sense of noble ease and hidden control in social life, Philip Dormer Stanhope, fourth Earl of Chesterfield, in a letter to his son written in 1765, advises: "Do everything in minuet-time; speak, think, and move always in that measure – equally free from the dullness of slow, or the hurry or huddle of quick, time" (1845, 2:405). To make such contrived movement and attitude appear supremely natural, however, required years of training beginning at a very young age. Only the most privileged would have the time and means to acquire such skills. Thus, the gestures of social dancing were politicized as a means of class identification and class exclusion.[2]

A broad knowledge of theatrical and ballroom dances, both historical and current, was considered essential for composers and performers alike. The music for each dance type had its own tempo, associated melodic gestures, and patterns of accentual stress, much of which was not notated in the score but part of its performance practice. To effectively compose and perform dance music one thus needed to understand the bodily basis of these musical characteristics. In a discussion on the superior quality of string players in Jean-Baptiste Lully's orchestra, Georg Muffat, for example, makes the observations that "to become acquainted with the proper tempo of the Ballets, what helps the most, other than regular practice with the Lullists, is an understanding of the art of the dance, in which most Lullists are well versed. That is why one should not be amazed at their exact observance of that tempo" ([1695] 2001, 42). Johann Philipp Kirnberger, writing some eighty years later, expresses a similar point of view. In the preface to his collection of dances, *Recueil d'airs de danse caractéristiques, pour servir de modele aux jeunes compositeurs et d'exercice à ceux qui touchent du clavecin*, Kirnberger articulates the value of a wide knowledge of dance types not only for the performance of dance music but also for the performance of nondance genres such as the fugue.

> How will the musician give the piece he performs the appropriate expression, which the composer conceived, if he cannot determine . . . exactly what sort of movement and what character are appropriate to each kind of measure? In order to acquire the necessary qualities for a good performance, the musician can do nothing better than diligently play all sorts of characteristic dances. Each of these dance types has its own rhythm, its phrases of equal length, its accents at the same places in each motif; thus one identifies them easily, and through repeated practice one unconscientiously becomes accustomed to distinguishing the proper rhythm of each dance-type, defin-

ing its motifs and accents, so that finally one easily recognizes in a long piece the various intermingling rhythms, phrases, and accents. . . . On the other hand, if one neglects to practice the composition of characteristic dances, one will only with difficulty or not at all achieve a good melody. Above all, it is impossible to compose or perform a fugue well if one does not know every type of [dance] rhythm. ([c. 1777] 1995, preface)

And in his treatise *The Art of Strict Musical Composition* Kirnberger reiterates the importance of dance for students of composition: "Every beginner who wants to become well grounded in composition is advised to become familiar with the disposition of all types of [dances], because all types of characters and rhythm occur and can be observed most accurately in them. If he has no skill in these character pieces, it is impossible to give a definite character to a piece" ([1771–79] 1982, 216n78).

While Kirnberger advocates that composers be familiar with the full range of ballroom dances in order to be conversant with a wide vocabulary of "characters and rhythm," it was the minuet that was most commonly used to teach the basic elements of musical composition. For music theorists and composition teachers such as Kirnberger, Joseph Riepel, and Heinrich Koch, the minuet offered several pedagogical advantages. It was a familiar and current genre: both as a dance type and as a musical type, its length could be relatively short, often no longer than sixteen bars, and it could be relatively simple in its melodic and harmonic designs. Thus, beginning composition students were able to start with something small and manageable but that contained all the essential elements of larger compositions. In other words, the minuet was appropriated as an *idealized* model for larger, more complex compositions.[3] For Riepel, "a minuet, according to its realization, is no different from a concerto, an aria, or a symphony. . . . [T]hus we wish to begin therewith, [with the] very small and trifling, simply in order to obtain out of it something bigger and more praiseworthy."[4] Koch echoes this sentiment: "The knowledge of these forms is useful to the beginning composer not only in itself but also with regard to the larger products of art; for these forms are at the same time representations in miniature of larger compositions" ([1787] 1983, 118). As Wolfgang Budday (1983) argues, the correlation between simple and more complex eighteenth-century musical forms and genres suggests that the minuet and other ballroom dances are integral to if not the basis of the Viennese Classical style.

A fallout of this pedagogical approach is that instead of considering the minuet repertoire in all of its diverse forms, composition teachers stripped it

down to its bare essentials and clothed it with elements that were considered
to be the ideal features of Classical composition: harmonic simplicity, proportional symmetry, periodicity, and a transparent melody and accompaniment
texture. This idealization led to the false notion that *all* minuets exhibit, or
should exhibit, these musical attributes, especially dance minuets, where a
regular and symmetrical 8 + 8 periodicity was until quite recently considered
an essential feature for it to be danceable. The research of Tilden Russell
(1983, 1992, 1999) has shown that minuets found in composition treatises as
well as dance treatises represent a repertoire very distinct from minuets composed for the ballroom dance floor, where it is not at all unusual to find a wide
range of formal organizations, levels of complexity, and, in some instances,
irregular phrase organizations.

For Bach, Mozart, and Chopin, the three art composers whose dance
music I examine in this book, dance was a part of their compositional pedagogy, both as students and as teachers. While little is known about Bach's
own musical education, it is likely that he used minuets and other dances
to teach composition and keyboard performance to his sons.[5] Leopold Mozart, who was an experienced pedagogue, required Nannerl and Wolfgang
to compose and perform minuets as elementary music exercises. Wolfgang
also employed this pedagogical technique with his students Barbara Ployer,
Thomas Attwood, and Franz Jacob Freystädtler, whom he taught in Vienna
in the mid-1780s.[6] Writing from Paris to his father six years earlier, in May
1778, Wolfgang provides an amusing account of his futile attempts to use the
minuet to teach the uninspired daughter of the duc de Guines.

> She did quite well in writing a bass line for the First Menuett that I had
> written down for her. Now she is beginning to write for 3 voices; she can
> do it all right; but she gets easily bored; and I can't help her there. . . . She
> simply has no inspiration of her own; nothing comes out of her; I have tried
> all sorts of methods. Among other things I tried the idea of writing down
> a simple Menuett to see whether she could do a variation on it? – Well,
> that didn't work. . . . Then I wrote down 4 bars of a Menuett and said to
> her – look, what a stupid fellow I am, I started a Menuett and can't even fin-
> ish the First part – please be so kind and finish it for me. (Mozart 2000, 154)[7]

Chopin's earliest surviving works, composed in 1817, when he was seven years
old, are polonaises, which are similar to the minuet in function and position within the hierarchy of Polish social dances. Either the minuet or the
polonaise was used ceremonially as the opening dance of a ball; and in both

the order of the couples was determined by their social position, with the highest-ranking couple dancing first, in the case of the minuet, or leading the other couples, in the case of the polonaise. In emphasizing the historical and cultural authority of the polonaise, Polish commentators were fond of drawing comparisons to the French minuet. Kazimiérz Brodziński observes that while the polonaise "can be called a serious knightly dance, the French *minuet* is the dance of an elegant court and of an educated society. The expression of grace in [the minuet] is formal and contractual: every movement is extremely calculated. . . . The polonaise is equally as the minuet a dance of dignified persons but has more freedom and is less theatrical" (1829, 85–86).[8]

Firsthand knowledge of ballroom dancing was important for composers for the simple reason that they were often called upon both professionally and informally within their social circles to provide music for dancing. Eighteenth-century residences of the aristocracy and royal courts, especially those of great wealth and influence, invariably included a ballroom, a resident retinue of musicians, a dancing master, and a court composer. Among other duties, the composer would be asked to provide dance music for formal balls and ballet productions, especially during carnival season. As a contractual part of their vocation, composers such as Haydn and Mozart thus had a professional relationship to ballroom dancing; to be successful, they needed to know what was in vogue on the ballroom dance floor and how to write music that was both beautiful and useful for dancing. Hummel, Schubert, and Chopin are the last major art composers who maintained an active, though, in the case of Schubert and Chopin, nonprofessional, relationship with ballroom dance music. Many accounts survive that speak of their unsurpassed abilities as improvisers of dance music at private social gatherings. The most interesting account of this type of improvisation that I have found comes from an entry in Louis Spohr's travel diary in which he describes a private musicale held in the home of one of his friends in 1814 during the Congress of Vienna. Late at night, just as the party was ending, "a few of the ladies" asked Hummel to provide some dance music.

> Gallant and accommodating as he always was toward the ladies, he seated himself at the piano and played the desired waltzes, at which point the young people in the next room began to dance. I and some of the other artists present gathered around the piano, our hats in our hands, and listened. No sooner had Hummel noticed this new audience than he began to

improvise freely, holding, however, to the steady waltz rhythm in order not
to disturb the dancers. He took the most striking themes and figures from
my own compositions and those of others that had been played in the course
of the evening's program and wove them into his waltzes, varying them more
fancifully with each repetition. Finally, he worked them into a fugue, giving
full rein to his contrapuntal wizardry, without ever disturbing the pleasure of the dancers. Then he returned to the gallant style and ended with a
bravura which was extraordinary even for him, still exploiting the themes he
had originally selected, so that the whole extravaganza had the character of
a fully rounded composition. The listeners were delighted, and thanked the
ladies whose passion for dancing had provided them with such a treat. (1961,
109–10)

Deeply rooted in the creative imagination of the eighteenth and nineteenth centuries, ballroom dance practices provided a rich and diverse language of musical devices, conventions, and gestures that composers drew
upon for all genres of music – both instrumental and vocal, secular and sacred.
Not only were the raw materials of concert music drawn from the ballroom
(phrase rhythms, thematic repetition schemes, and rhythmic patterns) but
also elements of expression. Music theorists and aestheticians considered music and dance to be intimately related – sister arts, whereby music mimetically
represented the physical motions and gestures of dance. It followed that the
correspondence between physical gesture and musical gesture was an important source of expression in music. As Newman Powell observes, Kirnberger
regarded rhythms of dance music "as the embodiment of an emotional state
or affect" (1967, 73). In his treatise on aesthetics, *Kalligone*, written in 1800,
Johann Gottfried Herder asserts that one can "scarcely avoid associating music with movement when he is deeply moved: his face, his posture, the way he
moves his body and beats time with his hands all express what he hears. The
dances of primitive peoples and of warm-blooded, vigorous races alike all take
the form of mime. This was true even of the Greeks, who spoke of music as
the 'leader of the dance,' a dance that involved every response [of which] the
soul was capable" ([1800] 1981, 255).

RESEARCH REVIEW

Although this dance survey has been brief, it is at least adequate, I hope, to
demonstrate the deep and penetrating influence of dance in the time period
of my study. Given its importance in social life, composition pedagogy, per-

formance practice, and music aesthetics as well as its pervasive presence in all genres of music, it is surprising just how little research has been devoted to the topic of dance-music relations. By research in dance-music relations, I mean studies that explore the dynamic and creative intersection between dance and music: How is the structure of music and its meaning shaped by the social contexts of the ballroom dance floor? How does one medium serve as an analogue for the other? And how are they different?

Perhaps not surprisingly, more attention has been given to dance-music relations of the eighteenth century. Powell's translation of and brief but thoughtful commentary to the preface of Kirnberger's *Recueil d'airs de danse caractéristiques* is the earliest scholarly work I am aware of that draws attention to the creative relationship between a composer's "knowledge of dance rhythms and the art of composition," a line of critical inquiry that, he observes, "has been almost totally neglected by twentieth-century musicians, even those especially interested in baroque style" (1967, 74, 72). Leonard Ratner is the first to answer Powell's call to arms. In his seminal 1980 text, *Classic Music*, Ratner interprets eighteenth-century dance types as part of an expressive vocabulary of musical topics, which he defines as characteristic figures that allude to well-known categories of music associated with different types of human activities (e.g., dance, ceremony, military, hunt) or musical styles (e.g., French overture, learned style, Turkish style, *galant* style). Ratner's book not only provided the beginnings of a critical framework in which to interpret dance topics in non-dance genres, but it also drew attention to the extent that dance topics were used in Classical music. Two important studies quickly followed: *Rhythmic Gesture in Mozart* (1983) by Wye Jamison Allanbrook and Sarah Reichart's 1984 dissertation, "The Influence of Eighteenth-Century Social Dance on the Viennese Classical Style." Allanbrook closely follows and develops Ratner's model of musical topics, exploring in greater detail the expressive rhythmic gestures and characteristic meters and tempos of social dance and their employment in two of Mozart's operas, *Le nozze di Figaro* and *Don Giovanni*. Reichart's dissertation is the first study to provide a detailed investigation into the social contexts, choreographies, and music of eighteenth-century ballroom dances; she then uses that information to identify and interpret dance allusions in the concert music of Mozart, Haydn, and their contemporaries. In their book *Dance and the Music of J. S. Bach* (1991), Meredith Little and Natalie Jenne follow a similar path from the ballroom dance floor to stylized dance music, first presenting the choreographic and musical characteristics of French court dances and then discussing Bach's interpretation of them in his instrumental dance works.

Tilden Russell, in his 1983 dissertation and two subsequent articles (1992 and 1999), provides sophisticated, in-depth studies of ballroom minuet music drawn from a wide range of sources, including dance treatises, published collections of dances (*recueils*), and manuscript tunebooks. Russell dismantles the myth of perfect correlation between the choreography and the music and in its place reveals a rich and diverse repertoire that not only lacked standardization but also often exhibited asymmetrical and irregular phrase organizations. Gretchen Wheelock (1992) and Melanie Lowe (1998, 2002, 2007) turn their critical gaze to the meanings of dance in Haydn's instrumental music. Wheelock's project investigates Haydn's minuet music for its artful jesting. After explaining current and eighteenth-century views and interpretations of wit and humor, Wheelock demonstrates how Haydn, by invoking Classical conventions of genre, style, syntax, and form, engages listeners in plays of expectations. In her dissertation, article, and book, Lowe provides rich and multifaceted explorations of the different expressive modes beyond wit and humor that are found Haydn's symphonic minuets and dance finales. Examining a wide range of primary sources and concepts drawn from semiotic theory (Hatten 1994) and topic theory (Ratner 1980; Allanbrook 1983; Agawu 1991), Lowe investigates how eighteenth-century listeners might have constructed meaning in response to Haydn's topical experimentations. David Neumeyer examines aspects of phrase organization in eighteenth-century ballroom contredanses. He interprets and applies the style information gleaned from his study to an analysis of finale movements from Mozart's and Haydn's concert music and concludes that William Caplin's (1998) distinction between "tight-knit" and "loose-knit" phrase organizations "may have a source in the active and expressive opposition of music for dancing and (instrumental) music for listening" (Neumeyer 2006, n.p.). And, most recently, Lawrence Zbikowski theorizes how music can represent the dynamic processes of the dance. Drawing on research in cognitive linguistics, Zbikowski treats music as a form of communication whose basic unit is what he calls the "sonic analogue." A sonic analogue "represents through patterned sound the central features of some dynamic process. One of the places sonic analogues are most evident," he believes, "is in music for dance" (2008, 286). Zbikowski applies his concepts to an insightful analysis of the finale of Haydn's String Quartet op. 76, no. 4, which progresses from a close correspondence between the music and dance to a state of contest that shifts the listener's attention away from the dance and redirects it to the "rhetoric of tonal forms" (2008, 305).

It is not unreasonable to argue that research in dance-music relations of the eighteenth century, while still a relatively young field with many unexplored areas, has established a strong and robust foundation of texts, especially when one adds to it research devoted principally to historical, social, or choreographic aspects of the ballroom dance, of which there is a fairly large body of works. There is a precipitous drop in similar research projects concerning dance-music relations in the first half of the nineteenth century. To date, there are only three published studies in English.

The cultural reasons for this neglect are complex and lie well beyond the scope of this brief introduction. Suffice it to say, though, that beginning in the nineteenth century, and most notably with the writings of Eduard Hanslick, music critics and aestheticians have devalued musical texts associated with pleasure, the human body, utilitarian function, and popular social entertainment. This can be seen most readily in the terminological distinction between popular music and concert music, which is typically expressed in negative and positive terms: popular music is referred to as low class, lowbrow, light, commercial, and trivial, while art music is referred to as high class, highbrow, serious, and cultivated.[9] Entrenched in musical academia during the past two centuries, these attitudes and prejudices have gradually begun to recede only in the last twenty years.[10] Interestingly, ballroom dance music of the eighteenth century has largely remained immune from such criticisms. Certainly, what has helped the case of eighteenth-century dance is that the majority of these dances originated in (or were influenced by) the French court of Louis XIV. Thus, they were in the service of the ruling class and were created for and danced by the aristocracy. The associations of prestige and high culture therefore are a defining part of their identity as dance and music. Furthermore, there is little substantive difference in the eighteenth-century compositional language between dance music and concert music. The same composer was responsible for composing a new set of minuets for a carnival ball as well as for writing a new ballet or symphony for his patron's name-day celebration. The popular music revolution of the nineteenth century created a market that could financially support a new class of composers who specialized solely in the production of ballroom dance music. And while the ballroom music of Lanner and Strauss Sr. is steeped in the conventions of Austro-German

Classical music, they developed a distinctly popular style that on some levels rubbed against those Classical conventions.[11]

Two of the three studies of dance-music relations of the nineteenth century are devoted to the waltz.[12] The relationship between waltz music and its ballroom contexts is front and center in Sevin Yaraman's book *Revolving Embrace: The Waltz as Sex, Steps, and Sound* (2002). Yaraman first establishes how the physical movements of the dance are reflected in the music. She then casts her net far and wide, examining how the stylistic features of the waltz and its associated cultural associations are adapted, transformed, and combined with other elements in the instrumental waltzes of Chopin, Brahms, Tchaikovsky, and Ravel and in the operatic waltzes of Verdi, Puccini, and Berg. Derek Scott's important book, *Sounds of the Metropolis* (2008), chronicles the emergence of popular music in four cities: London, New York, Paris, and Vienna. His discussion of popular music in Vienna, not surprisingly, centers on the waltz. One of Scott's goals is to define the "popular" in the Viennese waltz not only in terms of its reception but also in terms of the development of a new stylistic language distinct from "serious" music. Maribeth Clark (2002) examines the locus of embodied meaning, popular culture, and French opera in Parisian quadrilles of the 1830s and 1840s. Specifically, she is interested in quadrille music based on arrangements of operas and the meanings that are born from this collision of musical styles and genres.

MINUET AND WALTZ

The focus of my book is on the eighteenth-century minuet and the nineteenth-century waltz. Emblematic dances of their times, the minuet and waltz are often defined in opposition to each other in their choreography and in their expressive and cultural meanings. It is this opposition of identities and meanings that makes them such an appealing pair for a study such as mine. Born of the court of Louis XIV and known as the "queen" of dances, the minuet was a celebration in movement of all the accoutrements and bodily gestures of noble society. As a ceremonial spectator dance, the minuet both identified a person as part of the ruling class and indicated his or her hierarchical position within it. Technically difficult and requiring years of instruction to master, the choreography of the minuet is characterized by intricate step patterns performed by dancers in opposition to each other; the man and woman never embrace. Conversely, the waltz is an egalitarian dance that emerged from the lower-class peasant culture of Austria, Germany, and Bavaria. Less technical and easier to learn, the waltz is characterized by a constant rotating motion, using the same step pattern throughout the dance. The constant spinning motion of the waltz required the couple to embrace tightly, torso to torso, for the duration of the dance. The waltz celebrated individuality, physical pleasure, and freedom from aristocratic convention and was considered by many to be an immoral dance. Its ascendancy at the end of the eighteenth century as the most popular ballroom dance in Europe mirrored the social and political revolution of the time: the fall of the ancien régime and the rise of a politically powerful middle class.

What is often overlooked, however, is that, despite these considerable differences, in certain regards the minuet and waltz are also quite similar, and these similarities form a foundation of comparison that highlights their differences to a greater degree. Both dances are notated in triple meter; both dances employ a dance step of six beats, thus requiring two bars of music (most other ballroom dances employ steps requiring one bar of music); and both dances require as a minimum a single couple for their execution (as opposed to a group dance such as the contredanse or quadrille, which requires four or more couples). Furthermore, there is evidence that indicates that an early version of the waltz used dance steps that were similar to those of the minuet. In the first comprehensive English treatise to provide a full description of the waltz, Thomas Wilson uses "the word *bourée* (or *bourrée*) to describe the *enchaînement* of three steps used in the second measure of the waltz. This same basic *bourrée* sequence is used in the second measure of the minuet step as described by eighteenth-century dancing masters. Wilson points out that the waltz *bourrée* should be danced on the toes and does not include the 'sinks' (*pliés*) required in the *bourrée* of the minuet" (Strobel 2004, 6:360).

ORGANIZATION OF THE BOOK

My book is divided into six chapters: the first two are devoted to the minuet, and the remaining four are devoted to the waltz. Chapter 1 begins by attempting to answer the practical question: What makes ballroom minuet music danceable? The second part of the chapter explores the influence of the danced minuet in the minuets of Bach's French Suites. In chapter 2 I examine Viennese ballroom minuets from the second half of the eighteenth century. A defining feature of this repertoire is the marked contrast between the first and second minuet (commonly called the trio). Focusing on

Mozart's ballroom minuets, I consider why such sharp contrast might have
been desirable.

For the remainder of the book I turn my attention to the most important
dance genre of the nineteenth century – the waltz. The detailed study of the
minuet provided in chapters 1 and 2 allows me to define the waltz with greater
precision and to locate and discuss significant changes in dance practices from
the eighteenth century to the nineteenth century. For example, one cannot
fully appreciate the radical nature of the waltz's choreography (i.e., its close
physical embrace and constant spinning motion) without understanding how
it violated eighteenth-century dance practices and sensibilities. The manner
in which ballroom spectators viewed the dancers is another important area
of change.

Chapter 3 focuses on issues of reception, spectatorship, aesthetics, and
musical form in the ballroom waltzes of the two most important waltz composers of the first half of the nineteenth century: Joseph Lanner (1801–43) and
Johann Strauss Sr. (1804–49). Drawing on a wide array of literary sources,
the first part explores the Viennese waltz as a public spectacle: Who was
watching? How did they watch? What were they watching? The second part
considers how aesthetic properties drawn from the visual experience may have
influenced and shaped aspects of the waltz's thematic material and large-scale
formal design.

The final three chapters of the book are devoted to Chopin and the dance.
Chapter 4 provides an overview of social dancing in Warsaw from roughly
1800 to 1830 and discusses the reception of the waltz in Warsaw. In the second
part of this chapter, I examine Chopin's involvement with social dancing both
as a dancer and as a dance musician. In chapter 5 I endeavor to demonstrate
how Chopin translates the bodily gestures of the dance into musical gestures
and how these musical gestures serve as compositional source material whose
potential is developed on different levels of musical organization, from the
smallest to the largest. Another issue I develop during the course of this
chapter is the nature and function of the musical differences between the
waltzes Chopin chose to publish during his lifetime and those he intentionally left unpublished. In the final chapter I consider what influence Lanner
and Strauss Sr. may have had on Chopin's conception of the waltz. His unpublished Warsaw waltzes show little influence of Viennese practice. Chopin
was exposed to the waltz music of Lanner and Strauss Sr. during his two trips
to Vienna (1829 and 1830–31), and the two waltzes he composed during this
time can be read as intentional engagements with Viennese practice. My book

concludes with a quick glance at Chopin's remaining published waltzes. In these works Chopin combines features of the Viennese model with his own more Classically oriented formal sensibilities and with a bravura style that evokes a sense of masculine physicality. I argue that Chopin's adjustments of the Viennese model may be read as a critique that, to some extent, was motivated by his own anxieties with regard to performing, composing, and publishing in a popular music genre so strongly associated with femininity and unmitigated sensual pleasure.

1st

Influences of the Early Eighteenth-Century Ballroom Minuet on the Minuets from J. S. Bach's French Suites, BWV 812–817

Cadence, which is the indispensable regulator of the Minuet, is also a rock against which many are dashed.

GENNARO MAGRI

Because of the prominence of social dancing in eighteenth-century social life, it would seem likely that musical features of Baroque ballroom dance types, and especially of the minuet, carried over into nondance genres and in some way influenced the formation of the Classical style, especially in regard to aspects of Classical phrase organization, such as periodicity and symmetrical formal designs based on repeating four- or eight-bar units. Leonard Ratner observes that "dance topics saturate the concert and theater music of the classic style; there is hardly a major work in this era that does not borrow heavily from the dance" (1980, 18). But beyond citing apparent similarities between dance music and Classical music, it becomes difficult to pinpoint the exact nature and level of the dance's influence. Certainly, dance was not the only player in the formation of the Classical style. As Charles Rosen and others have pointed out, vocal music – both folk and art – also had a tremendous impact and may have influenced the formation of the Classical style as much or even more so than the dance.[1] Furthermore, many functional dances in the first half of the eighteenth century exhibited irregular phrase organizations, and we now know that in some social settings dancers did not even pay heed to the music's melodic organization, let alone coordinate their footwork to it.[2] If this is true, then one cannot argue as convincingly for the practical necessity in dance music of one particular type of phrase organization over another. This, in turn, weakens the position that dance music provided the principal model for the development of phrase organization in Classical music.

Questions emerge. Just what was required of the music to make it danceable? How did the practical necessities of the dance affect the phrase organization of the music? And, perhaps most important, what might composers have learned from composing dance music? In addressing the first of these questions, this chapter begins by focusing on the practical aspects of one of the two most important social dances of the eighteenth century, the minuet – specifically, the ballroom version of the minuet, the *menuet ordinaire*.[3]

THE MINUET AS DANCED

The most common form of the social minuet (as opposed to theatrical minuets) was the *menuet ordinaire*, which was in vogue from the court of Louis XIV through to the end of the eighteenth century.[4] The organizing component of the *menuet ordinaire* – and of all French court dances – is the "step-unit": a collection of individual steps, hops, or springs involving at least two changes of weight from one foot to another. In the minuet, the principal step-unit is the *pas de menuet*, which contains four changes of weight, always beginning with the right foot (RLRL).[5] The *pas de menuet* requires six beats in ¾ time to complete and begins on the upbeat with a bending of the knees. The bending of the knees, often referred to as a "sink" or *plié*, prepares the dancer for a rise or spring on the downbeat.

Step-units were combined to form symmetrical floor patterns called "figures," typically comprising four to eight step-units and thus requiring eight to sixteen bars of music to complete. Figure 1.1 reproduces a plate from Kellom Tomlinson's 1735 treatise *The Art of Dancing*.[6] It illustrates the standard succession of six figures for the *menuet ordinaire*: (1) the introduction, (2) the S reversed, (3) the presenting of the right arm, (4) the presenting of the left arm, (5) the S reversed, and (6) the presenting of both arms and conclusion.[7] Each of the figures shown comprises eight dance steps, which Tomlinson has numbered (in very small print) within the figures. Since each figure comprises eight step-units, and the step-unit involves two bars, the eight-bar musical strains composed by Tomlinson for each figure would need to be repeated to conform to the sixteen-bar figures. Thus, in this particular diagram the large-scale melodic design is congruent with the figures of the dance. The entire dance is preceded by and concluded with reverences to the highest-ranking personages (seated at the top of the hall or dancing space) as well as to one's partner. Tomlinson does not provide music for these gestures.

WHAT MAKES THE MUSIC DANCEABLE?

Most dance scholars are of the opinion that for minuet music to be danceable there needs to be some congruence between the musical organization and the choreography of the dance. Just where that congruence lies varies from scholar to scholar. On the one hand, Julia Sutton (1985, 125) believes that there was complete congruence between the music and the dance at all levels of structure. Tomlinson's diagram of six minuet figures given in Figure 1.1 would appear to support her position. Assuming each of the eight-bar musical strains is repeated, the music and dance are closely aligned. Others, such as Wendy Hilton (1981, 293), Sarah Reichart (1984, 167), and Meredith Little and Natalie Jenne (1991, 69–70), allow for large-level conflicts between dance figures and musical strains while maintaining the need for congruence between the minuet's steps and a consistent two-bar grouping in the phrase organization of the music. Tilden Russell (1983, 64), however, believes that "there was no

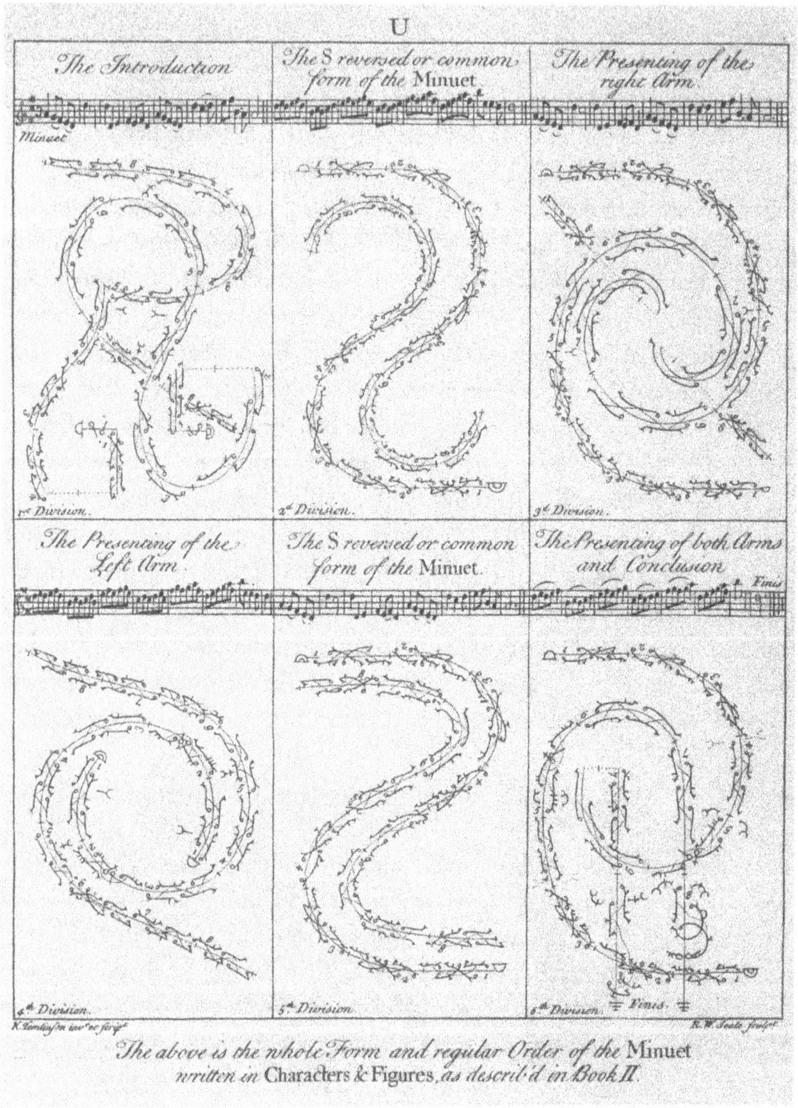

FIGURE 1.1. Kellom Tomlinson's diagram of the standard six figures
for the *menuet ordinaire* (*The Art of Dancing*, London, 1735, Plate U).
Reproduced with the permission of Rare Books and Manuscripts,
Special Collections Library, the Pennsylvania State University Libraries.

one-to-one relation between the dance and the [phrase organization of the] music." Echoing an earlier study by Karl Heinz Taubaut (1968, 169), Russell maintains that "the music provided a metrical rather than formal basis for the dance" (1983, 61–62). In a later article, Russell takes an even more extreme position, stating that "if asymmetry and irregularity are present in dance minuets at all structural levels, then presumably discrepancies were created with the dance at all structural levels, too, from the step to the figure to the length of the completed dance" (1999, 419).

In considering dance-music relations of the minuet, however, one must first consider the function and context of the dance: theatrical, pedagogical, ceremonial court balls, or more informal balls held outside of court.

As a general rule, when the dance and music were composed for a specific occasion or when a dancer was given prior notice as to what music would be played, there often was, as Sutton claims, complete agreement between the music and the dance. This situation would arise in the case of theatrical dances as well as many dances performed at formal court balls, where almost nothing was left to chance. Typically, only a select few of the invited guests were permitted to dance at formal balls; and as part of the preparations, a dancing master would choreograph and compose new dances for the ball and distribute them to the designated dancers for them to practice beforehand (Brainard 1986, 164). Clothing and, on occasion, even hairstyles were prearranged for the dancers as well (Harris-Warrick 1986, 44).

Although there were exceptions, minuets included in pedagogical treatises were almost always choreographed to fit the music exactly, as Tomlinson's diagram illustrates.[8] Here the six dance figures are accompanied by a tune in simple binary form (A:‖:B) repeated three times, yielding a six-part design (A:‖:B, A:‖:B, A:‖:B) that perfectly matches the six figures of the dance. In a series of fourteen ornately engraved plates, Tomlinson, within the same treatise, provides a beautiful and detailed iconographic display of the minuet's choreography, combining dance notation, musical notation, and depictions of dancers at specific points in the choreography of the minuet's figures.[9] Figure 1.2 reproduces one of the plates. The tune that provides the accompaniment for the dancers in the series of plates, like the tune in Figure 1.1, is cast in simple binary form (A:‖:B) and repeated three times in order to match the six figures (A:‖:B, A:‖:B, A:‖:B). After depicting the opening reverences, for which Tomlinson scores a musical fanfare, most of the plates depict either the first half or the second half of one of the six figures. As shown by the

FIGURE 1.2. Kellom Tomlinson's depiction of the minuet (*The Art of Dancing*, London, 1735, Plate XII). *Reproduced with the permission of Rare Books and Manuscripts, Special Collections Library, the Pennsylvania State University Libraries.*

small numbers below the music of Figure 1.2, Tomlinson indicates the precise coordination of the four individual two-bar steps of the dancers to the music: each step – without exception in the entire series of plates – begins on an odd-numbered measure.[10] Another way to think about the dance-music relations exhibited in Tomlinson's multimedia display is that not only is there complete congruence between the dance figures and melodic organization, but, on a lower level, the minuet's dance steps are also perfectly coordinated with the music's two-bar hypermeter.[11]

There are two likely reasons for the close coordination of dance and music found in Tomlinson's treatise and other eighteenth-century dance treatises. No doubt, dancing masters did not want to introduce any unneeded complexity that might overwhelm or confuse their students. Dancing masters typically accompanied their students with a violin or a pochette, which was a small, pocket-size violin that easily allowed the dancing master to play a dance tune while demonstrating the steps or keeping a close eye on his students' footwork. The ability to provide musical accompaniment thus enabled dancing masters to exercise control over all aspects of their teaching environment, which in many cases, as with Tomlinson, included the composition of their own dance tunes. The strong pedagogical association established between the minuet and a particular tune, however, could prove problematic. While visiting Paris in 1762, Leopold Mozart observed that "in the whole town there are about two or three favourite minuets, which must always be played, because the people cannot dance to any save those particular ones during the playing of which they learned to dance" (1966, 40–41).

The second reason for congruence between music and dance is that dancing masters likely approached the dances in their manuals as they did theatrical dances, where, given the opportunity to choreograph a dance to a specific tune, their natural inclination was to mold the dance around the tune or vice versa for those dancing masters who composed their own music. For example, in 1700 the dancing master Raoul-Auger Feuillet advertised in the preface to his *La pavane des saisons* that for a fee he would provide an appropriate choreography to any tune sent to him. Moreover, it was an aesthetic presupposition of the time that dance music should translate some element of the physical motion of the dancers into its musical organization, not only to "hold out a helping hand in order to bar with greater precision the character and movement of the dance" (Batteux [1746] 1981, 55) but also, in doing so, to provide a unified artistic work whose whole is greater than the sum of its parts.

Tomlinson hints at such a synergistic notion in a poem, which he apparently penned, that precedes his visual display of the minuet.

> Whilst Tuneful *Music* gives the Ear Delight,
> And Graceful *Dancing* charms ye ravish'd Sight;
> They give a double Force to Cupid's Dart;
> Which through ye Eye, makes Passage to ye Heart. ([1735] 1970, opening
> unnumbered page of Book II)

At less formal court balls and at public balls held outside of the court, however, which accounted for the majority of dance events, there was little opportunity for dancers to know beforehand what music would be played. While eight-bar phrases are common, there are many examples of dance minuets containing six-, ten-, or twelve-bar phrases. Thus, because there was no standard phrase length for minuet music or, as we shall see, for any of its dance figures or succession of figures, it would only be by sheer coincidence that the dancers' choreography would fit the phrase organization of the music (Russell 1992, 125–26). Interestingly, the lack of congruence does not appear to have distracted the dancers or caused displeasure. Quite to the contrary, it is possible that, at least for some experienced dancers and observers in the side galleries, some sort of conflict between dance and music was desirable, a point I will return to later.

From the perspective of the dancers, there are two factors that could lead to conflicts between the dance and the music, the first and most important being the improvisatory nature of the *menuet ordinaire*, for it was considered in good taste for the man to add embellishments, within the bounds of proper decorum, at will. Not only could flourishes be added to the steps, but also steps could be added to increase the lengths of the figures.[12] Thus, the length of the dance and of its component parts could be altered "according to the dancer's pleasure" with apparently little concern over the relation of the dance to the musical accompaniment (Tomlinson [1735] 1970, 140). Tomlinson summarizes:

> In Effect [the minuet] is no more than a voluntary or extempory Piece of
> Performance, as has already been hinted, in Regard there is no limited Rule,
> as to its Length or Shortness, or in Relation to the Time of the Tune, since
> it may begin upon any that offers, as well within a Strain as upon the first
> Note or commencing thereof. It is the very same with Respect to its ending,
> for it matters not whether it breaks off upon the End of the first Strain of the
> Tune, the second, or in the Middle of either of them, provided it be in Time
> to the Music. ([1735] 1970, 137)

One final matter that would result in noncongruence is the opening reverences. After the dancers have made their bows to the highest-ranking personages present in the hall and to their partner, Tomlinson instructs them not to wait for the opening of the next strain to begin the dance. Instead, they should "begin upon the first Time that offers, in that it is much more genteel and shews the *Dancer's* Capacity and Ear in distinguishing of the Time, and from thence begets himself a good Opinion from the Beholders, who are apt to judge favourably of the following Part of his Performance; whereas the attending the concluding . . . of a Strain has the contrary Effect" (Tomlinson [1735] 1970, 124). Thus, within the same treatise Tomlinson presents two very different approaches to the issue of dance-music coordination. On the one hand, in the two complete minuet choreographies presented with illustrations and music, he constructs complete congruence between dance and music. As I suggested, one may think of such carefully considered dance-music relations as a theatrical ideal, well suited for staged minuets but not for the unpredictable environment and performance practices of the public ballroom. And, as we have seen in his discussion of the minuet as danced, Tomlinson is quite clear that such congruence is not only impractical but also undesirable.

The first chapter of Joseph Riepel's trailblazing treatise *Anfangsgründe zur musikalischen Setzkunst* (1754) contains an interesting bit of evidence in support of the desirability of noncongruence between dance and music. The text is written in Socratic style as a dialogue between a teacher and his student. During the course of Riepel's discussion on the use of asymmetrical phrases, the young student interrupts his teacher with an observation drawn from his own life experiences: "I am thoroughly familiar with all the German dances that are played in our beer halls. If there is one with two four-measure phrases, the people are happy but a little subdued, but as soon as they hear one with two three-measure phrases, they all begin to jump around as if they were crazy."[13] While the story is fictitious and does not speak specifically of a minuet, and, in any case, it would be unthinkable for a minuet couple to begin to "jump around as if they were crazy," Riepel does draw attention to the aesthetic virtues of noncongruence. As Russell observes in regard to the minuet, "it may have been precisely the inevitable incongruities between music and the steps (as well as the occasional, unpredictable concinnities) that made the minuet so interesting and delightful an experience, for both the dancers and the spectators" (1999, 419).

"TIME"

From the evidence cited above, it is obvious that dancers – at least experienced dancers in public ballroom settings – were little concerned with coordinating their dance steps with a minuet's phrase organization; this may account for the rather high percentage of irregular phrases found in dance minuets, especially in the time period before 1770. If dancers did not require synchronicity between their minuet figures and the music's melodic organization, then there was no practical need for the standardization of the minuet's melodic organization or, for that matter, of the minuet's choreography as well. Indeed, the very lack of the requirement for synchronicity allowed for greater flexibility in both music and dance and in the relationship between the two. In contrast to the minuet, the contredanse did require dancers to coordinate precisely the beginnings and ends of their figures to the beginnings and ends of phrases. As a result, contredanse music on the whole exhibits a much higher degree of structural uniformity and is rooted in what David Neumeyer calls the "quadratic syntax," that is, formal designs that employ four-, eight-, or sixteen-bar units (2006, 1). As we shall see in chapter 2, though, by the last quarter of the eighteenth century, a quadratic syntax had become a defining feature of Viennese ballroom minuets.[14]

If dancers did not listen to the melodic organization, then what exactly did they attend to in the music beyond a basic pulse and tempo? Would any audible music in triple time at an appropriate tempo serve equally well as an accompaniment to the footwork of the dancers? Or are there any other bases of congruence that may have shaped and influenced the development of the minuet as a musical genre?

According to Tomlinson and other dancing masters of the eighteenth century, an important aspect to dancing a minuet in *bon goût* was the dancer's ability to coordinate his or her dance steps with the minuet's time. "Time" was a term commonly used in the eighteenth century to refer to a piece's metrical organization (Hilton 1981, 82–83). In general, Tomlinson instructs the dancer to "mark the time" of any dance by rising from a sink to the first note of a bar. In doing so, the dancer gesturally marks the downbeats of each bar, thereby visually (from the spectator's point of view) and physically (from the dancer's point of view) supporting the notated meter. For the minuet, however, Tomlinson ([1735] 1970, 148–49) observes that a dancer is not to mark the downbeats of each bar but of every other bar. By rising from a sink to the first note of every two bars, the dancer marks not only downbeats but potential hypermetrical downbeats as well.

Thus, to dance the *menuet ordinaire* effectively, dancers would need only attend to the minuet's hypermetrical organization. By gesturally marking the downbeats of every other bar, dancers provided a potential basis of congruence between their step-unit and a two-bar hypermeter. Composers of functional minuets generally responded to the dancers' cueing requirements by providing in their music a clear and consistent two-bar hypermeter. Although a two-bar hypermeter can also be found in the music of other dance types, its prominence in music specifically composed to accompany the minuet dance establishes it as a defining feature of the genre and provides a basis of congruence beyond pulse and tempo.[15] In the language of Batteux, which I quoted earlier, this congruence fulfills a basic requirement of dance music that it "must conform to the thing that it expresses, being the dress tailored for the body" ([1746] 1981, 50).

Although Tomlinson is perhaps the most explicit of all eighteenth-century writers on the metrical relationship between the minuet as danced and minuet music, he is not alone. For example, in order to feel two bars of the minuet as one metrical unit, dancing masters often instructed their students to count in $\frac{6}{4}$ rather than in $\frac{3}{4}$, despite the moderate tempo.[16] Reflecting this practice, many early minuets – especially those used in dance treatises – either were notated in $\frac{6}{4}$ or used a dotted line to indicate metrically weak bars.[17] In conducting their students, dancing masters and music teachers reinforced the hypermeter by beating down on the first bar (the *bonne mesure*) and up on the second bar (the *fausse mesure*).[18] Later in the century, the Italian dancing master Gennaro Magri reiterated the importance of time in the minuet. He described the two-bar metrical unit not only as the minuet's "real substance" and "indispensable regulator" but also as "a rock against which many are dashed" ([1779] 1988, 188–90).

In eighteenth-century dance sources, discussions of two-bar metrical units only occur in connection with the minuet. Why were two-bar metrical units so important to the minuet as compared to other dances? For the simple reason that the minuet is the only court dance, aside from the passepied (a close relative of the minuet), that employed a two-bar step-unit.[19] All other dances contain step-units that are no longer than one bar.[20] With one-bar step-units, the downbeat of every bar is equally marked by the dancer's movements by a rise from a sink. So long as dancers know where the downbeats are,

FIGURE 1.3. Pierre Rameau's 1725 depiction of a royal ball presided over by Louis XV (*Le maître à danser*). *Reproduced with the permission of Rare Books and Manuscripts, Special Collections Library, the Pennsylvania State University Libraries.*

they will be "in time" with the music. Because of this, there was no practical reason for dancers to hear metrical levels above the notated meter. With a step-unit duration of two bars, however, it is critical for dancers to hear a consistent two-bar hypermeter, especially when they first begin to dance. For if, as Tomlinson says, the dancers "should happen to begin out of Time, it is a thousand to one if they ever recover it throughout the dance . . . and not being able to recover it afterwards, they dance the whole Minuet out of Time" ([1735] 1970, 124). An anonymous writer of a short dance treatise published in the *Lady's Magazine* in 1785 agrees: "If he sets off out of time, he must be some time before he can recover it, and the minuet is spoiled."[21] Certainly, the incentive to keep track of the two-bar hypermeter was enhanced by the fact that the *menuet ordinaire* was danced by only one couple at a time while everyone else watched. Figure 1.3 provides Pierre Rameau's 1725 depiction of a ceremonial court ball with Louis XV presiding on his throne at the top of the hall. Within the dancing space the same couple is shown twice: first as they make their reverences to the king and then as they stand side by side ready to begin their dance. In such an environment, any mistake certainly would have been noticed and would have resulted in some loss of reputation.

The insistence of Sutton, Hilton, Reichart, and others on the practical necessity of two-bar groups stems from a common confusion between melodic organization and metrical organization. While they correctly identify the presence of two-bar units as a defining feature of minuets, they mistakenly attribute those units to the melodic organization rather than to the metrical organization. The melodic organization may indeed support the metrical structure, thus resulting in a succession of two-bar groups. This type of congruence, however, is not essential to the minuet, and, in fact, minuets comprised entirely of two-bar segments are exceedingly rare. One scholar, tightly holding on to the notion of symmetrical, duple-length phrases as the norm in the minuet, suggested the fantastic notion that through some quirk in historical preservation, only the exceptional irregular minuets have survived (Goldmann 1956, 17).

I agree with Taubaut's and Russell's position that in order to dance the *menuet ordinaire* it was not necessary for the music's phrase organization and the dancer's choreography to be completely congruent at any level. While I also agree with their position that the minuet's music provided a metrical rather than a formal basis for the dance, that basis can be refined as a two-bar hypermeter.

THE MINUETS FROM BACH'S FRENCH SUITES

Although there is debate over the provenance of the posthumously applied modifier "French" in the title French Suites, both the use of French dance titles and the simpler, more elegant *galant* melodies and less discursive and contrapuntal treatment of the dance music, especially in comparison to Bach's earlier English Suites and later Partitas, do suggest a connection to the dances of the French court. This avenue of influence is circumstantially supported in that Bach, as Little and Jenne (1991, 3–15) have shown in their book on Bach's dance music, was well acquainted with the social dances of his time, especially those of the French court. In the period of reconstruction after the devastation of the Thirty Years' War (1618–48), many German cities, including Leipzig, Dresden, Celle, Württemberg, Köthen, and Weimar, embraced French culture as a means of alleviating wartime strife. And the majority of the German courts employed French dancing masters, preferably Parisian, to teach not only dance but all aspects of deportment (Little and Jenne 1991, 9). Certainly, Bach encountered French culture while he was a student at the Michaelisschule in Lüneburg (1700–1702), where he shared room and board with students from the nearby Ritterakademie. According to Karl Geiringer,

> the [Ritterakademie] was a center of French culture. French conversation, indispensable at that time to any high-born German, was obligatory between the students; and Sebastian with his quick mind may have become familiar with a language which he had no chance to study in his own schools. There were French plays he could attend and, what was more important, French music he could hear[;] as a pupil of Lully, Thomas de la Selle taught dancing at the Academy to French tunes. Most likely it was de la Selle, noticing the youth's enthusiastic response, who decided to take Bach to the city of Celle, where he served as court musician.[22]

But perhaps the most compelling evidence for Bach's knowledge of French court dance is that Bach was personally acquainted with two French dancing masters, Pantaleon Hebenstreit (1667–1750) and Jean-Baptiste Volumier (c. 1670–1728) (Little and Jenne 1991, 14). Hebenstreit supported himself as a dancing master while living in Leipzig, Weissenfels, and Eisenach. In 1714 he took a position in Dresden as a court violinist and pantaleonist (a keyboard instrument of his own invention). Volumier, a composer, dancing master, and exceptional violinist, was *Konzertmeister* of the Dresden orchestra from 1709 to 1721.

  Although the various dance types appearing in Bach's French Suites were not specifically intended for dancing, it would be a mistake to assume that they are unsuitable for dancing. Depending on the degree of stylization, some are clearly more suited to the ballroom floor than others. As a general rule, older dance types that were out of fashion as social dances were subject to greater stylization. Allemandes and gigues, for example, are among the oldest dances contained in the suites and were dances that were rarely, if at all, used as social dances at the time Bach wrote them. In Bach's suites they are among the most stylized. They serve a structural function within each suite as a whole: the allemandes, metrically very free and improvisatory, assume the role of opening preludes, whereas the gigues, with their weighty and extended contrapuntal passages, serve effectively as closing movements.

Out of all the dances contained in the French Suites, the minuets are among the least stylized, showing little substantive differences from functional minuets of the time. In her *New Grove* article on the minuet, dancer and dance historian Meredith Little observes that "Bach's minuets are extremely well suited to dance accompaniment" (1980, 356). The ballroom character of these minuets is not surprising, given that the minuet was among the newest and by far the most popular of the social court dances included in the suites. Thus, there were fewer opportunities for either idealized reminiscence or stylistic corruption from external influences. Moreover, since Bach's minuets were performed without dancing, it was particularly important for the music "to conform to the thing that it expresses" in order for the listener to perceive it as minuet music (Batteux [1746] 1981, 50). This may be another reason why the form and phrase lengths of minuet music meant for listening tend to be a bit more standardized and formulaic than what is found in the repertoire of ballroom music, at least during the first half of the eighteenth century. In other words, in the ballroom one immediately knows it is minuet music by its direct association with the dancers. For minuet music *sans* dancing to be immediately recognized as minuet music, Bach and other composers needed to instill in it a well-defined – perhaps even exaggerated – sense of "minuetness." And there was no better place to turn to for an ideal representation of the minuet than the pedagogical minuets of dance treatises, which, as I have discussed, are characterized by quadratic phrase structure and complete congruence between the music and the dance.

Like the minuets composed for the court ballrooms of Paris, for his minuets Bach favored simple textures of two or three voices, a clearly articulated phrase organization comprised mostly of four- or eight-bar phrases, and a breezy and nonchalant melodic style. Overall the music captures the key aesthetic qualities of the minuet as danced: artful simplicity, gracefulness, and noble ease. But while Bach's minuets are eminently danceable and recognizable as minuets, they are generally on a higher artistic level than minuets found in published dance manuals and *recueils*. On the whole, Bach's keyboard minuets are marked by a more sophisticated contrapuntal design between the melody and the accompaniment, a wider range of harmonies and key areas, and a much more unified motivic design. Finally, Bach's minuets were conceived for the keyboard and as such frequently use idiomatic keyboard passagework that is uncharacteristic of ballroom minuets, whose melodies were typically written for the violin.

Bach's practical knowledge of the minuet as danced is evidenced by the presence of a strong, unambiguous, and consistently held two-bar hypermeter in every minuet of the suites. This musical characteristic sets Bach's minuets apart from the other dance types of the French Suites – both new and old. While his other dances may at times project a strong sense of hypermeter, very few do it as clearly or as consistently as the minuets.

Bach employed a variety of techniques to project a two-bar hypermeter. In general terms, it is achieved by consistently placing some sort of "phenomenal accent" on the downbeats of every other bar. A phenomenal accent is created by any musical event that "gives emphasis or stress to a moment in the musical flow" (Lerdahl and Jackendoff 1983, 17–18).[23] Sudden changes in dynamics, register, contour, texture, and timbre are some examples. Most typically, though, Bach created phenomenal accents by locating the inception of an "event" of relatively long duration at the beginnings of every other bar. The event may be a pitch, harmony, texture, pattern of articulation, or some combination thereof. The beginnings of such durations receive an accent; when they are consistently placed two bars apart, a two-bar hypermeter emerges.

BWV 812

Example 1.1 presents the opening section of Bach's minuet from the French Suite in D Minor, BWV 812. Between the staves is a hypermetrical analysis (represented by arabic numbers), and beneath the music is a grouping analysis (represented by brackets). At the bottom I have listed the phenomenal accents or "cues" used by listeners to extrapolate the beginnings of each two-bar hypermeasure.

In this example Bach employs a consistent pattern of phenomenal accents brought about by changes in texture, contour, register, and harmony to establish a two-bar hypermeter. The first beat is marked as a downbeat by all voices entering simultaneously with $\hat{1}$, in the outer voices.[24] It is also strongly articulated by the relatively long durations that begin on the first beat: the

Hypermeter

Dm: i   iv⁶   V   i⁴   Am: V   i⁴ iv V   i

phrygian half cadence   perfect authentic cadence

Grouping Structure   d c b a

Phenomenal Accents

• long duration of a pitch	• change of harmony and initiation of	• return of the tonic	• change in contour
• long duration of a harmony	a cadential progression	• change of texture	• initiation of a cadential progression
• long duration of texture	• change of texture	• long duration of a pitch	• dissonant resolution into a more
• stable bass and soprano	• change in register in the soprano		stable harmony
	• new motivic material		

EXAMPLE 1.1. Minuet from J. S. Bach's French Suite in D Minor, BWV 812, bars 1–8.

opening harmony, bass note, and texture are sustained until the downbeat
of bar 3. The downbeat of bar 2 receives some emphasis through a sudden
change in the soprano's register, a change in contour in the inner voice, and
the sequential repetition in the top voice. But this downbeat is less strongly
articulated than the downbeat of the first bar and serves as the second hypermetrical beat.

A two-bar hypermeter is unequivocally established by the strong emphasis given to the downbeat of bar 3. Particularly important is the change
of harmony – harmonic rhythm is one of the most important perceptual in-
puts in the establishment of meter. As part of a Phrygian half cadence, the
iv⁶ not only effects a harmonic change but also initiates the beginning of a
two-bar cadential progression that provides durational emphasis as well. In
the remainder of the excerpt similar events verify and reinforce the two-bar
hypermeter established in the first four bars.

Another more effective way Bach projects a two-bar hypermeter, in this
example and in his minuets in general, is through the use of a particular
type of phrase organization in which new groups are consistently initiated
every other bar. This technique establishes a strong durational accent at the
beginnings of odd-numbered bars, thereby supporting a two-bar hypermeter.
William Rothstein refers to the correspondence between initiation points of
melodic groups and strong beats in the metrical organization as "the rule of
congruence" (1995b, 173). The remainder of this chapter focuses on the use of
such phrase organizations as a means of establishing the minuet's practical
necessity.

By saying that in Bach's minuets new groups are consistently initiated
every other bar, I do not mean that Bach's minuets consist entirely of two-bar

groups, as some have suggested. Through the technique of overlap, the end of one group may also serve as the beginning of another, thus resulting in a three-, five-, or seven-bar group. In the present example, the first half of the minuet is comprised of one eight-bar phrase divided into two smaller four-bar phrases. At the next level of phrase organization, level *c*, the four-bar phrases are further subdivided into two subphrases. Notice that the second four-bar phrase, which leads to a perfect authentic cadence in the dominant minor, is segmented into two subphrases proportioned 3 + 2. The first subgroup of the second phrase is extended into bar 7, overlapping with the beginning of the second subphrase. This overlap is accomplished by the prolongation of the modulating dominant (bar 6) and its resolution at the downbeat of bar 7. The resolution of the dissonance in conjunction with stepwise motion in the outer voices carries the subphrase into the next bar. Thus, it can be seen that groups of asymmetrical length do not interfere with the establishment of a two-bar hypermeter so long as the inception of groups occurs on odd-numbered bars.

Sentence Form

Certain patterns of thematic repetition figure very highly in Bach's minuets. In contrast to the predominant use of simple binary in the other dances (A:‖:A), rounded binary (A:‖:BA) is used in three out of seven minuets.[25] Parallel periods are common, as are phrases built out of contrasting subphrases. But by far the thematic pattern used most often in Bach's minuets is "sentence" form.[26] In its normative form, a sentence is an eight-bar phrase composed of two subphrases: (1) the first subphrase, itself divided into two groups, contains the presentation of a basic idea (two to three bars long, depending on whether or not overlap is present) followed by a literal or varied repetition of the basic idea beginning in the third bar; (2) the second subphrase, beginning in the fifth bar, contains a continuation to a cadence. The continuation is typically marked by thematic fragmentation, a faster harmonic rhythm, and a registral climax, followed by a linear descent into an authentic or half cadence. As a result of fragmentation, the continuation itself may exhibit the sentence's characteristic grouping structure in miniature (1 + 1 + 2).

Bach's minuets are exceptional in their imaginative and varied sentences; they represent a musical compendium of sorts in which every time a sentence form occurs, Bach utilizes a different constructive principle. Especially noteworthy, as we shall see, is Bach's treatment of the repetition of the basic idea. Furthermore, by initiating a new group at the beginnings of the first, third, and fifth bars of each phrase, the eight-bar sentence is an ideal means for supporting a two-bar hypermeter. Thus, it is not surprising to see it used so often not only in Bach's minuets (after 1720) but in the minuets of other eighteenth-century composers as well.[27]

Returning to Example 1.1, the opening refrain of this minuet is organized as a modulating period: the first four-bar phrase ends with a half cadence; the second four-bar phrase modulates to A minor, the key of the minor dominant, and ends with a perfect authentic cadence. Now observe that each four-bar phrase is organized as a small sentence: 1 + 1 + 2 and 1 + 2 + 2. The odd math of the second four-bar phrase (1 + 2 + 2 = 4) is a result of the overlap between the second and third groups, whereby bar 7 is counted twice. In both phrases the repetition of the basic idea, first stated in the top voice, is restated in the same voice but at a different pitch level and with a different harmonization.

BWV 815

The entire first half of the minuet in E♭ major, BWV 815 (Example 1.2), consists of one eight-bar phrase organized as a sentence in which the basic idea is imitated by the bass an octave below. The underlying tonal motion supporting the basic idea is a descending linear span in the soprano, E♭–D♭–C–B♭–A♭–G, which, beginning with the C in bar 2, is doubled a tenth below. The arrival of the G in bar 3 not only concludes the linear descent but also effects a voice exchange between the second beat of the first bar and the downbeat of bar 3, as shown by the crossed lines in Example 1.2 (the second beat of bar 1 also effects a voice exchange between the first beat of bar 1). The end of the basic idea, as defined by these tonal motions, also serves as the beginning of the varied repetition of the basic idea. The same linear descent, E♭–G, now in the left hand, extends the repetition of the basic idea to the downbeat of bar 5, which also serves as the beginning of the continuation. Thus, the technique of overlap in conjunction with nonduple groups (3 + 3 + 4) not only supports a two-bar hypermeter but gives it more prominence through the conjunction of both a beginning and an ending boundary.

The continuation itself exhibits sentence form but on a smaller scale: 1 + 1 + 2. Although in this regard the continuation group itself is a self-contained motivic structure with a well-defined beginning, middle, and end, on a higher level it also effectively serves the function of "continuation to a cadence." The contraction in the size of the groups and the increase in chord

EXAMPLE 1.2. Minuet from J. S. Bach's French Suite in E♭ Major, BWV 815.

changes per bar provide a rhythmic acceleration to the perfect authentic cadence in bars 7–8.

The second half of this minuet (bars 9–16) also exhibits sentence form with overlapping groups (3 + 3 + 4). Here the repetition of the basic idea is achieved through varied transposition of the right hand's melody. Thus, in this minuet structural uniformity as derived from the opening material – a hallmark of Bach's compositional style – is achieved not only motivically but in terms of the phrase organization as well.[28]

BWV 814

Thirty-six bars long without repeats, the minuet from the French Suite in B Minor, BWV 814, is one of the longest minuets of the French Suites. Its length, however, is not indicative of a digressive treatment of its motivic material. Quite to the contrary, it is a model of elegance, restraint, and hidden control. The first half, shown in Example 1.3, consists of a sixteen-bar parallel period in which the consequent modulates to the relative major. Both the antecedent and the consequent exhibit "sentence within sentence" organizations. And, as in the previous minuet, the use of overlapping groups in conjunction with regularized patterns of thematic repetition helps establish and accentuate a consistently held two-bar hypermeter.

EXAMPLE 1.3. Minuet from J. S. Bach's French Suite in B Minor, BWV 814, bars 1–16.

In the opening phrase, the basic idea – a very plain, arpeggiated melody with very little linear or harmonic motion – is repeated (almost) literally in bars 3–5. The propelling force for this rather mundane and static opening four bars is an overarching bass arpeggiation that extends from the downbeat of bar 1 to the downbeat of bar 5 (refer to the voice-leading graph in Example 1.3).

In the continuation segment of the phrase, a tremendous drive to the cadence is achieved by three means: (1) an increase in harmonic rhythm through a descending fifths progression; (2) the inception of the first substantial linear motions of the piece, both in the bass and in the soprano; and (3) the use of sentence form in smaller proportion. As a result, the dominant in bar 8 is achieved with great force, both linearly and harmonically. In order to avoid a jolting pause, Bach dissipates the tonal tension by increasing the rhythmic motion in the bass and by providing an upward arpeggiation in the left hand, which lifts us back to the opening of the consequent phrase.

The simplicity of the opening arpeggiated melody enables Bach to use it as an accompanimental figure in the opening of the second half of the minuet (Example 1.4).[29] Above it he presents an entirely new eight-bar melody, one with no strong internal divisions. In fact, this type of melody would be stylistically antithetical to the minuet were it not for the very regularized and predictable accompaniment below. Bach thereby avoids what could have been a banal repetition of the opening melody (including repeats, this is the fifth time we have heard it) both by providing it with a different textual function and by crafting a new melody above it.

In the final phrase Bach gives us yet another variation of sentence form. There are two noteworthy features. First, the repetition of the basic idea

EXAMPLE 1.4. Minuet from J. S. Bach's French Suite in B Minor, BWV 814, bars 17–36.

is achieved through a rising 5–3 voice-leading sequence. Second, the continuation group (bars 29–36) of this large sentence is itself organized as a sentence – not a four-bar sentence, which would balance the four-bar-long presentation, but rather a full eight-bar sentence. In order to insure that the start of the proportionally larger continuation does not function too strongly as a new beginning, Bach exaggerates the presentational function of the basic idea and its repetition (bars 25–28) and downplays the presentational aspect of the continuation's basic idea and repetition (bars 29–32).

I shall first discuss the presentation aspect of bars 25–28. An opening agogic accent in the melody and a closing agogic accent in the bass clearly segment the basic idea and its repetition, thus setting it apart from what comes before and after. Except for cadential notes, these are the longest held notes in the piece. Segmentation, and hence presentation, is further emphasized by the quarter rest in bar 28, the only rest in the entire minuet. Finally, a new rhythmic diminution in the melody coupled with the rising sequence of the repetition draws attention to itself. Bach often reserves the rising sequence to signal sectional or global closure; the ascent allows the music to build to a climax that will "fall down" into the final cadence. Its use here highlights its role as part of the final phrase of the minuet.

Although the continuation (bars 29–36) is itself organized as a sentence, Bach maintains its overall function as a continuation to a cadence (i) by continuing the registral ascent initiated by the basic idea and its repetition, (2) by shifting into a constant stream of eighth notes in the right hand and quarter notes in the left hand, and (3) by beginning the continuation with an enlarged V–I progression that not only replicates the descending fifth progression of the basic idea (bars 25–26) but also reestablishes the tonic, thereby allowing time to prepare for the final cadence.

In sum, every phrase of this minuet, like the minuet in E♭ major previously discussed, is a sentence. Each sentence, however, employs a different constructive principle. The opening parallel period uses (almost) literal repetition. The phrase beginning the second half recontextualizes the opening melody as an accompanimental sentence over which a melody with very little internal division is played. The final sentence of the work utilizes the typically Baroque procedure of sequence in the repetition of the basic idea. Its continuation is then expanded through the use of a "sentence within a sentence."

BWV 817

In the final suite of the set, Bach presents another minuet consisting entirely of sentences (Example 1.5).[30] Structural uniformity is further obtained through motivic consistency: the entire piece is derived from the opening two-bar idea. That a piece is generated from a single musical idea is certainly not extraordinary for Bach. The motivic fabric of most of his works is drawn from material presented in the opening bars. What is striking about this minuet is that in the face of all the repetitions, none involve the techniques of imitative counterpoint. All of the repetitions are in the service of a particular type of phrase construction: sentence form.

The high degree of structural uniformity within the phrase organization together with an almost complete agreement between the phrase organization and the metrical organization result in a highly segmented musical surface. Segmentation is further emphasized by the use of solo texture to begin groups and the abandonment of eighth-note motion at the ends of groups, which is quite unusual for Bach. I shall use this minuet – the last minuet I will discuss – to show how Bach, in the face of such severe compositional restraints, overcomes the danger of creating an overly rigid and predictable piece of music. Three factors provide the dynamic impetus both to hold this piece together and to drive it forward: the binding unity of *Stufen*, rhythmic displacements, and constructive conflicts between the dance as kinesthetically felt and the music as heard.[31]

EXAMPLE 1.5. Minuet from J. S. Bach's French Suite in
E Major, BWV 817.

Stufen

Two unusual but related features of this minuet, especially noticeable in the
first and last eight-bar phrases, are the scarcity of bass notes and the slow
harmonic rhythm. The first phrase is supported by the progression I–V,
the last phrase V–I. As the voice-leading sketch shows, in the first phrase,
the opening tonic triad is gradually unfolded by an ascending arpeggiation,

$\hat{3}$–$\hat{5}$–$\hat{1}$–$\hat{3}$. This arpeggiation, together with the bass's pedal E, tonally fuse bars 1–5 together as the expression of a single harmony – the tonic *Stufe*. Only after the bass E becomes transformed into a dissonance in bar 6 is it finally dislodged from its pedal point function into a cadential progression tonicizing the dominant.

Although the harmonic rhythm of the second phrase increases somewhat at the musical surface, at the middleground it is essentially static, consisting of one harmony, the dominant. Established at the end of the previous phrase, the dominant is composed-out by means of a double-neighbor/bass motion, B–C#–A–B, that both unifies bars 9–16 as one voice-leading unit and establishes a large-level manifestation of the neighboring motion first presented in bar 2 in the upper voice. And, at a deeper level, bars 1–16 are heard as the progression of just two *Stufen*, I–V.

Bar 17 marks the return of this minuet's opening material, thereby establishing it as a rounded binary form. Bach avoids a literal return of the opening material and provides global closure by reversing the progression of the opening phrase, I–V, to V–I. Thus, what initially sounds like a tonic return in bar 17 turns out to be the inception of an elaborated dominant. This dominant is prolonged until it resolves into the final tonic of the last bar. The use of the dominant to begin the phrase, as opposed to the tonic, undercuts the stability of the thematic return and helps propel the music onward to its final resolution.

Rhythmic Displacements

The delayed entrances of the bass within the phrase structure create staggered beginnings in which the bass and soprano are out of phase with each other. While the use of solo texture helps signal the beginning of each group, the absence of a bass voice weakens the stability of the opening bars of each group, giving them the character of an upbeat. Nonetheless, I interpret the opening bar of each group as a hypermetrical downbeat for two reasons. First, danced minuets typically begin on the first beat of the bar without the use of upbeat figures; eighteenth-century listeners would therefore hear the downbeat of the first bar as hypermetrically strong. Second, while the bass does enter in bar 2, it enters on the weak part of the first beat and concludes with a descending octave leap that strongly emphasizes the third beat. As such, the bass's role, at least in the first two subphrases of each phrase, is to support intermediate closure.

EXAMPLE 1.6. Bass line added to the opening phrase of the minuet from J. S. Bach's French Suite in E Major, BWV 817.

As Example 1.6 so clumsily illustrates, Bach could easily have composed a bass line to the opening bar of each group. Not only does the added bass line take away much of the ambiguity and tension that resulted from its absence, but it also provides too much stability at the beginning of each group. Also notice that the added bass support for the dominant in bar 3 overemphasizes closure in bar 4: the soprano's î feels too much like the goal of a complete phrase rather than an intermediate step along the way. The net result is a loss of continuity across overly predictable phrase boundaries.

Perhaps the most complicated phrase of this minuet is the middle eight-bar phrase. Although harmonically it prolongs a single chord, the dominant, its upper voice is composed-out by means of a linear descent (F♯–E–D-♮–C♯–B) in which all pitches of the descent are rhythmically delayed or antici-pated. The diagonal lines in the voice-leading sketch indicate some of these displacements. Out of all the displacements, the delay of the E in bar 13 causes the greatest disturbance, resulting in an overlap between the second and third groups of the phrase.

Since the middle phrase begins as a transposed version of the first phrase, it is natural to hear the opening phrase as a model upon which to base our ex-pectations. In bar 12 it is the right hand that deviates from the expected course of action and is thus heard as thematically unstable. The right hand's descend-ing run lands on the wrong note (B♯), forcing another attempt in which it gets it right. In terms of the voice leading, the wrong note is part of a chromaticized ascent in an inner voice (B–B♯–C♯). The delay of the C♯ through the B♯ helps alleviate the effects of the middleground parallel octaves between the inner voice and the bass. Example 1.7 reconstructs one possible model from which the surface can be heard to deviate. Although, as an abstraction, Example 1.7 may represent a more normal version of the second eight-bar phrase, in reality the second phrase's position within the form demands some sort of destabilization and greater continuity. By delaying both the E and the inner voice C♯, Bach achieves both.

EXAMPLE 1.7. Recomposition of bars 9–16 of the minuet
from J. S. Bach's French Suite in E Major, BWV 817.

Conflicts between the Dance and the Music

Finally, one must keep in mind that eighteenth-century listeners would most likely be imagining and kinesthetically feeling the dance as danced while the music was being played. In terms of the functional dance, the six-beat-long minuet step always begins on the upbeat with a "rise from a sink." Thus, the last beat of every other bar would be felt, physically, as a pickup into the downbeat of the next bar. This conflict between the dance and the music provides a sense of continuing motion across the phrase boundaries, which always begin on the downbeat.

CONCLUSION

The consistent emphasis on a two-bar hypermeter both in the choreography of the dance and in the music is a defining feature of the *menuet ordinaire,* one that helps distinguish it from other court dances. The compositional challenge of providing a consistent two-bar hypermeter gave composers experience in the manipulation and control of metrical levels above the notated meter. To meet the practical requirement of a two-bar hypermeter, Bach, in the minuets of the French Suites, relied on a type of phrase construction that is more characteristic of Classical works than Baroque: sentence form within a predominantly homophonic texture.[32] Sentence form is found in all but one of the seven minuets, and of the six minuets that employ it, five make use of it in every phrase throughout the piece. The one minuet where it is absent serves as "second minuet," where some sort of contrast was perhaps desired.

The forward-looking approach to phrase construction exhibited in Bach's minuets is very different from the more contrapuntal phrase techniques commonly found in his other works, even within the French Suites. For example, the allemande from the French Suite in D Minor, BWV 812, is characterized by a continuous outpouring of material based upon an opening motive set within a polyphonic texture. The absence of any regularized motivic contrast or repetition, the lack of congruity between the voices, the almost obsessive rhythmic continuity, the polyphonic texture, and the fact that the motivic contents are not bounded within the bars result in a hierarchically shallow, irregular, and thus unpredictable phrase structure. In sharp contrast, the minuets, by enlarging the basic motivic unit from two or three beats to two or three bars and by employing standard patterns of melodic repetition (here sentence form) within a predominantly homophonic texture, have a hierarchically deeper, more regular, and thus more predictable phrase organization. To borrow a term from Erwin Ratz (1973), the phrases contained in Bach's minuets are much more "tightly knit" than those contained in other dances.

I believe the principal motivation for such highly articulated and regulated phrase organization was to project the characteristic two-bar hypermeter of the minuet as danced. That hypermeter is a defining feature of the minuet is in line with what the eighteenth-century ballroom minuet embodied: natural grace, noble simplicity, and restrained elegance. As Magri observes: "The minuet needs hidden control which corresponds to the gracefulness which is sought in it" ([1779] 1988, 187).[33] It is my contention that hypermeter musically provided much of that "hidden control."

This study sheds new light on Edward T. Cone's observations concerning a fundamental shift between late Baroque and Classical styles (1968, 57–78). According to Cone, the primary metrical level for the majority of Baroque music is the beat: "The beat seems to form a pre-existing framework that is independent of the musical events that it controls" (1968, 70). While the beat is still maintained in Classical music, its presence is not "as persistently obvious to our ears . . . for it is the measure, rather than the beat, that is the fundamental unit in Classical music" (Cone 1968, 72). The minuet provided eighteenth-century composers a vehicle to explore higher metrical levels beyond the notated meter and in doing so facilitated and thus may have influenced this shift to some degree. That the minuet was congruent with changing compositional sensibilities was perhaps one reason why it was adopted over other French court dances as the preferred dance movement in multimovement works.

As a final point, Table 1.1 illustrates that Bach's early minuets seldom employ sentence form at the beginning, where it would be most useful in establishing a two-bar hypermeter. The turning point seems to come in a set of three minuets, BWV 841–43, composed around 1720. Karl Geiringer (1966, 270) has suggested that these minuets served as compositional exercises for

Bach's son Wilhelm Friedmann, in which the first was written by Wilhelm Friedmann alone, the second jointly by father and son, and the third by J. S. Bach alone. The first two are of a simpler nature and do not employ sentence form. The third, the longest and most elaborate of the three, employs sentence form from beginning to end. It is as if Bach, in wanting to communicate to his son the temporal essence of the minuet as danced, seized upon the one particular phrase organization that best suited this purpose. And from that point on, the use of sentence form became a standard feature of Bach's minuets.

TABLE I.I. BACH'S SURVIVING MINUETS

BWV	WORK AND INSTRUMENT	DATE	PLACE	NUMBER	OPENING SENTENCE	COMPLETE USE OF SENTENCES
1033	Sonata in C (flute)	?	?	1	no	
				2	no	
822	Suite in G Minor (*Klavier*)	?	?	1	no	
				2	no	
				3	no	
820	Overture in F Major (*Klavier*)	1708–14 or earlier	Weimar	1	no	
				2	no	
1071	Sinfonia in F Major (orchestra) (early version of BWV 1046)	1713	Weimar	1	no	
				2	yes	no
809	English Suite no. 4 in F Major (*Klavier*)	by 1715–25	Weimar/ Leipzig	1	no	
				2	no	
1006	Partita no. 3 in E Major (violin)	1720	Cöthen	1	no	
				2	no	
1007	Suite no. 1 in G Major (cello)	c. 1720	Cöthen	1	no	
				2	no	
1008	Suite no. 2 in D Minor (cello)	c. 1720	Cöthen	1	no	
				2	no	

TABLE I.I. (CONT.) BACH'S SURVIVING MINUETS

BWV	WORK AND INSTRUMENT	DATE	PLACE	NUMBER	OPENING SENTENCE	COMPLETE USE OF SENTENCES
841	Minuet no. 1 (*Klavier*), W. F. Bach Clavier-Büchlein	c. 1720	Cöthen		no	
842	Minuet no. 2 (*Klavier*), W. F. Bach Clavier-Büchlein	c. 1720	Cöthen		no	
843	Minuet no. 3 (*Klavier*), W. F. Bach Clavier-Büchlein	c. 1720	Cöthen		yes	yes
929	Trio in G minor (*Klavier*) W. F. Bach Clavier-Büchlein	1720	Cöthen		yes	no
1066	Suite in C Major (orchestra)	by 1724–25	Cöthen/ Leipzig		no	
812	French Suite no. 1 in D Minor	1722–25	Cöthen/ Leipzig	1	yes	yes
				2	yes	yes
813	French Suite no. 2 in D Minor	1722–25	Cöthen/ Leipzig	1	yes	no
				2	no	
814	French Suite no. 3 in D Minor	1722–25	Cöthen/ Leipzig	1	yes	yes
				2	no	
815a	French Suite no. 4 in E♭ Major	1722–25	Cöthen/ Leipzig		yes	yes
817	French Suite no. 6 in E Major	c. 1724	?Leipzig		yes	yes
818a	Suite in A Minor (*Klavier*)	c. 1722	Cöthen		yes	yes
819	Suite in E♭ Major (*Klavier*)	c. 1722	Cöthen	1	yes	yes
				2	yes	no
825	Partita no. 1 in B♭ Major (*Klavier*)	1731	Leipzig	1	yes	yes
				2	no	

BWV	WORK AND INSTRUMENT	DATE	PLACE	NUMBER	OPENING SENTENCE	COMPLETE USE OF SENTENCES
827	Partita in A Minor (*Klavier*)	1731	Leipzig		yes	yes
828	Partita no. 4 in D Major (*Klavier*)	1731	Leipzig		no	
1069	Suite in D Major (orchestra)	c. 1729	Cöthen/ Leipzig	1	no	
				2	yes	no
1067	Suite in B Minor (orchestra)	c. 1738–39	Leipzig		yes	yes

Source: The chronological and geographical listing of Bach's minuets given here is based on a listing given in Little and Jenne (1991, 207–208).

2nd

Mozart in the Ballroom: Minuet-Trio Contrast and the Aristocracy in Self-Portrait

❈

Madame Mozart told me that great as his genius was, he was an enthusiast for dancing, and often said that his taste lay in that art rather than music.

MICHAEL KELLY

In the first half of the eighteenth century, minuets, and especially danced minuets, were not typically paired with second minuets in a *da capo* ABA form.[1] When they were, there was no standard practice as to the type or degree of contrast between the two minuets. It was not until the second half of the eighteenth century that marked contrast between first minuets and second minuets – by now commonly called "trios" – became standard practice (see Russell 1983, 225). And it was Viennese composers who were most fond of this form of association. The type of contrast was confined within a rather narrow and predictable range: minuets were loud, employed the full orchestra, and tended to use walking bass lines predominantly in quarter-note motion; trios were soft, employed a reduced orchestra, and were characterized by a simpler texture with fewer bass notes. One might imagine that this contrast was in some sense designed to fit the minuet's function as dance music for social consumption. This chapter explores the purpose and nature of the contrast, focusing on Mozart's orchestral minuets written for the ballroom.[2]

The chapter is divided into four parts. In part 1, which builds on material from the previous chapter, I determine whether or not there is any choreographic basis for the sharp musical contrast that defines Viennese minuets and trios. In part 2 I explore the aesthetics of the dance and the mental attitudes of minuet dancers as described and depicted by contemporary writers and artists. In the third part I examine the types of musical textures and rhythms that Mozart uses in his trios and how they correlate to the physical motions of the dancers. I conclude by considering how the cultural associations of the minuet and the architecture of dancing spaces may have played a role in shaping specific qualities of the minuet-trio contrast.

THE RELATIONSHIP BETWEEN CHOREOGRAPHY AND MUSIC

The minuet was the last couple dance (*danse à deux*) to emerge from the French court of Louis XIV. While other French court dances fell from use in the eighteenth-century ballroom, the minuet continued to be danced until the beginning of the nineteenth century.[3] Its popularity, however, began to decline after 1750. During the second half of the eighteenth century, minuets would be retained as the opening ceremonial dance of balls, after which would commence the more energetic and popular contredanse. Although less complex in its choreography than other court dances, the minuet was fiendishly difficult to master and was considered the true test of aristocratic behavior. "The greatest difficulty in performing the minuet," observes Wendy Hilton, "impressively lies in its apparent simplicity," in which "the ultimate aim was to appear supremely natural" (Allanbrook and Hilton 1992, 144). As Richard Leppert explains, this naturalized physical attitude "involved precise control over the entire body, from the carriage and turn of the head to the position of the arms, wrists, hands, legs and feet" (1988, 89). The technique thus required to dance the minuet effortlessly was considerable and speaks to the strong choreographic connection of French court dancing to French court ballet.

In exploring the relationship between the minuet as danced and the music that accompanied it, one thing is certain: there is no choreographic basis for the sharp, sectional musical contrast between minuets and trios that appears after midcentury. As I discussed in chapter 1, the evidence strongly suggests that experienced dancers at social balls outside of the court did not attempt to coordinate their figures to the music's melodic organization. One of the factors that prevented dance-music congruence was that there was no standardization of phrase lengths; thus, only in the unlikely case that dancers knew beforehand what music would be played could they coordinate their figures to the music. But, as is made clear by dancing master Kellom Tomlinson, lockstep congruence between the minuet music's melodic organization and the minuet's choreography was not an aesthetic aim of a minuet performance. What distinguished a remarkable minuet dancer from a less inspired one was a dancer's ability to improvise. Tasteful flourishes could alter the internal lengths of the individual figures, thereby creating noncongruence (or reestablishing congruence, as the case may be) between the dance and the music. Moreover, the minuet's principal figure – the S reversed – could be repeated at will, thus altering the dance's large-scale proportions. Additionally, the length of the opening reverences was at the discretion of the dancers. If, for example, the person presiding over the ball was of very high rank, the reverences would be more elaborate and thus take more time. Moreover, after the completion of the opening reverences the dancers were not obligated to wait for the opening of the next phrase to begin their dance.

Once the basic components of the *menuet ordinaire* were standardized at the beginning of the eighteenth century, its choreography remained remarkably consistent throughout the eighteenth century, with very little substantive changes. Thus, the dramatic change in musical style after midcentury does not correspond to a shift in choreographic style. The minuet as a dance is characterized by a controlled consistency and homogeneity of movement throughout the dance, and, while there are sectional divisions between the succession of the minuet's figures, there is no overall tripartite organization. As I suggested in chapter 1, congruence between the music and the dance operates on a metrical rather than a melodic basis. All that dancers required from the music were a proper tempo, audibility, and a clear and consistent two-bar hypermeter. To be "in time" with the music, dancers coordinated their two-bar minuet steps with the music's two-bar hypermeter.

MOZART'S BALLROOM MINUETS AND THE
AESTHETICS OF THE MINUET AS DANCED

As a child prodigy, Mozart dazzled aristocratic audiences with his technical virtuosity. But Mozart was also groomed by his father to charm audiences with his aristocratic appearance and refined manners, for part of the fascination with child prodigies in Mozart's time was the uncanny juxtaposition of child appearance and adult behavior. By an early age Mozart was fluent in several languages; he had had instruction in horseback riding and fencing; he had refined and expensive tastes in clothing; and he was passionate about dancing. According to his wife, Constanze, he was especially skilled at dancing the minuet.[4]

Table 2.1 provides a list of all surviving orchestral dances Mozart composed for the ballroom. Several observations can be made: first, by a large margin, minuets outnumber all other dances; second, Mozart turned his creative energy toward the composition of dance music during carnival season (the Viennese celebrated carnival from 7 January to Ash Wednesday); and third, Mozart only began composing the newer spinning dances, the *Deutscher* and the *Ländler*, during the last four years of his life. This last point will have bearing on the oft-cited observation that Mozart frequently uses *Ländler* elements in the trio sections of his minuets, a point I shall return to later.

TABLE 2.1. MOZART'S ORCHESTRAL DANCES FOR THE BALLROOM

SALZBURG DANCES (C. 1768–78)

1768	In a "directory of everything this 12-year-old boy composed since he was 7 years old," Leopold Mozart lists "many minuets with all kinds of instruments."					
1769	26 January	Salzburg	7	Minuets	oom-pah-pah	K. 65a
1770	13 or 14 April	Rome	1	Contredanse		K. 123
1770	August	Bologna	1	Minuet in E♭ Major (without trio)		K. 122
1770	autumn	Salzburg	6	Minuets	oom-pah-pah	K. 104
1771–72		Salzburg	6	Minuets	oom-pah-pah	K. 105
1771–72		Salzburg	6	Minuets	oom-pah-pah	K. 61h
1772	early summer	Salzburg	19	Minuets	oom-pah-pah	K. 103
1772	June	Salzburg	6	Minuets	oom-pah-pah	K. 164
1773	December	Salzburg	16	Minuets	oom-pah-pah	K. 176

TABLE 2.I. (CONT.) MOZART'S ORCHESTRAL DANCES FOR THE BALLROOM

SALZBURG DANCES (C. 1768–78)

1776	Carnival	Salzburg	4	Contredanses		K. 101
1777	Carnival	Salzburg	4	Contredanses		K. 267
1778		Salzburg	8	Minuets	oom-pah-pah	K. 315a

EARLY VIENNESE DANCES (1782–87)

1782?		Vienna?	3	Minuets (without trios)		K. 363
1784		Vienna	6	Minuets		K. 461
1784	January	Vienna	6	Contredanses		K. 462
1784	January	Vienna	2	Quadrilles		K. 463
1787	6 February	Prague	6	*Deutsche* with Coda		K. 509

REDOUTENSAAL DANCES (1788–91)

1788	14 January	Vienna	1	Contredanse		K. 534
1788	23 January	Vienna	1	Contredanse		K. 535
1788	27 January, 6 December	Vienna	12	*Deutsche* with Coda	oom-pah-pah	K. 536 and K. 567
1788	24 December	Vienna	12	Minuets	oom-pah-pah	K. 568
1789	21 February	Vienna	6	*Deutsche* with Coda	oom-pah-pah	K. 571
1789	December	Vienna	12	Minuets	oom-pah-pah	K. 585
1789	December	Vienna	12	*Deutsche* with Coda	oom-pah-pah	K. 586
1789	December	Vienna	1	Contredanse		K. 587
1791	23 January, 5, 12 February	Vienna	12	Minuets	oom-pah-pah	K. 599, 601, and 604
1791	January 29, February 5, 12	Vienna	12	*Deutsche* with Coda	oom-pah-pah	K. 600, 602, and 605
1791	5 February	Vienna	2	Contredanses		K. 603
1791	28 February		6	*Ländler* Dances	oom-pah-pah	K. 606
1791	28 February	Vienna	1	Contredanse		K. 607
1791		Vienna	5	Contredanses		K. 609
1791	6 March	Vienna	1	Contredanse		K. 610

Overall total: 120 minuets, 48 *Deutsche*, 27 contredanses, 6 *Ländler*, and 2 quadrilles

Although contrast between minuets and trios is found in all of Mozart's danced minuets, from his earliest to his last, it is most prominent in his late minuets written for the Imperial Ballrooms (Redoutensäle) of Vienna.[5] As a preliminary example, I turn to the third minuet of Mozart's K. 599, written for the carnival season of 1791 (Example 2.1). Both the minuet and the trio are organized as simple binary forms (A:‖:B) symmetrically divided into two eight-bar phrases, a characteristic shared by almost all of Mozart's Viennese minuets and trios.[6] More specifically, the first part of the minuet is in sentence form (2 + 2 + 4) and ends with a half cadence in the tonic key; the beginning of the second part introduces four bars of new material over a dominant pedal; and the final four bars are a varied restatement of bars 5–8, which comprises the continuation part of the opening sentence. This type of thematic design, in which the cadential segment of the first part is used to end the second part, is often referred to as "balanced binary," which is a subcategory of simple binary form. The trio is similarly organized, although the continuation part of the first section is articulated with a perfect authentic cadence in the tonic key. When bars 5–8 return at the end of the second part, Mozart varies the bass line and second violin part in order to provide a stronger sense of closure (the cadential V is now preceded by a ii^6, whereas in bar 8 it was preceded by a I^6).

The music of the opening minuet is loud, forceful, and majestic, evoking a sense of monumental grandeur through several means: the dynamic marking is *forte* throughout; the violins' melodies are characterized by arpeggiation, often involving very large leaps; there is prominent use of flourishes, trills, and march rhythms; the harmonic language is entirely diatonic and in the major mode; and the texture is predominantly homophonic. This is generic aristocratic music that speaks of social, historical, and political power and authority. It is also music that today is most often thought of as exemplary of Viennese minuet music of the late eighteenth century.

These grandiose Redoutensäle minuets and others like them ironically subverted the essence of what the minuet as a dance was intended to represent and display. For Jean-Jacques Rousseau, the minuet's core character is "noble and elegant simplicity" (1751–72, 10:346). C. J. von Feldtenstein observed in 1767 that the minuet "appears to have been invented by the Graces themselves" and provides "the occasion for displaying everything beautiful and charming in nature which a body is capable of employing."[7] Johann Georg Sulzer describes the minuet as possessing an affect of "noble and pleasing propriety, but joined with simplicity."[8] For Giovanni Andrea Battista Gallini,

EXAMPLE 2.1. (*above and facing*) Mozart's third minuet from K. 599.

the chief aim of the minuet is to "bring forth the natural graces, and not to smother them with the appearance of study and art" ([1762] 1967, 146). The simplicity of nature, he argues, is "the great fountainhead of all the graces; from which they flow spontaneous, when unchecked by affection, which at once poisons and dries them up" (Gallini [1762] 1967, 167). The appearance of too much study, it was thought, detracted from the natural beauty and grace of the dancers. As a warning, Gallini cites the proverb: "No gentleman can be said to dance well, who dances like a dancing-master" ([1762] 1967, 169–70). Writing in 1779, Gennaro Magri summarizes the attributes of a good minuet performance: "The Minuet needs hidden control which corresponds to the gracefulness which is sought in it. It needs a languid eye, a smiling mouth, splendid body, unaffected hands, and ambitious feet" ([1779] 1988, 187).

Thus, according to eighteenth-century commentators on the dance, the two most important aesthetic attributes of the minuet are natural grace and noble simplicity.[9] These two qualities were joined together in a physical and mental attitude of self-assured nonchalance – what was often referred to in dancing manuals as "complaisance."[10] For John Weaver, complaisance entails an "artful carelessness, as if [dancing] were a natural emotion, without a too curious and painful practicing. . . . To dance too exquisitely is, I must own, too laborious a Vanity."[11] Attitudes, postures, and gestures of constraint were morally based and motivated by the highly valued virtues of modesty, forbearance, self-control, and a disdain for revealing one's inner feelings. When mastered, the attitude of complaisance created an aura of genteel refinement and unflappable inner calm.

This attitude of behavior had long been a distinguishing feature of aristocratic conduct. In his 1528 *Il libro del cortegiano*, Baldassare Castiglione offers the reader a "universal rule which seems to apply more than any other in all human actions or words: namely, to steer away from affections at all costs,

EXAMPLE 2.2. Voice-leading sketch of the third trio,
K. 599, bars 1–8.

as if it were a rough and dangerous reef, and . . . to practice in all things a
certain nonchalance which conceals all artistry and makes whatever one says
or does seem uncontrived and effortless. . . . Intense application and skill robs
everything of grace" ([1528] 1976, 67). In observing the ill effects of an overly
affected dancer, Castiglione cautions the reader that nonchalance can be carried too far. "We clearly see him making every effort to show that he takes
no thought of what he is about, which means he is taking too much thought."
This overly careless attitude "is contrary to that pure and charming simplicity
which is so appealing to us all" ([1528] 1976, 68). Complaisance in the physical
realm is characterized by suave and relaxed body motions, the look of floating
weightlessness, and controlled vitality. Dancing masters sharply criticized any
signs of exuberance, excess of body motions, gestures of strength, and shows
of virtuosity. The tranquil center of all movement was the torso, which was at
all times to remain relatively still and upright.

Returning to Example 2.1, one sees how well the music of the trio section
reflects the aesthetics of the minuet as danced. Framed within the majestic
music of the minuet, the music of the trio is soft, placid, and effortless. The
simple, cantabile melody is characterized by gentle twists and turns and by
artful variation. The opening descending two-bar motive is answered by
an ascending variation – essentially, a figurated tonal inversion. Winds are
added in the restatement of bars 1–2 in bars 5–6. The final two bars of the
eight-bar phrase are an expanded variation of the descending fifths of bars 2
and 6. As the voice-leading sketch given in Example 2.2 illustrates, the surface
intricacies of the melody are imbued with a sense of inner composure and
continuity by an evenly paced serpentine line, G–F–Eb–F–G–F–Eb. In bar
7 the inner-voice pedal Bb is registrally transferred to the upper voice, where
it then gently floats down a figurated fifth onto the cadential tonic.

Supporting the melody, a murmuring accompanimental pattern provides rhythmic regularity and continuity, elegant simplicity, and a refined

sense of control. Notice how all the voices of the accompaniment circumscribe gently winding contours. Especially noteworthy in this trio is Mozart's innovative orchestration. The doubling of the melody in the first four bars by the horn and first violins imbues the melody with a sense of sonic depth and warmth. In the second reprise, the woodwinds expand the basic two-bar motive of the opening phrase into a four-bar curvaceous flourish in parallel thirds. This is simple yet sophisticated music – what I recognize as "artful simplicity" in opposition to "artless simplicity," which is, as we shall see, a defining characteristic of Mozart's *Deutsche* and *Ländler*. And finally, the melody is comprised of clearly demarcated two-bar groups. This consistent melodic grouping, together with the harmonic progression in which the tonic is stated in every other bar, firmly establishes the two-bar hypermeter needed by the dancers.

The placidity and ease of the trio is accentuated by the overt physicality of the minuet. Much of the perceived power and strength of the minuet stem from the listener's mimetic motor response in imagining or watching the performers (or imagining themselves) producing the music. In comparison to the music of the trio, the minuet music requires a great deal more physical exertion to perform: the *forte* dynamics demand more air pressure from the winds and more bow pressure from the strings; the violins' double-stops are technically difficult to perform and require greater bow speed; the staccato articulation in the violins requires a jerky, stop-and-go bow arm motion; and finally, the large leaps require greater arm speed and greater shoulder movement. Physical exertion is at its most extreme in the final four bars, which are a variation of bars 5–8. After arriving on the high C in bar 14, the melody plunges to the lowest range of the violin. The leap from the high C to the low A♭ not only necessitates a shift in hand position from third position to first position but also involves crossing over two strings. In the final gesture, the violin returns to the upper register and concludes with two triple-stops, which in performance would be played with two successive down-bows.

Minuet and Nature

Wrapped up with the image of the minuet dance as an embodiment of noble simplicity and natural grace was the commonly accepted notion that the minuet was a descendent of a French peasant dance, the *branle de Poitou*.[12] Michael Praetorius in his *Terpsichore* was perhaps the first to cite a folk source for the minuet ([1612] 1971, Bd. 15:x). The folk connection quickly gained widespread acceptance and was repeated in the eighteenth-century writings of Sébastien de Brossard ([1740] 1966, 51), Jean-Jacques Rousseau (1751–72, 10:346), and Charles Compan ([1787] 1974, 231), among others. Writing in the time of Mozart, Gennaro Magri reports that the minuet "is of Rustic origin. It was born among the Peasants of Anjou, a province of France. They danced it artlessly, but with a natural simplicity, just as the Rustics of today dance the regional and national dances. Hence little by little it was improved and under Louis the Great met with approbation and a happy fate: it was put into better order and, by degrees, perfected, it came to occupy the principal place among Ballroom Dances" ([1779] 1988, 179).

Conceptually, the minuet, by imitating the natural movements of an imagined ancient peasant dance, was tied to an arcadian image of nature. Eighteenth-century dance commentators were also engaged in the construction of a type of "cultural rescue" myth: the peasant class was incapable of perfecting their own rustic dance, and it was only with the intercession of dancing masters and high culture that the artless simplicity of the peasant minuet could become transformed into the artful simplicity of the aristocratic minuet. The supposed folk origins of the minuet shaped not only its image as the embodiment of natural grace but also its value as an artistic work. A central doctrine of eighteenth-century Enlightenment aesthetics is that art is defined and justified as the imitation of the beautiful in nature. The rooting of the minuet in rustic peasant culture (in other words, nature) thus provided aesthetic justification for the minuet as an art form. According to dancing masters, the signal achievement in the development of the minuet and in its successful performance on the ballroom dance floor was the seamless and balanced combination of art and nature. As Gallini cautions, "nature does not refuse cultivation, but she will not bear being forced" ([1762] 1967, 168).

The associations of the minuet with grace and simplicity and with the God-given beauty of nature are found in eighteenth-century visual depictions of minuet dancing. It was a common ploy for artists and engravers to situate minuet dancers outdoors in the midst of a beautiful pastoral setting. Figure 2.1 presents perhaps the best-known eighteenth-century pastoral idealization of the minuet. In this painting, the French Rubenist painter Antoine Watteau (1684–1721), famous for his scenes of elegant society, beautifully balances the portrayal of aristocratic power and wealth with the graceful ease and simplic-

FIGURE 2.1. Antoine Watteau's painting *Les plaisirs du bal* (1715–17). *By kind permission of the Trustees of Dulwich Picture Gallery.*

ity of noble behavior. A group of young courtiers are casually assembled in an architecturally stunning courtyard complete with massive columns and classical statues. With a bust of Zeus presiding high above, a young couple dances a minuet against the backdrop of nature. The gracefully arching branches of the trees and the gentle flow of a water fountain form a perfect complement to the natural(ized) movement of the dancers. In this painting and others like it, the positioning of minuet dancers in the presence of nature does not denote a lower, more rustic style but rather accentuates and elevates the minuet's graceful character and natural expression.[13]

So how does one reconcile the aesthetic image of the minuet as danced – drawn from contemporary dance treatises, dictionaries, encyclopedias, and artwork – with the actual music? I propose that in the Viennese ballroom during the second half of the eighteenth century, there emerged two very different musical interpretations of the minuet dance (though both versions, as we shall see, maintain and share an essential feature of functional minuets: a clearly emphasized two-bar hypermeter). The music of the minuet depicts the political, social, and historical power and authority of the minuet dance and of the aristocratic participants. The music of the trio embodies the natural grace and noble simplicity exhibited by the dancers on the ballroom dance floor.

In Watteau's painting, the monumental architecture provides a frame that allows the interior space to resonate with the quiet grandeur of timeless power. Indeed, the past seems to come to life in the form of female statues who gaze down upon the activities of the courtiers. Far above, overlooking all, Zeus remains supremely aloof and uninterested. The grand architectural frame, with its reference to Greek mythology, brings into focus the dynamic contrast between the opposing aesthetic forces of power and grace as well as the perceived relationship between past and present. (The beauty of the minuet dancers would have been framed not only by the architecture but also by an ornately carved Rococo picture frame.)[14] In much the same way, the powerful music of the minuet, with its references to an older style of composition (walking bass line) and to the topic of the military (dotted rhythms of the march, fanfares, frequent use of the trumpet, horn, and timpani), frames the graceful music of the trio, which with its more contemporary *galant* style of accompaniment focuses on the present tense of the dancers on the ballroom floor.

Many of Mozart's ballroom minuets and trios fall within the oppositional categories of power and grace – but not all of them. In several of Mozart's early minuet trios, for example, musical contrast between the two is not particularly well defined. Another more common situation involves the mixing of styles within an individual movement. Many of Mozart's minuet movements, for example, alternate back and forth at the phrase level between the expressions of power and grace. While this is common with minuet movements, rarely does Mozart mix styles within a trio movement, although exceptions may be noted, as I shall explain below.

Mid-Eighteenth-Century Aesthetic Notions of Beauty

The aesthetic qualities that contemporary writers ascribe to the minuet dance are also found in the writings of eighteenth-century commentators who sought to define universal qualities or impressions of the beautiful. The painter and engraver William Hogarth, in his 1753 treatise *The Analysis of Beauty*, defined beauty in the empirical terms of the Enlightenment. Operating from the premise of the objective existence of beauty, Hogarth believed that all things beautiful possessed similar traits that could be observed and analyzed. For Hogarth, all questions about beauty are ultimately questions about lines, since all objects are composed of them. The most beautiful lines, the ones that exhibit and optimize classical qualities of beauty, are those that contain gentle, undulating curves. Lines that are too angular or circular result in expression ranging from barbaric crudeness to humor. Conversely, the "serpentine line," as Hogarth calls it, is an essential quality of all that is beautiful. In the course of his treatise, he proceeds to trace the appearance of serpentine lines from nature, as exemplified by the female body, to classical sculpture and painting, to the ordinary and mundane (e.g., chair legs, candlesticks, and clothing).

Hogarth identifies two types of serpentine lines: for serpentine lines in two-dimensional space, he uses the term "line of beauty," while for those in three-dimensional space, he uses the term "line of grace." Beauty extended into the realm of physical motion thus results in grace, which, as Hogarth argues, is best exemplified by the dance. "The perfection of all dancing," for Hogarth, is the minuet, because it displays "the greatest variety of movements in serpentine lines imaginable" ([1753] 1997, 109–10).[15] As can be seen in Kellom Tomlinson's diagram of minuet figures previously shown in Figure 1.1, minuet dancers circumscribe a series of ever-winding serpentine paths on the ballroom dance floor. Hogarth makes special mention of the most characteristic figure of the minuet, the S reversed, which is the purest representation of the serpentine line ([1753] 1997, 109). He also finds the serpentine line in the minuet's dance step, the *pas de menuet*: "The ordinary undulating motion of the body in common walking (as may be plainly seen by the waving line, which the shadow [of] a man's head makes against a wall as he is walking between it and the afternoon sun) is augmented in dancing into a larger quantity of *waving* by means of the minuet-step, which is so contrived as to raise the body by gentle degrees somewhat higher than ordinary, and sink it again in the same manner lower in the going on of the dance" (Hogarth [1753] 1997, 109). Finally, Hogarth finds the line of grace in the "turns of the head and the twist of the body in passing each other, as also gentle bowing and presenting hands" ([1753] 1997, 110). In this way, Hogarth observes these lines of grace within several dimensions of the minuet as danced: in the winding paths of the figures, in

FIGURE 2.2. Print No. 2 from William Hogarth's *Analysis of Beauty* (1753).
*Reproduced with the permission of Rare Books and Manuscripts, Special
Collections Library, the Pennsylvania State University Libraries.*

the undulating motions of the steps, and in the various movements of the
dancer's hands and head.

Figure 2.2 presents Hogarth's second of two prints contained in his *Analysis of Beauty*. Hogarth contrasts the physical expression of beauty (grace), as
depicted by the first couple on the left dancing the minuet, with the expression
of the ridiculous and the grotesque, as depicted by the rest of the crowd, who
are engaged in a rowdy country dance. Notice the languid eyes of the minuet
dancers, their serene countenances, the gentle twists of their heads, the turning out of the gentleman's legs, and, perhaps most striking when compared to
the rest of the dancers, the balanced and graceful positioning of their arms
and hands. Hogarth highlights the eminence of the minuet couple not only by
the graceful and controlled manner of their movement but also by their clothing (he wears a sash), the artistic lighting, which brightly illuminates them,
their position in the room in relation to the musicians, and their position in

the print in relation to us, the viewer. In shorthand notation, Hogarth, in the upper left-hand corner (his Figure 71), analyzes the entire line of dancers, from left to right.

Four years later, in 1757, Edmund Burke, in his widely influential treatise *A Philosophical Enquiry into the Origins of Our Ideas of the Sublime and Beautiful*, provides a more detailed account of beauty, which he defines in opposition to the sublime. In contrast to the objectivist approach, in which beauty is defined as a self-subsistent entity, Burke defines it largely in terms of its emotional effects upon the perceiver. Beauty, for Burke, elicits the softer virtues such as easiness of temper, compassion, and kindness, while the sublime excites stronger emotions such as admiration, fear, joy, sadness, and awe.

Burke's definition of grace resonates both with Hogarth's conception of the minuet as beautiful and with dancing masters' descriptions of proper minuet dancing:

> Gracefulness is an idea belonging to *posture* and *motion*. In both [of] these, to be graceful, it is requisite that there be no appearance of difficulty; there is required a small inflection of the body; and a composure of its parts, in such a manner, as not to encumber each other, nor appear divided by sharp and sudden angles. In this ease, this roundness, this delicacy of attitude and motion, it is all that the magic of grace consists, and what is called its *je ne sais quoi*. ([1757] 1958, 119)

In the representation of beauty, all the arts were believed to share common aesthetic principles and attributes.[16] For Hogarth, it is the ever-present serpentine line tempered with fitness, composed variety, simplicity, and intricacy. For Burke, attributes of beauty common to all art, including music, are smallness, softness, delicacy, winding surfaces, unbroken continuities, and easy and gradual gradations. Speaking specifically of music, Burke observes that loudness and strength of sounds are not qualities of beautiful sounds, nor are quick transitions from one bar to another or any sudden or surprising event. Such sounds will excite "mirth, or other sudden and tumultuous passions; but not that sinking, that melting, that languor, which is the characteristical effect of the beautiful" (Burke [1757] 1958, 122–23).

Thus, the aesthetics of the minuet as danced were closely tied to eighteenth-century notions of beauty, grace, and nature. The attributes of these aesthetic categories, I would suggest, find their corollary in the music of Mozart's ballroom trios.

TABLE 2.2. ATTRIBUTES OF NATURAL GRACE AS EXEMPLIFIED BY THE MINUET

simplicity (tempered with variety)

tranquility

small inflections of the body

composure of the body

delicacy of attitude and motion

roundness of motion

weightlessness

restraint and hidden control

effortlessness – no appearance of difficulty, pretension, study, art, or affectation

physical and mental attitude of complaisance (artful carelessness)

Hogarth's line of grace (serpentine line)

    gentle, undulating curves

    no sharp or sudden angles

    unbroken continuity

MOZART'S BALLROOM TRIOS

Mozart's consummate skill as a dancer allowed him, to a degree far greater than Haydn and Beethoven, to compose music that translated the character and movement of the dance into musical motion, thus making his trio music beautiful yet useful for dancing. This correspondence of qualities of attitude, gesture, and motion between dance and music is a basic tenet of functional dance music. Indeed, as Herbert Dieckmann has noted (1973–74, 201), the degree of utility – that is, the suitability and aptness of the music to the dance – was considered an important aspect of its beauty in eighteenth-century aesthetics. In his treatise *Les beaux-arts réduits à un même principe*, Charles Batteux observes that "if the dance is to be pre-eminent[,] the music must not be distractingly brilliant. It should merely hold out a helping hand in order to bar with greater precision the character and movement of the dance" ([1746] 1981, 55).

Table 2.2 provides a summary of the attributes of grace referred to in the previous discussion. For Hogarth, dancing masters, and other commentators, the minuet reflected, more than any other social dance of the time, the highest expression of grace. In support of the notion that it is the music of Mozart's trios (rather than his minuets) that reflects the aesthetics of the dance and the quality of motion and attitude exhibited by the dancers, this section takes a closer look at the types of musical motion and texture that characterize Mozart's trios.

Rhythmic Ease

Mozart effectively translates several of the aesthetic attributes of grace – simplicity, the appearance of ease, and a delicacy and roundness of motion – into a well-developed sense of what I shall call "rhythmic ease."[17] In general, rhythmic ease is the result of compositional techniques that provide continuity, transparency, and a sense of musical lightness. Much of Mozart's rhythmic ease derives from his deployment of musical textures. Hence, whereas Mozart's minuets typically employ an older-style figurated chorale texture with a walking bass line in predominantly quarter-note motion, his trios most often employ a more modern, *galant*-style melody and accompaniment texture with a slower harmonic rhythm, fewer bass notes, and more rests. The outcome is a texture that is simpler, more transparent, and less bottom-heavy.

Murmuring Accompaniments

A large percentage of Mozart's trio melodies are supported by murmuring accompaniments.[18] Murmuring figures, almost always played by the violins, are the most characteristic feature of the accompaniment's upper voices. The murmuring upper voices will either repeat the same pitches or, more commonly, perform some sort of oscillating pattern.[19] Murmuring accompaniments also feature a sparse bass line that typically articulates only the downbeats of each bar. The bass notes may be held for three beats or, as in the trio shown in Example 2.1, for one beat followed by a two-beat rest. The constant stream of eighth notes provides the trio with uninterrupted continuity, while the contour of the motion circumscribes the gentle, undulating curves of the serpentine line. The sparse bass line lightens the texture and provides transparency, which enables the listener to hear more readily both inside and through the texture.

Much of the perceived stability and ease of a murmuring accompaniment is a result of its repetitive and thus predictable nature. As a result, it takes less effort on the part of the listener to discern the metrical organization, thereby allowing one to reflect more readily on other aspects of the music.

EXAMPLE 2.3. The second minuet and trio from his collection of six minuets, K. 461.

Another factor contributing to the sense of rhythmic ease is a metrical shift in the primary beat level that occurs between the minuet and trio. The minuet's characteristic walking bass line and dotted-eighth/sixteenth rhythms focus the listener's attention on the metrical level of the quarter-note beat. And while other metrical levels are active, including a two-bar hypermeter, it is the primacy of the quarter-note level that distinguishes the music of the minuet rhythmically from that of the trio and contributes to a sense of metrical weight and stately ploddingness. As Edward Cone (1968, 66) has observed, the primacy of the quarter-note beat is a defining feature of much Baroque music. This metrical characteristic and the walking bass line are examples of a continuing presence of Baroque compositional practices within the evolving tradition of minuet music. These older compositional practices give the minuet a sense of historical weight and authority. In the murmuring accompaniment of the trio, the walking bass line gives way to a supportive bass line marking off downbeats and chord changes. This newer, *galant*-style accompaniment pattern shifts the metrical focus from the quarter note to the bar, which consequently provides the music with a slower, more leisurely (i.e., nonchalant) pace.

For an example of the contrast provided by a murmuring accompaniment, consider the second minuet and trio of K. 461 (Example 2.3). Composed in early 1784, this collection of six minuets was Mozart's first minuet set written for the Viennese ballroom. The second minuet opens with a dramatic downward leap in the violins that, in violation of standard eighteenth-century rules of melodic writing, continues in the same direction after the leap, eventually bottoming out on the lowest note of the violins (G). The remaining part of the eight-bar melody gradually arpeggiates back up to the original register before falling to a cadence on the dominant. This is a strong, forceful melody marked by effort and self-determination. A conventional walking bass line supports the melody and focuses the listener's attention on the metrical level of the quarter note. The second half begins with a variation of the opening four bars; however, this time the melody is given to the lower voices, which increases the minuet's sense of gravity and weight.

In clear contrast, the trio inhabits an interior space of effortless beauty. The murmuring second violins gently animate the texture, while the sparse bass line and the legato slurs in the second violins shift the focus of the listener from the metrical level of the quarter note to the dotted half note. A simple but elegant eight-bar melody, composed of clear two-bar groups, winds its way in a leisurely manner from $\hat{5}$ down to $\hat{1}$. The second four bars of the melody are a rhythmic variation of the first four bars. Notice how in bar 5 Mozart resists restating the exact rhythms of bar 1 (e.g., the melody could have moved to B♭ on the third beat of bar 5). Typically, a varied restatement will elaborate upon its model in a way that provides more content and activity. Here, Mozart does the reverse. He simplifies an already straightforward rhythmic motive by sustaining the G for the entire bar. This slight adjustment not only gives the melody a sense of melancholy restraint but also allows the entrance of the bass, which now assumes a melodic role, to be heard more clearly. Mozart elaborates bar 6 rhythmically, which together with the fluid bass line provides a gentle push to the cadence.

The two-bar motive that begins the second reprise of the trio is a variation of the trio's opening two-bar motive. In the varied restatement, the low B♭ on the downbeat of bar 9 delays the first melodic note D. Importantly, one does not hear the succession of these two notes (B♭–D) as a melodic leap, as one does the first two notes of the minuet. Rather, the two pitches belong to different strands of the texture. The opening B♭ reinforces and doubles the pedal B♭ of the second violin part, whose voice is given greater emphasis by the staccato markings on the downbeats of bars 9 and 11. The melody's *fp* on the second beat weakens any sense of melodic connection between the two pitches. In the final four bars, Mozart enlivens the varied restatement of the opening melody with chromaticism (notice the unexpected upward turn from B♮ to C in bar 14) and with staccato articulation in the accompanying second violins.

Such artful variation of simple melodic material is, as we have seen in this trio and in the one previously shown in Example 2.1, a defining feature of Mozart's ballroom trios. The tasteful variation of two-bar motives corresponds especially well to the minuet as danced. Commenting on the minuet's potential for variation, Wendy Hilton observes that "the absolutely unique characteristic of the menuet among the other *danses à deux* is its flexibility" (1997, 292). The "plain straight steps" of the two-bar *pas de menuet* may be performed forward, backward, and sideways to the left or right (Tomlinson [1735] 1970, 103). Furthermore, it was considered in good taste to add to the *pas de menuet* flourishes and steps of embellishment, the choice of which would have been governed by current fashion. Kellom Tomlinson ([1735] 1970, 103–105, 113–23, 139–41), for example, discusses at length four possible embellishments of the basic minuet step.[20] And finally, extemporized movements of the dancer's arms and hands, which might include gestures involving fans and hats, provided further means of variation. Tomlinson summarizes the varied and improvisatory nature of the minuet:

> [The minuet] is no more than a voluntary or extemporary Piece of Performance. . . . The said *Dance* and its Steps, as I have already observed, altogether depend on Fancy, and are in their Performance various and uncertain; for it is left to the Pleasure of everyone to perform them in the Order here set down, in any better Method of their own, or without any [embellished] Steps. Indeed, it must be confessed that the [embellished] Steps well performed in a *Minuet* are great *Ornaments* to that *Dance*, in filling it with Variety. ([1735] 1970, 137, 141)

In several trios Mozart highlights the murmuring quality of the accompaniments by omitting a functional bass altogether. The accompaniment of the trio from the fourth minuet of K. 461, shown in Example 2.4, is almost entirely based on the murmuring line played in unison in the violins, cello, and bass. At the onset, the listener's focus is on the woodwinds' melody, which, in the first four bars, evokes the pastoral topic of the horn call. In bar 3, however, Mozart unleashes the murmurs, which rise up to a high point in bars 4–5 and then recede to the cadence. Both the melody and the murmuring accompaniment circumscribe large, eight-bar arches beginning and ending with $\hat{1}$. Each line, however, reaches its structural apex at a different time: as shown in the following voice-leading sketch (Example 2.5), the melody reaches its high point in bar 3; the accompaniment's serpentine line crests two bars later in bar 5. The continuous eighth notes and the arrival of the accompaniment's high point in bar 5 together undercut the sense of melodic caesura in bar 4, thereby providing continuity across the melody's two four-bar segments. Furthermore, as the voice leading illustrates, there is no cadence and hence no strong tonal articulation between bars 4 and 5. Such fluidity and continuity of musical motion is a defining feature of Mozart's trios and is a characteristic that sets them apart from his minuets.

Oom-pah-pah

The trio from the eighth minuet of K. 176, shown in Example 2.6, dates from December 1773. Mozart's Salzburg minuets generally share the same characteristics as those he composed for Vienna – his minuets are loud and forceful and his trios simple and graceful. As is to be expected, the overall quality of these early works is not as refined or as inventive as his Viennese dances, nor is

EXAMPLE 2.4. The trio from the fourth minuet of Mozart's K. 461.

EXAMPLE 2.5. Voice-leading sketch of the opening
phrase of the trio from the fourth minuet of K. 461.

the contrast in aesthetic forces of power and grace as sharply defined. Nevertheless, the qualities of motion found in his early minuets support the notion
that it is the trios that reflect the aesthetics of the minuet as danced – noble
simplicity and natural grace.

One reason for introducing a Salzburg minuet trio at this point is to illustrate the early use of another standard trio accompaniment pattern that
provides rhythmic ease, namely, the oom-pah-pah accompaniment. In this
trio, Mozart combines the murmuring violins with the oom-pah-pah of the
low strings, bassoon, and oboes. Oom-pah-pahs and murmuring accompaniments are related in that they are both characterized by a sparse bass line,
which draws the listener's ear to the upper voice(s) of the accompaniment
texture. Even the basic rhythmic character of the oom-pah-pah is latent in

EXAMPLE 2.6. The trio from the eighth minuet of Mozart's K. 176.

the murmuring accompaniment because the pitch pattern of the murmur most often, as in the present case, emphasizes beats 2 and 3. Overall, this remarkable little trio is held together in exquisite suspension by an intricate interplay of different rhythmic patterns. Against the constant flow of the second violins' eighth notes, the other three voices alternate entrances on each beat of the bar. Moreover, the legato grouping slurs of the second violins' eighth notes create a different durational pattern (half note + quarter note). The articulative use of silence provides a transparent texture in which each voice can be clearly heard. And finally, a clear two-bar hypermeter, initially established by the two-bar harmonic rhythm, is maintained throughout the dance.

Example 2.7 reproduces the trio from the sixth minuet of K. 104, written in late 1770 or early 1771. Here an oom-pah-pah accompaniment played by the second violins and lower strings runs the entire course of the trio. In the first half, a simple but charming melody played by the first violins and piccolo inscribes a melodic contour of winding arches.[21] The trio's opening progression begins on a dominant chord, which resolves to the tonic in bar 3. Often referred to as an "auxiliary progression," this is a compositional technique that Mozart commonly uses in his trios, and it is an important means of establishing continuity in the tonal motion from the end of the minuet to the beginning of the trio.[22] When both the minuet and trio are in the same key, as is the case here, the end of the minuet always ends with a structural tonic, which normally would be directly followed by the opening structural

EXAMPLE 2.7. The trio from the sixth minuet of Mozart's K. 104.

tonic of the trio. The immediate succession of two structural tonics, however, creates a highly segmented boundary that emphasizes the beginning of the trio. The use of an auxiliary progression, however, harmonically destabilizes the trio's opening bars, thus softening the articulative impact of its initial boundary.[23] It begins up in the air, so to speak, and the resulting sense of continuity and lightness correlates well with the continuity and lightness of motion exhibited in the dance. When we examine the Viennese waltz, we will find that auxiliary progressions are a signature technique of Lanner and Strauss Sr.

The trios from K. 104 and K. 176 are early examples of Mozart's minuet music, written when he was a teenager living with his family in Salzburg. Example 2.8 presents the first half of a trio from his last published collection of minuets, K. 599, written for the carnival season of 1791. Here, beneath an imitative duet of the oboe and first bassoon, we see a more refined use of the oom-pah-pah accompaniment. The pah-pahs on the second and third beats are slurred together in consistently ascending arpeggiations that counterbalance the descending lines of the oboe and bassoon. Mozart provides the accompaniment with a sense of line, wholeness, and continuity not only through the large arch of the bass line but also through the ascending linear progression (F–G–A–B♭), which remains somewhat hidden in the afterbeats of the first violin (see the stemmed notes in the score). This line provides a counterpoint to a slower-paced ascending third (B♭–C–D, with registral transfer) in the oboe. Also noteworthy is the imitative exchange between the

EXAMPLE 2.8. The first half of the trio from the fourth minuet of Mozart's K. 599.

oboe and first bassoon. As I shall explain below, such melodic dialogues are a characteristic feature of Mozart's trios.

The oom-pah-pah pattern, however, is most often associated today with the *Deutscher*, the *Ländler*, and the waltz, lower-class spinning dances that emerged as popular ballroom dances in Vienna only by the end of the eighteenth century. Indeed, so strong is the association that many assume the mere presence of the oom-pah-pah automatically indicates a lower-class spinning dance. As was shown in Table 2.1, however, Mozart used the oom-pah-pah as a standard accompaniment pattern in his trios long before he began composing *Deutsche* and *Ländler*. Furthermore, Mozart does not even use the oom-pah-pah in his first collection of *Deutsche*, nor is it used with any great consistency in his subsequent *Deutsche* and *Ländler*.[24] In reference to the early history of spinning dances, Eduard Reeser observes that the oom-pah-pah "only occurs sporadically before about 1815" (1949, 38). In the last two decades of the eighteenth century, there was no standardized practice for these newer dances. In his own *Deutsche* and *Ländler*, Mozart drew on a wide variety of accompanimental textures, including those commonly found in minuets.

Mozart was not alone in the practice of using the oom-pah-pah in ballroom minuet trios. This accompaniment pattern can also be found in the minuet trios of Michael Haydn, Joseph Haydn, Carl Maria von Dittersdorf, and Franz X. Süssmayr, among others. The earliest occurrence of this texture that I have found is in the trio of a minuet by J. C. Bach written around 1750.[25] As shown in Example 2.9, the trio, as sophisticated as it is in its harmonic and contrapuntal organization, is entirely set within an oom-

EXAMPLE 2.9. The trio from an early minuet by J. C. Bach (c. 1750).

pah-pah texture. For Mozart and his contemporaries, the oom-pah-pah was one of several means used in trios to depict musically the exalted qualities of artful simplicity, natural grace, and noble ease. By itself, the oom-pah-pah was not tethered to a single genre. Much like the Alberti bass, it was an accompaniment texture that could be used within a variety of genres and expressive contexts. It is the oom-pah-pah *in combination* with other musical elements that defines the music as a particular dance type. While Mozart's minuets are marked by artful simplicity, his *Deutsche* and *Ländler* are marked by artless and naive simplicity. Overall, they are characterized by repeated rhythmic and motivic patterns that contain little or no variation, a highly segmented melodic organization, extremely simple counterpoints, and simple harmonic progressions.

Only with the explosion in popularity of the waltz in the opening decades of the nineteenth century did the oom-pah-pah become indelibly linked to a single genre. This broader definition of the oom-pah-pah accompaniment runs against current thought, which promotes a very narrow topical range for the oom-pah-pah. While the topic of the *Ländler* or the *Deutscher* is evoked by some late eighteenth-century minuet trios not intended for dancing, especially those within the minuets of Haydn's quartets and symphonies, one should not automatically assume the presence of a different, lower-style dance based solely on the presence of the oom-pah-pah accompaniment, and especially so if the music was intended for minuet dancing. Let us not forget that Mozart was an accomplished minuet dancer and a connoisseur of aristocratic behavior; he knew very well what type of music was appropriate for the occasion, for the social position of the dancers, and for their dancing pleasure.

EXAMPLE 2.10. The opening of the trio from the seventh *Deutsche*
of Mozart's K. 567.

Artless Simplicity

Many commentators have interpreted the simpler melodies and textures of
Mozart's trios as an indicator of the "lower" style of a spinning dance.[26] I have
instead interpreted Mozart's simplicity in the context of eighteenth-century
notions of beauty as manifest in the high and noble grace (ideally) exhibited
by minuet dancers on the ballroom floor. To distinguish more subtly between
high and low styles of simplicity, it may be helpful to compare the artful
simplicity of Mozart's trios with the artless simplicity of his *Deutsche*. Rarely
will Mozart's artless simplicity apply to all parameters of music; it will typically be clearly apparent in only one or two areas of the composition. Example
2.10 shows the opening phrase of a *Deutscher* trio from a collection of twelve
Deutsche dated 6 December 1788. The music is soft, gentle, and flowing, but
it lacks the sophistication of his ballroom minuet trios. First, there is no
functional bass and, as a result, no outer-voice counterpoint; the murmuring

second violins are grounded by an unrelieved, pulsating quarter-note pedal in the cello and bass that is sounded throughout the entire piece. Second, the accompaniment texture, rhythm, and melodic design are all marked by repetition and uniformity with very little variation or variety. In Hogarth's opinion, "simplicity, without variety, is wholly insipid" ([1753] 1997, 30). The only subtle compositional touch is the early entrance of the timpani in bar 8, which accentuates a hypermetrically weak beat and creates a timbral overlap between the two eight-bar phrases. Compare this *Deutscher* with the minuet trios previously given in Examples 2.1 and 2.3, which also contain murmuring accompaniments. The simplicity of Mozart's *Deutsche* is characterized by banality, uniformity, and predictability. Variety, artifice, and singularity, on the other hand, characterize the simplicity of his minuet trios. Especially noteworthy in the minuet trios is Mozart's continuous and artful variation of an opening two-bar motive.

The trio of the first *Deutscher* from a collection of six *Deutsche*, K. 571, is reproduced in Example 2.11. These Redoutensäle dances were composed for the carnival season of 1789. Here we see an example of the oom-pah-pah accompaniment within the context of a lower-class spinning dance. As I suggest, it is the context of the oom-pah-pah and not the oom-pah-pah itself that defines this dance as a *Deutscher*. Specifically, this piece demonstrates four *Deutscher* features that are not found in minuet trios that similarly employ oom-pah-pah accompaniments:

· While the tonal organization of this dance is both interesting and sophisticated, the motivic fabric is banal – the same motive is repeated throughout the entire work with little rhythmic or articulative variation. Such continuous repetition with little or no variation, while typical of a *Deutscher*, is seldom found in minuets or minuet trios.

· The motive is one bar long. Repeating one-bar motives are a common feature of Mozart's *Deutsche*. Two bars, corresponding to the two-bar minuet step, are the standard length of motives in minuets and minuet trios.

· The music lacks a clear and consistent two-bar hypermeter. The consistent appearance of *forte* tuttis on even-numbered bars establishes an accentual pattern that challenges a two-bar hypermeter beginning in bar 1. Even-numbered hypermetrical schemes, hypermetrical disruption, and hypermetrical ambiguity are not

uncommon in Mozart's *Deutsche*. In minuets and minuet trios, a clear
and consistent two-bar hypermeter, beginning in the first bar, is a
practical requirement on behalf of the dancers.

· Registral transfers in the second violins' afterbeats result in a very
fragmented and disjunct line. For example, in bars 1–5 a descending
line, G–F♯–E–D, is split between two registers. The registral
transfers at the beginning of the second half are even more severe.
While such jagged melodic lines are not uncommon in *Deutscher*
accompaniments, fluency and composure are signature characteristics
of Mozart's minuet-trio accompaniments, as seen in the minuet trio
shown in Example 2.8.

EXAMPLE 2.11. The trio of the first *Deutsche* of Mozart's K. 571.

Duets

One final characteristic of Mozart's minuet trios deserves mention: melodic duets. Melodic duets never occur in the music of the Mozart's minuets (nor in his *Deutsche* and *Ländler*), but they abound in the music of his minuet trios. If, as I have argued, we consider Mozart's trios as a musical vision of the minuet as danced – as capturing not only the aesthetics of the dance but also its spectacle – then duets assume programmatic significance as a musical representation of the two dancers on the ballroom dance floor. The minuet was the last remaining *danse à deux* from the court of Louis XIV to be danced in the public ballroom. In its standard form, it was performed by a single couple while everyone else watched. And what they watched was "a refined expression of ritualistic courtship. The dancers face each other almost continually; they approach, pass, and retreat, and their only physical contact is holding hands at arm's length while circling" (Hilton 1998, 4:432). Because they perform the dance figures in opposition to each other, the two dancers do not merge within a single line of motion, as in the spinning dances, but rather maintain their own spatial, physical, and expressive identities throughout the dance. As Shirley Wynne (1970, 26) observes, an important element of connection between the minuet dancers was their eye contact, which, within the boundaries of proper decorum, could be quite flirtatious. Throughout the entire minuet, the dancers were to "always turn their heads towards whoever they are dancing with, along whichever line they follow, and the less they can take their eyes from each other, the more grace will be added" (Magri [1779] 1988, 183). Within this seductive play between the man and the woman, according to Curt Sachs, "the erotic is stylized to the last degree" (1952, 398–99).

Example 2.12 presents the trio from the second minuet of K. 176. Here the second violin is paired with the first violin largely in parallel thirds, sixths, and fourths but in a slightly less elaborate rhythm and with more legato articulation. The subtle rhythmic and articulative variation allows the two violins to be heard as a duet rather than as a single voice that is doubled. The duet can be compared to two dancers performing the same steps and figures but in a slightly different manner. One could even suggest gender associations with the musical protagonists, based on how the dancers moved across the dance floor and the way in which their appearance was highlighted by the clothing they wore.[27] The first violin assumes the role of the male dancer: it leads melodically with a quarter-note anacrusis; it is rhythmically more active; and it is more active in articulation, using more bows per bar. With its legato rhythms

EXAMPLE 2.12. The trio from the second minuet of Mozart's K. 176.

and subservient registral and melodic position, the second violin represents the female dancer. Notice how in the opening four-bar phrase of the second reprise, hemiola is achieved by the fourfold repetition of the dotted quarter note + eighth note. This rhythmic pattern defies the gravitational pull of the $\frac{3}{4}$ meter, creating a sense of floating weightlessness.

A far more common type of duet found in minuet trios, as seen previously in Example 2.8, is the duet based on dialogue texture, most often imitative in nature.[28] In the trio from the first minuet of K. 176, shown in Example 2.13, the first and second violins converse back and forth at one-bar intervals. At the beginning of the second half, they come together in contrary motion (bar 9) and parallel motion (bar 10). Bars 13–16 are a varied and condensed restatement of bars 3–8. Especially noteworthy is this trio's motivic fabric: it begins with a statement and varied imitation of the motive; in bars 3–5 the motive is inverted; and the contrary motion of bar 9 is based on a combination of a varied retrograde and retrograde inversion of the opening motive. Mozart thereby tempers the uniformity of this trio with variety and considerable craft, despite which it remains artfully simple.

Mozart's trios written for the carnival balls at the Imperial Palace are exceptional in their rich and subtle scoring of melodic dialogues. The trio from the ninth minuet of K. 568, shown in Example 2.14, is exemplary. Within the

EXAMPLE 2.13. The trio from the first minuet of Mozart's K. 176.

confines of a sixteen-bar trio, Mozart gives us a miniature instrumental seduction aria of extraordinary beauty.[29] The seduction is played out over the gentle
pulsations of a murmuring string accompaniment. The oboe enters first with
a four-bar melody comprising two two-bar groups. The second group (bars
3–4) is a varied transposition of the first group. The opening leap of a fourth is
filled in with diatonic and chromatic passing tones, giving the melody a greater
sense of fluidity and directed motion. The upwardly resolving appoggiaturas
in bars 2 and 4 provide the melody a sense of questioning or hesitancy. Notice
that in bar 4 Mozart simplifies the rhythm; how easy it would have been to
repeat the two eighth-note/quarter-note rhythmic patterns of bar 2. Instead,
he rounds off the opening four bars with two quarter notes, a gesture that
gracefully tempers and restrains the eighth-note motion that arises in bar 3.
The bassoon answers the questioning oboe with a confident, undivided four-
bar melody that modulates from the tonic to the dominant.

In the second half, the entrances of the oboe and bassoon are separated
by only one bar. Mozart also brings the two voices closer together conceptually by combining motives from both the bassoon's and the oboe's melodies – namely, the bassoon's forceful rising seventh motive (bar 5) and the
oboe's questioning appoggiatura motive (bar 2). Once again the oboe begins,
and the bassoon follows its motivic lead but ignores its harmonic outlook,
whose dominant seventh on B♭ suggests a resolution to the subdominant E♭.
Instead, the bassoon reasserts its active harmonic role by rather abruptly re-
directing the tonal motion from the flat side of the circle of fifths to the sharp

EXAMPLE 2.14. The trio from the ninth minuet of Mozart's K. 568.

side and initiating a descending fifths progression that ultimately leads to the subdominant E♭ in bar 14.

In bar 13 both voices join together in sweet thirds. Just as in bar 4, Mozart here obtains a sense of restraint and inner composure by slowing the composite rhythm from the eighth-note pulse of bars 11–12 to a quarter-note pulse. The excitement of their union is, however, disclosed by the high, repeated staccato B♭ in the first and second violins. The musical climax of their union is marked by the couple's simultaneous sforzandi on the downbeat of bar 14, which is texturally exposed and highlighted by the absence of the bass (the first and only time where the bass does not articulate the downbeat). Thus, the gender imagery and sexual drama that are tangible within the dance hall are articulated particularly clearly in this little duet, albeit within the bounds of the trio's simple and elegant style.

Mixed Styles

In a number of Redoutensäle minuets, Mozart experiments with contrasts of power and grace *within* each movement of the minuet-trio set. Very often Mozart introduces the contrasting style in the first four bars of the second

Minuet: Power   :‖:   Grace   Power

Trio: Grace   :‖:   Power   Grace

Minuet: Power   :‖:   Grace   Power

DIAGRAM 2.1. Pattern of contrast in Mozart's late minuets.

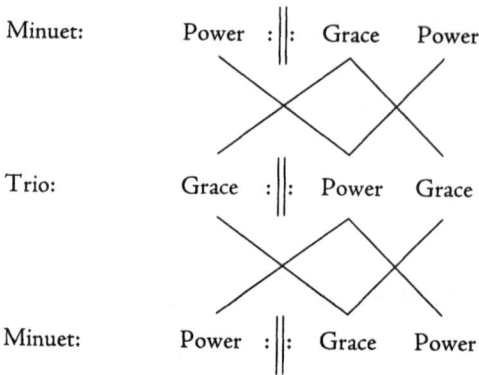

EXAMPLE 2.15. (*above and facing*) The third minuet and trio
of Mozart's K. 601.

reprise, what Leonard Ratner (1980, 213) refers to as the X section of a rounded binary form layout. In the minuet collections K. 568 and K. 585, composed in 1788 and 1789, respectively, Mozart uses this pattern of contrast within his minuets but not his trios.[30] In his last collection of minuets composed in 1791, however, contrasting styles are featured on a consistent basis within both the minuet and the trio. As Diagram 2.1 illustrates, when both the minuet and the trio exhibit this pattern of contrast, they have an inverse relationship to each other.

As an example, I turn to the third minuet and trio of K. 601, shown in Example 2.15. The minuet opens with loud, majestic music complete with march rhythms, fanfare flourishes, and a walking bass line. A clear two-bar hypermeter is quickly established by the two-bar harmonic rhythm, the 2 + 2 + 4 motivic design (sentence structure), and the first violins' triple stops on the downbeats of bars 1, 3, and 5. The dotted and syncopated rhythms drive the music forward forcefully toward the perfect authentic cadence in bars 7–8. After the double bar, the music suddenly shifts into the music of the beautiful. For the accompaniment, Mozart combines both the murmuring and oom-pah-pah patterns. A gently curving melody floats effortlessly above. The powerful music resumes in bar 13 with an abbreviated version of bars 1–8.

The tranquil music of the X section of the minuet returns as the motivic basis of the music of the trio. Bar 1 of the trio is a smoother rhythmic variant of bar 9 of the minuet; bar 2 reproduces both the rhythm and contour. Mozart underscores simplicity by paring down the accompaniment to just the oom-pah-pah of the lower strings. In the second four bars, an eighth-note serpentine line in the second violins animates the accompanimental texture while the melody gently falls onto a perfect authentic cadence. Placid tranquility is boldly interrupted in bar 9 by a varied return of the majestic minuet music. The sense of power and authority is exaggerated by the expansive triple stops in both violin parts and by the addition of the timpani, which was not used in the minuet. A shortened and varied version of the opening phrase restores peace and brings the trio to a close, completing a symmetrical pattern of power and grace.

THE MINUET AS A CULTURAL AND HISTORICAL ICON

The foregoing discussion has examined in some detail the correspondences between the minuet as danced and the music of the trio. In its textures, rhythms, and melodic designs, the soft, flowing, and gentle music of Mozart's ballroom trios mirrors the grace exhibited by the dancers as they execute the serpentine figures of the minuet dance on the ballroom floor. By contrast, the loud, powerful, and forceful music of the minuet portrays the social and political status of the dance and of its participants. Culturally understood, the trio music reflects *what* the two individual dancers are doing on the dance floor, whereas the minuet music represents *who* they are collectively.[31] This section considers further motivations for the pompous and grandiose style of Mozart's minuets and, hence, for the contrast between the two styles.

By Mozart's time the minuet was considered an ancient dance. It had emerged in the court of Louis XIV a hundred years earlier and quickly assumed the position as the "queen of all dances" (Feldtenstein 1767, 37). As the eighteenth century wore on and other aristocratic court dances fell aside, the noble associations of the minuet increased. In the process, the minuet became a cultural and historical icon representing the power and authority of the ruling class, the ancien régime. The ancien régime throughout Europe was increasingly coming under attack as the ideals of liberalism and republicanism spread. In the face of such social and political unrest, the minuet was used as social ritual that glorified and reaffirmed the divinely ordained order and power of the Hapsburg monarchy and aristocracy.[32]

As the historian Jeroen Duindam observes, "the court of Vienna was reputedly one of the most ceremonial courts in early modern Europe" (2003, 197). All public occasions in which the nobility took part were carefully prescribed with detailed rules and regulations; very little was left to chance. As the opening dance of the Viennese ball, the minuet held a privileged place. It was the oldest dance, the most difficult dance to learn, and considered the true test of genteel behavior. In anticipation of the public display, great preparation went into the dancers' clothing, cosmetics, and coiffures. The order of the dancers was determined by their social status, with the highest-ranking couple dancing first. And the entire dance was preceded and concluded with reverences to the highest-ranking personages in attendance as well as to one's partner. Thus, in the context of the entire ball, the minuet functioned not only as a dance but also as a courtly introduction and processional.

It is important to remember, as recorded by Otto Jahn (1882, 3:217), that Mozart's Redoutensäle minuets were commissioned by the emperor of Austria, and it was not uncommon for Joseph II and his family to attend these imperial balls. Unlike much of his other music, Mozart's minuets were art in the direct service of the emperor and were thus integrated into the very fabric of Viennese social life. To accentuate the minuet's royal patronage, ceremonial function, and cultural and political associations, Mozart and other Redoutensäle composers fortified their minuets with fanfares, brass and timpani, march rhythms, and rhythms drawn from the Polish polonaise. The melodic element was severely restricted, thereby reducing the music's sense of voice and individuality. The result was loud, majestic music that evoked an enlarged sense of time and space of the sort appropriate for ceremonial functions. Much like the architecture in Watteau's painting, Mozart's minuet music speaks of the collective experience of the aristocracy – their political power, historical lineage, and exalted position within society.

Représantation de la Grande Sale des Redoutes et du Bal Masqué

FIGURE 2.3. Depiction of a masked ball in the Grosser Redoutensaal by Markus Weinmann, 1760. *Reproduced by permission of the Wien Museum.*

A Matter of Being Heard

As Mary Sue Morrow (1989, 102) relates, in the five years between 1747 and 1752, two large rooms in the Imperial Palace were lavishly remodeled in Rococo style as two ballrooms: these became known as the Grosser and Kleiner Redoutensäle. Figure 2.3 shows a print of the larger of the two ballrooms a few years after it was completed. Especially noteworthy is the architectural prominence given to the dance orchestra situated in the central balcony.[33] Imperial Viennese balls held in the Redoutensäle were less exclusive than their French counterparts: during carnival anyone with a mask could enter the ball by paying an entrance fee.[34] Yet, as Daniel Heartz (1995, 66) explains, while Maria Theresa restricted entrance during her reign to nobility, councilors, and the military, her liberal-minded son, Joseph II, reopened the balls in 1772 to the general public.

With more people of different classes gaining access to the ballroom, the ballroom dance floor became more crowded. The monarchy in Vienna was particularly accommodating to the swell of dancing feet. In response to the larger crowds, larger dance halls were built and large existing rooms were

FIGURE 2.4. Anonymous engraving of a masked ball in the Grosser Redoutensaal, c. 1780. *Reproduced by permission of the Wien Museum.*

remodeled as ballrooms. In addition to the Kleiner and Grosser Redouten-säle, both Imperial Theaters (Burgtheater and Kärntnerthortheater) were routinely appropriated during carnival season as dance halls, their parterres raised to the level of the stage in order to create one large dance floor. As Heartz (1995, 65) further relates, the Imperial Riding School (Spanischen Hofreitschule) was transformed on special occasions into a gigantic ballroom that could accommodate up to eight thousand people. Figure 2.4 shows the large Imperial Ballroom as it appeared during a masked carnival ball c. 1780. Although more clearly seen in Figure 2.3, the dance orchestra is again situated in the balcony to the left of the main staircase.

In 1787, the year Mozart began his duties as imperial court composer, the publishing firm Artaria & Co. issued the fourth installment of Johann Pezzl's printed description of Vienna. Pezzl provides a vivid description of carnival madness in the Imperial Ballrooms:

> In one wing of the Imperial Castle are two enormous rooms, dedicated to Comus and Bacchus. From 7 January to the morning of Ash Wednesday they are open, at first once a week, then twice a week, and throughout the three final days of carnival. One alights at an iron gate, passes through the

ranks of fifty moustached grenadiers, who with their bearskin hats and bay-
onets terrify any shy girl as, with palpitating heart, she enters the famous
Redout for the first time on the arm of her lover. When you have pressed
through this entrance hall and climbed a flight of stairs, all of a sudden
you are in the great magical room. The light from many thousands of wax
candles reflected in the great crystal chandeliers and from the pyramid-like
candelabras arranged in symmetrical rows dazzles the eye; one's ears are
enchanted and captivated by fanfares of trumpets and drums, intermingled
with the softer tone of a hundred musical instruments; instinctively the
youthful foot joins in one of the delightful dances. . . . The entertainment
begins at ten in the evening and goes on until six in the morning. . . . If only
a thousand people attend, it feels too lonely; 1,500 dancers make a nice Redout, and with that number there is still enough room to dance. With 2,000
there is no longer room to dance properly, and in the last few days, when
there may be up to 3,000 pleasure seekers, it is a real squeeze. The orchestra
plays its minuets and German dances in vain, for there isn't room to take
three formal steps; everyone is jammed together, making a great awkward
mass of people for whom only a slow wave-like motion is possible.[35]

As a means of comparison with earlier French dance practices, refer back
to Figure 1.3, which reproduces Pierre Rameau's 1725 depiction of a royal ball
presided over by Louis XV. The two dancers are represented twice in time
lapse, first in the center of the room as they give reverences to Louis XV,
who is seated in the most elevated position at the top of the hall, and then at
the bottom of the room as they prepare to begin the minuet. The ladies, in
splendid adornment, are seated; the gentlemen stand behind them. A dance
orchestra of at least eighteen musicians is seated at the bottom of the hall.
The research of Rebecca Harris-Warrick (1986, 41–49) confirms the visual
depiction shown in Figure 1.3: courtly dancing spaces in France, from the end
of the seventeenth century into the second half of the eighteenth century,
were relatively small. For example, most of the balls held at Versailles during the reigns of Louis XIV and Louis XV were held in the Salle de Mars.
The size of the floor is 1,650 square feet. In contrast, the floor of the Grosser
Redoutensaal is 7,500 square feet.

Thus, to characterize the Viennese carnival ball scene in the second half
of the eighteenth century, what we have are large dancing spaces, amply sup-
plied with food and alcohol and crowded with men and women of various
social classes who were out to have a good time. Over the noise of the crowd,
the minuet and trio music, for it to be properly danced to, had still to be heard.
The audibility of the music was subject to other environmental conditions,

such as where one was situated within the hall in relation to the musicians, how many people were in the hall, what time of night it was, how much alcohol had been consumed, and whatever else was taking place inside the hall. For example, if, at the beginning of the ball, it so happened that a member of the royal family or some well-known dignitary decided to participate in the minuet, then the crowd noise would presumably be relatively low, since most people would be watching the spectacle. The important point is that the noise level would fluctuate during the course of the night.

A steady stream of music at one unchanging dynamic level (even a *forte* level) could easily lose its active presence in a changing acoustical environment with so many competing sounds. The loud-soft alteration of Mozart's minuets and trios were conceived, I believe, with these specific conditions in mind. The alternating entrances of the grandiose minuets, with their *forte* dynamics, driving arpeggiations, and full orchestral force, were necessary so that the music could punch through the din of the crowd and thereby reclaim its active presence. In a crowded ballroom, the bass and timpani could be heard more easily than the treble melody. Accordingly, the bass assumes greater importance in marking the beginnings of every other bar, which dancers needed to hear in order to execute their two-bar step-units in time with the music. A standard rhythmic pattern of bass lines as found in Redoutensäle minuets is five quarter notes followed by a quarter rest. The quarter rest silence effectively highlights the beginnings of the repeating two-bar pattern. Once the two-bar hypermeter is firmly established in the minuet, the composer could turn to the softer music of the trio. If the dancers should lose their footing because of an increase in crowd noise, they only needed to wait for the return of the minuet in order to regain it. The alternation of loud and soft thus serves two purposes: it supports the opposition of power and grace, and, in cases where the crowd noise swells above the level of the soft trio music, it insures the audible and active presence of the dance music.[36]

CONCLUSION

In a time of social change, upheaval, and revolution, the late eighteenth-century Viennese aristocracy tightly embraced the minuet as a potent symbol of their position in society. As a type of musical propaganda, the minuet establishes the historical authority, political power, and social status of participants of the dance. In contrast to the minuet, which focuses upon the collective experience of the aristocracy, the trio is artistically centered on the

TABLE 2.3. SUMMARY OF CONTRASTS BETWEEN MINUETS AND TRIOS

MINUET	TRIO
collective experience of the aristocracy	individual experience of the dancing couple
ceremonial and processional	*danse à deux*
past tense (or timeless)	present tense
older musical style (Baroque)	contemporary musical style (*galant*)
stock, generic music	heightened musical individuality
powerful music	graceful music
grandiose	artfully simple
loud	soft
tutti	concertino
disjunct melodies	conjunct melodies
rhythmically heavy and plodding	rhythmic ease (flowing and light)
dense texture	transparent texture
chordal	melody and accompaniment texture
	murmuring and oom-pah-pah

individual couple on the ballroom dance floor. Table 2.3 summarizes the different functions and aesthetic qualities of the minuet and trio. Perhaps more than any other major composer since Jean-Baptiste Lully, Mozart was acutely sensitive both to the ideological needs of his royal patrons and to the practical requirements of the minuet dancers on the ballroom dance floor. The dual interpretation of the minuet (class representation versus the representation of the individual couple) resulted in a sharply defined contrast between the opposing forces of power and grace.

As a hermeneutic device, one may think of Mozart's grandiose minuets as gilded frames surrounding serene centers – by its contrast, the minuet accentuates the beauty of the trio and provides a historical and social context in which to interpret it. Gilded frames were much in vogue throughout the eighteenth century, especially in the framing of royal portraits.[37] The subject of the portrait was typically depicted in a graceful, unaffected pose with an expression of utmost serenity bordering on an air of "sprightly vacancy."[38] To enhance the sense of noble ease and natural grace, the subject was often situated outdoors or in view of the outdoors. Commissioned by rulers and nobility, court frames "represent an essential, and long underestimated, component of the arts employed for propaganda purposes and as a status symbol, expressed through grandeur, luxury and sculptural magnificence. . . . Its glowing, reflective properties have endowed the frame with a special significance, literally highlighting the picture it contains as well as harmonizing with surrounding furnishings" (Mitchell and Roberts 1999, 11:372–74). Thus, the gilded frame was used to establish the authority, power, social status, and wealth of the subject, while the natural setting, when used, complemented the graceful qualities of the subject's physicality, attitude, and character. Accordingly, as one moves from the frame to the center of the portrait, one traverses a conceptual space from the general and objective to the individual and subjective.

In eighteenth-century western European society, the imaginative concept of the frame pervaded all human endeavors – social, artistic, intellectual, and architectural. And nowhere was it more evident than in the ballroom: in the music the majestic minuet provided a frame around the graceful trio; each minuet dance was preceded by and concluded with reverences; the spectators formed a social frame around the dancing couple; and the ubiquitous frame was also found in the architecture (windows, doorframes, wall paneling, ceiling molding, balconies, etc.) and in the furnishings of the ballroom, of which the mirror was an essential fixture. Besides their primary function of casting reflective light, gilded mirrors provided noble dancers with ready-made portraitures of their splendid selves.

As a final note, the accompanimental textures commonly associated with the *Ländler, Deutsche,* and waltz were used first in minuet trios – not to invoke a "low" style but rather to approximate musically the high sentiments of artful simplicity, natural grace, and noble ease. The artful simplicity of Mozart's trios is to be distinguished from the naive and artless simplicity of his spinning dances. Nevertheless, because of its simpler melodic style and accompaniment texture, scholars often mistakenly assign the trio a subordinate position within the minuet-trio matrix. Josef Gmeiner (1979, 116, 133) explains the contrast between the minuet and trio as a social reflection of an increasing democratization of society and individualization of the middle class, which is musically represented by the integration of upper- and lower-class musical styles. Eric Blom (1941, 173–76) also interprets minuet trios as embodying a low style, which led him to the fantastic hypothesis that the trio was once a lower-class dance. Tilden Russell suggests that the "trend to simplicity may have been encouraged by the popularity of the *Ländler*" (1983, 222–23, 230). The present research suggests a reversal of the minuet-trio hierarchy in which Mozart's ballroom trios are heard as the essence of the minuet as danced – as a pure, sparkling gemstone set within a golden crown.

3rd

The Musical Visions of Joseph Lanner and Johann Strauss Sr.

Lanner and Strauss senior did not create the waltz, they were only particularly receptive to the wishes of a musically tuned body which moves in inner harmony with the modulations. The spark springs from the motions of the dancers over to the musicians, and induces them to play the correct musical strains, the true musical vision. The vision carries the amplified spark back to the dancers, and the festival of motion can begin.

VICTOR ZUCKERKANDL

For much of the eighteenth century the minuet reigned supreme as the "queen of all ballroom dances; the test of every dancer who wants to acquire a reputation; . . . and . . . the best occasion for displaying everything beautiful and charming in nature which a body is capable of employing."[1] While the minuet certainly was the most esteemed of all ballroom dances of the eighteenth century, it was not the most popular dance. The considerable technique required to perform the minuet excluded many from attempting it at public balls, especially since it was designed as a spectacle to be danced by a single couple while others watched. Furthermore, as the eighteenth century progressed, more and more bourgeoisie were gaining access to public ballrooms, and in most cases members of this social class were not trained in dance from their early childhood, as were the nobility; the minuet simply was not part of their repertoire. Thus, to accommodate the rather wide range of technical skill and social classes among the dancers, midcentury balls in France, Germany, and Austria typically began with a set of minuets and then continued the remainder of the night with French contredanses, which technically were much simpler and allowed for a greater number of participants and a greater degree of social interaction among the participants.[2]

After midcentury there was even greater change to come. For along with the political and social upheavals that were sweeping across Europe, another revolution of sorts was taking place on the ballroom dance floor. While the immense popularity of the contredanse has been interpreted as "analogous with the rise of bourgeois society and the decline of the aristocratic culture" (Sachs 1952, 398), another dance, much more radical in its opposition to the minuet and to the culture of the French court, would complete the ascendancy of bourgeois in the ballroom: the waltz, the emblematic dance of the nineteenth century.

The origins of the waltz are obscure.[3] In the regions of southern Germany, Bavaria, Austria, and Bohemia, new couple dances in triple meter emerged from the lower classes – dances that required the man and woman to spin on a tight axis while embracing each other. *Deutscher, Walzer, allemande, Dreher, Schwäbische Tanz, Schleifer, Strassburger,* and *Ländler* were all geographic, choreographic, or rhythmic terms used, some interchangeably, to refer to these new spinning dances (Allanbrook 1983, 59). By the first decade of the nineteenth century, one of these simple, unsophisticated spinning dances – the *Walzer* (waltz) – quickly ascended the terpsichorean ladder as the most popular ballroom dance in Europe and beyond.[4] A fast, whirling dance of circles, the waltz met the needs and passions of the emergent middle class: it was relatively easy to learn and therefore did not require years of expensive lessons from a dancing master; it allowed for a greater number of dancers on the floor; the sensation of spinning was a source of physical and psychological pleasure; and it was scandalous.[5] Although it may seem tame by today's standards, the waltz created a social outrage, for it was the first ballroom dance that permitted dancers to embrace face to face, torso to torso, for an extended period of time. Moreover, the centrifugal force created by the spinning motion required a firm grasp. The constant spinning motion visually blurred the couple's perception of the world around them – the only objects they could see clearly were each other. Thus, dancing couples were able to construct an intimate and private world within a crowded public space.

Mozart brilliantly captures this moment of change in the history of ballroom dancing in the famous dance scene at the conclusion of act 1 of *Don Giovanni* (1787). The salacious nobleman Don Giovanni, after stumbling upon the wedding procession of two young peasants, Masetto and Zerlina, and attempting to seduce the bride, offers to host a celebration for the wedding party at his castle. This, he believes, will give him another opportunity to seduce Zerlina and, he hopes, several other peasant girls. Once the festivities begin, it is the minuet that opens the dancing, as would be customary at balls. Mozart's stage instructions indicate that the minuet is to be danced, quite appropriately, by the opera's representatives of the noble class, Donna Anna and Don Ottavio, who arrive at the ball wearing capes and masks so as not to be recognized by Don Giovanni. Don Giovanni then begins his seduction by inviting Zerlina to dance a contredanse, a dance in which the mixing of social classes was a common affair. In an attempt to keep the suspicious Masetto at bay, Leporello, Don Giovanni's servant, forces him into a raucous, low-class *Deutscher*, the final dance that is introduced. The tight embrace required by the *Deutscher* enables Leporello physically to restrain Masetto, and the spinning motion reduces Masetto's ability to focus on what is going on around him. With Masetto effectively disposed of, Don Giovanni whisks Zerlina out of the ballroom into an adjoining room. Mozart thereby presents the three most important ballroom dances of the eighteenth and nineteenth centuries in quick succession – the aristocratic minuet, the more boisterous and bourgeois contredanse, and the crude and vulgar spinning dance, the *Deutscher*, which, as Daniel Heartz notes, "Mozart renders even more vulgar by using the Viennese dialect to label it 'Teitsch'" (1990, 190). Thus, the past (minuet), present (contredanse), and future (*Deutscher*) of dance are unfolded in this one scene.[6]

This chapter marks a shift in focus from the minuets of Bach and Mozart to dance-music relations of waltzes composed by Lanner, Strauss Sr., and Chopin. Part 1 explores the Viennese waltz as a public spectacle: Who was watching? How did they watch? What were they watching? From this section I sketch out four important aesthetic properties of the visual experience: repetitive continuity, self-containment, feminine beauty, and variety. Part 2 considers how the aesthetic properties drawn from the visual experience may have influenced and shaped aspects of the waltz's thematic

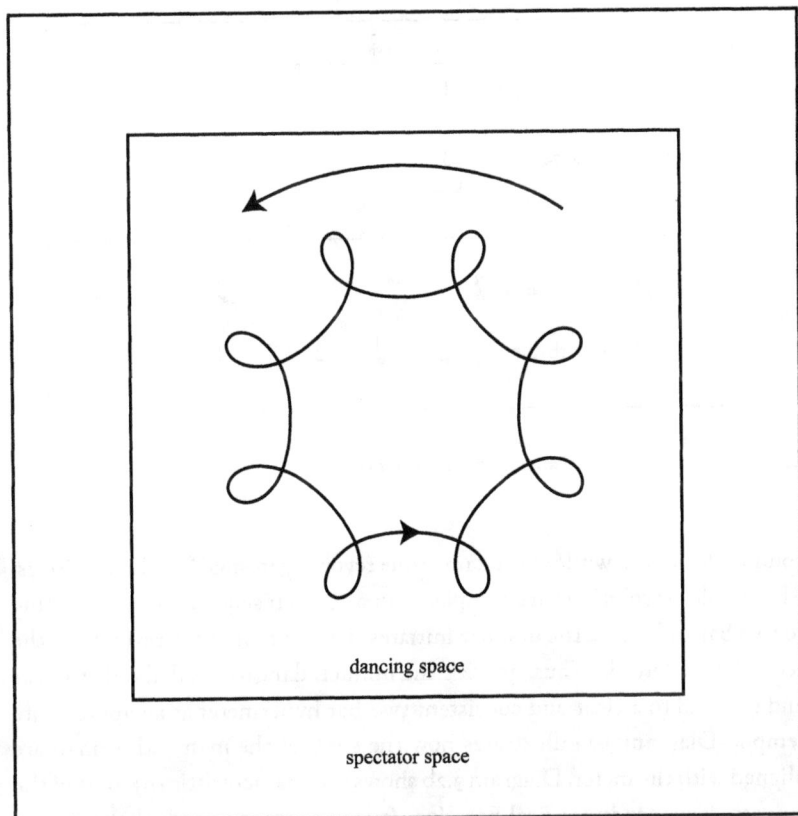

dancing space

spectator space

DIAGRAM 3.1. The spiraling path of the *valse à trois temps*.

material and large-scale design in the early Viennese waltzes of Lanner and Strauss Sr. I argue that Lanner and Strauss Sr. capture the image of the (female) human body by translating the visual spectacle into appropriate musical corollaries that are artistically developed on different levels of musical organization.

WALTZ AS DANCED: 1815–1840

The standard dance form of the waltz that held sway on European dance floors from about 1815 to 1840 was the *valse à trois temps*. As shown in Diagram 3.1, it requires the dancers to traverse the dance floor in large circles,

a.

	twirl				3 steps		
man's dance step:	1	(2	3)	|	3	4	5
woman's dance step:	3	4	5	|	1	(2	3)
	3 steps				twirl		

b.

man's dance rhythm: $\mathbf{2 \atop 4}$ 𝅗𝅥. | ♩   ♩   ♩

woman's dance rhythm: $\mathbf{2 \atop 4}$ ♩   ♩   ♩ | 𝅗𝅥.

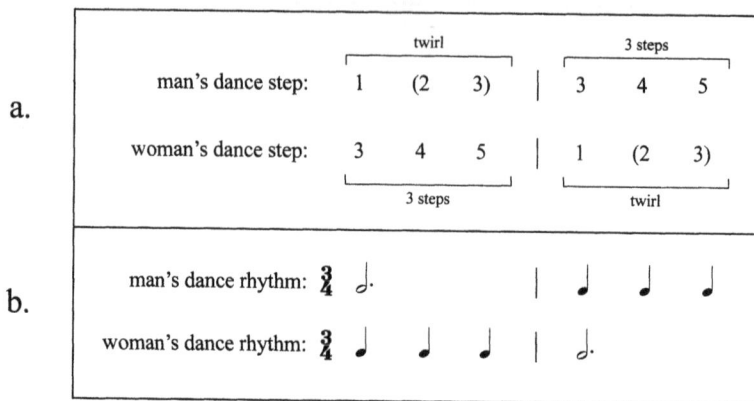

DIAGRAM 3.2. The metrical alignment of the dance steps.

counterclockwise, while at the same time revolving in small clockwise circles. The smaller revolutions are completed in a six-step sequence corresponding to two bars of music: the first bar initiates the first half of the revolution, the second completes it. Thus, as with the minuet, dancers needed only to hear and respond to a clear and consistent two-bar hypermeter at an appropriate tempo.[7] Diagram 3.2a illustrates how the steps of the man and woman are aligned with the meter. Diagram 3.2b shows the characteristic rhythms of the six-step sequence in musical notation. It is important to note that the man and woman *do not* perform the same steps at the same time. In the first bar, the man executes a pivot turn or twirl, as it is sometimes called. The second bar is completed with three clearly articulated steps. The woman reverses this two-bar pattern: she first performs three steps and then follows with a twirl. The defining feature of the *valse à trois temps* is the twirl; it is what distinguishes it from other styles of waltzing. As such, the twirl is conceptually marked in relation to the more commonly found three-step sequence. In his dance treatise, *Fashionable Dancing*, the French dancing master Henri Cellarius provides instructions for the twirl: "[On the first beat,] the gentleman sets off with the left foot. . . . [On the second beat,] [h]e slides the right foot, slightly crossed, behind the left . . . [and] [a]fterward, he turns upon his two feet, on the toes" (1840, 30).

While it appears that the gentleman performs the twirl in two steps, it actually only involves one true step (as defined by a change of weight from one foot to another). Once the dancer steps on his left foot, his body weight remains on that foot for the remainder of the bar. It serves as the pivot for the turn. That is why in Diagram 3.2a I enclose the second and third steps of the twirl in parentheses and in Diagram 3.2b I notate the twirl with a dotted half note. I will return to the rhythmic implications of the waltz's dance steps in chapter 4.

WATCHING WALTZERS WALTZ

Dance historian Elizabeth Aldrich observes that in contrast to the minuet, "the waltz was danced not primarily for the pleasure of a viewing audience, but, rather, for the pleasure of the dancers themselves – because it felt good" (1990, 30). One of my central arguments, however, is that while it is true that the waltz was not designed and performed as a presentation dance, the audience nonetheless did take great pleasure in watching waltzers waltz, but in a radically different manner than was possible with the minuet and other earlier ballroom dances.

A defining element of the dancer-spectator relationship is the dancers' awareness of the spectators' gaze. As I discussed in chapter 2, the minuet, at its core, is a ceremonial presentation dance (usually the opening dance of a ball) performed by two dancers alone on the dance floor willingly and knowingly before a viewing audience. Indeed, before the minuet dance began and after it ended it was customary for the dancers to acknowledge the highest-ranking member(s) of the audience with reverences. During their performance the couple – in their dress, countenance, mannerisms, and coded bodily movements – conveyed to the audience all the accoutrements of courtly behavior, the most important of which were natural grace, artful simplicity, and noble ease. In his description of a minuet performance in Rome during the carnival season of 1788, Johann Wolfgang von Goethe captures this intentional and transparent relationship between the dancers and the audience: "Scarcely anyone will venture to dance unless he has learned to do so correctly; especially the minuet is considered a true work of art, and only a few pairs act it out, so to speak. Such a pair is then encircled by the rest of the company and receives applause at the end" (1994, 6:411). Indeed, writing in 1779, the Italian dancing master Gennaro Magri declares that it is the moral duty of minuet dancers to keep the audience in mind: "He who dances in public must aim not only in satisfying himself but must consider himself obliged to give pleasure to the Spectators and, in order to please in the *Minuet*, nothing less than perfection is possible" ([1779] 1988, 189).

With the waltz there was no such mutual contract between the audience and the dancers. As Aldrich notes, waltzers did not perform intentionally for an audience but rather to satisfy themselves for their own pleasure.
Furthermore, as previously mentioned, the constant whirling motion of the
waltz creates a perceptual umbrella around the dancing couple. Dancers were
thus largely unaware of their surroundings and the peering eyes that might
have been following them around the dance floor. Again I turn to Goethe,
whose novel *The Sorrows of Young Werther* (published in 1774) contains one
of the earliest literary passages that describes the perceptual effects of the
waltz's spinning motion. Werther, in a letter to his friend Wilhelm, recounts
his experience at a ball in a small country village where, much to his delight,
he finds himself dancing with Lotte, the woman (married to his friend) with
whom he has tragically fallen in love.

> We began, and first delighted in joining arms according to the usual variety
> of patterns. With what charm, what ease she moved! When the waltz
> started, and the dancers whirled round each other like planets in the sky,
> there was some confusion, since some of the dancers were fairly clumsy.
> We kept back, allowing the other dancers to wear themselves out, and
> when the most awkward dancers had left the floor, we joined in and kept
> it up with one other couple – Audran and his partner. *Never have I moved
> more lightly. I felt myself more than human, holding this loveliest of creatures in
> my arms, flying with her like the wind, till I lost sight of everything else;* and –
> Wilhelm, I vowed at that very moment that a girl whom I loved, or for
> whom I felt the slightest attachment, should never waltz with another, even
> if it should be my end! You understand what I mean. (Goethe 1988, II:17,
> italics added)

Having been smitten with his beautiful dancing partner – who was also
an exceptionally good dancer – certainly played some role in Wilhelm's flight
of imagination, but, more practically speaking, the extinction of the external
world was due to the couple's constant rotary motions. While Wilhelm and
Lotte were one of only two couples on the ballroom dance floor, they were
oblivious to the presence (and gaze) of the audience around them. Werther's
admonition to himself that never should a woman he loved waltz with another man underscores the physical and emotional intensity of the waltzers' intimate embrace. The constant circling motion creates a physical bond
uniting the two dancers as one self-enclosed body of motion – as a spinning
orb. Because of the implicit sexual nature of this embrace, many critics of the

FIGURE 3.1. One of the underground ballrooms at the Elysium Tanzpaläst.

time, quite unsuccessfully, urged that, if the waltz was to be danced at all, only married couples should do it.[8]

While the *valse à trois temps* was not designed or performed as a presentation dance, its spectators, standing off to the side and often separated from the dancers by a rope or banister, peered into these intensely private, physically intimate, and self-contained social spheres, often with great enthusiasm. The act of doing so constituted a type of voyeurism – gazing into private spaces for pleasure.[9]

Nineteenth-century visual depictions of ballroom waltzing invariably include a gallery of interested spectators, typically male. Figure 3.1 presents a print of one of the luxurious underground ballrooms at the Elysium Tanzpaläst, a popular Viennese venue where Lanner and Strauss Sr. regularly performed. Notice how the spectators, who are gathered at the perimeters of the dancing space and in the gallery above, gaze upon the dancers. The most intense gazes come from the gentlemen on the bottom left and right sides of the print who appear to be entranced by the spectacle. Also notice the prominent and elevated position of the dance orchestra, with a violin-ist, presumably the orchestra leader, standing facing outward, observing the

FIGURE 3.2. J. J. Grandville, *Valtz au Colisée, 1830*.
Reproduced by permission of Musée des Beaux-Arts, Nancy, France.

waltzers.[10] Such prominent depictions of an orchestral leader, which become increasingly common in the early nineteenth century, not only foreground the presence of music in this scene but also draw attention to the creative connections between the dance and music: the musicians' music inspires the dancers, and the spectacle of the dancers inspires the musicians.

The illustrator who best captures the intentional social activity of watching waltzers waltz is J. J. Grandville. In a series of unpublished sketches dating from 1829 to 1830 of Parisian ballrooms, Grandville gives almost as much attention to the spectators as he does the dancers.[11] The Grandville prints presented in Figures 3.2 and 3.3 depict waltzing in a middle-class Parisian ballroom. In Figure 3.2 a group of men assembled shoulder to shoulder behind a banister take delight in the spectacle. Grandville effectively captures the single-minded intensity of their gaze – all of their heads are fixed forward; none engage in polite conversation among themselves. Figure 3.3 presumably depicts the same room but from a different angle. Here we see the dance orchestra situated in a loge above the dancers. The couples on the left appear to

FIGURE 3.3. J. J. Grandville, *La valse*, 1829/1830.
Reproduced by permission of Musée des Beaux-Arts, Nancy, France.

have just entered the dance floor and are preparing to waltz. Off to the right we again see a gallery of spectators, including a woman.

Why did watching waltzers waltz become such a popular activity at public balls? Just what was it about the waltz that held the spectator's gaze? What was the aesthetic nature of that experience? The choreography of the *valse à trois temps* is marked by unending repetitions of a single step pattern. Throughout the waltz, the couple continually circumscribes small clockwise circles embedded within larger counterclockwise circles. Once the dance begins, there are no changes in direction, no changes in steps, and no intermediary beginnings and endings, as there are with most other ballroom dances. Repetitive continuity is thus an aesthetic hallmark of the waltz's choreography. As a spectacle, however, this uniformity of motion was not what enthralled the spectator; rather, it was the constantly shifting, kaleidoscopic appearance of waltzing couples passing before the onlooker's eyes as he or she gazed from a fixed position in a side gallery. And, as we shall see in the selected quotes that follow, in the vast majority of written accounts of waltzing, the onlookers' eyes were fixed upon the swirling parade of women. Uniformly, the authors of these accounts describe the visual experiences as pleasurable, and to varying degrees of specificity they attempt to describe the aesthetic nature of their experience.

Christoph Friedrich Nicolai (1733–1811), a Berlin philosopher who wrote a parody on Goethe's *Werther* titled *The Joys of Young Werther,* also wrote a travel diary in which he recorded his firsthand impressions of the Viennese waltz: "The dance consists of a continuous turning in circles, often performed by twenty persons in succession. It is, however, a very moderate movement, and as women in Vienna have good figures and beautiful faces, this dance is really a pleasant sight. But the fact that the dancers can continue these slow and monotonous movements for many hours at a time without finding them dull indicates the almost inborn love of Austrians for leisurely comfort."[12] Thus, for Nicolai, in spite of the waltz's monotony of movement, there is beauty to be found in the feminine form. Michael Kelly, a friend of the Mozarts, agrees: "The ladies of Vienna are particularly celebrated for their grace and movements in waltzing, of which they never tire" ([1826] 1968, 202). In his memoir of the Vienna Congress of 1814–15, Auguste-Louis-Charles, comte de La Garde-Chambonas, describes in somewhat greater detail the activity of watching waltzers waltz.[13] His account is important not only for his description of the visual experience but also for his account of the druglike effect the music had upon both dancers and spectators.

> After the departure of the sovereigns the bands struck up a series of waltz tunes, and immediately an electric current seemed to run through the immense gathering. Germany is the country that gave birth to the waltz; it is there, and above all in Vienna that . . . that dance has acquired all the charm inherent in it. It is there that one ought to watch the apparently whirl-like course . . . in which the man sustains and carries away his companion, while she yields to the spell with a vague expression of happiness tending to enhance her beauty. It is difficult to conceive elsewhere the fascination of the waltz. As soon as its strains rise upon the air, the features relax, the eyes become animated, and a thrill of delight runs through the company. The graceful gyrations of the dancers, at first somewhat confused, gradually assume accurately timed movements, while the spectators whom age condemns to immobility beat time and rhythm, mentally joining in the pleasure which is bodily denied them.
>
> The pen fails to reproduce that enchanting scene of beauteous women covered with flowers and diamonds, yielding to the irresistible strains of

the harmony and being carried away in the strong arms of their partners until sheer fatigue compelled them to pause. The pen fails to reproduce the magnificent sight, to which daylight streaming through the windows put an end. (La Garde-Chambonas 1902, 40)

For La Garde-Chambonas, it is both sight and sound that stir the imagination: the feminine beauty of the spectacle is beyond description, and the music behaves like an "electric current" that sends "thrills of delight" through the crowd. Also of note is his account of older spectators who, physically unable to dance, gain pleasure by vicarious participation.

By the first decade of the nineteenth century, the waltz had evolved from a regional Austro-German dance to a cosmopolitan dance enjoyed by all levels of society throughout Europe. Although there were some notable differences, there was broad uniformity in the social dance practices of the upper classes from the major urban centers of Europe (London, Paris, and Vienna). In his novel *A Daughter of Eve* (published in 1838), Honoré de Balzac describes in vivid detail the dizzying display of variety found in upper-class Parisian ballrooms.

The salons presented a magnificent spectacle to the eye, – flowers, diamonds, and brilliant head-dresses; all jewel-boxes emptied; all resources of the toilet put under contribution. The ball-room might be compared to one of those choice conservatories where rich horticulturists collect the most superb rarities, – same brilliancy, same delicacy of texture. On all sides white or tinted gauzes like the wings of the airiest dragon-fly, crêpes, laces, blondes, and tulles, varied as the fantasies of entomological nature; dentelled, waved, and scalloped; spider's webs of gold and silver; mists of silk embroidered by fairy fingers; plumes colored by the fire of the tropics drooping from haughty heads; pearls twined in braided hair; shot or ribbed or brocaded silks, as though the genius of arabesque had presided over French manufactures, – all this luxury was in harmony with the beauties collected there as if to realize a "Keepsake."

The eye received there an impression of the whitest shoulders, some amber-tinted, others so polished as to seem colandered, some dewy, some plump and satiny, as though Rubens had prepared their flesh; in short, all shades known to man in white. Here were eyes sparkling like onyx or turquoise fringed with dark lashes; faces of varied outline presenting the most graceful types of many lands; foreheads noble and majestic, or softly rounded, as if thought ruled, or flat, as if resistant will reigned there unconquered; beautiful bosoms swelling, as George IV admired them, or widely parted after the fashion of the eighteenth century, or pressed together, as Louis XV required; some shown boldly, without veils, others covered by those charming pleated chemisettes which Raffaelle painted. The prettiest feet pointed for the dance, the slimmest waists encircled in the waltz, stimulated the gaze of the most indifferent person present. The murmur of sweet voices, the rustle of gowns, the cadence of the dance, the whir of the waltz harmoniously accompanied the music. A fairy's wand seemed to have commanded this dazzling revelry, this melody of perfumes, these iridescent lights glittering from crystal chandeliers or sparkling in candelabra. This assemblage of the prettiest women in their prettiest dresses stood out upon a gloomy background of men in black coats. (1899, 54–56)

Balzac's gaze is fascinated with all the features of the female form: her face, her body, her clothing, her jewelry, her movement, and her synesthetic relationship with the music as "a melody of perfumes." During the course of his account each woman is anatomically broken up into her constituent parts only to be reassembled as an object of ideal sentimental beauty – as a "keepsake." In capturing the aesthetic singularity of each woman's beauty, Balzac tacitly postulates the infinite variety of feminine beauty. And because the waltz offers the spectator an unending rotation of feminine visions, it is the ideal vehicle to display and view such variety. It is also apparent from Balzac's account that within the patriarchal conventions of the ballroom, women assume an exhibitionist role. Their appearance was intended to have a strong visual impact so that they attracted and held the controlling and imaginative gaze of the audience.[14] Nonetheless, while women drew visual attention to themselves by their constructed appearance, those gazes generally remained beyond the field of their perception.

As if trying to match Balzac's virtuosic account of waltzing Parisian women, the English travel writer Frances Trollope provides a similar account of sensual variety as displayed by Viennese women at a ball held on the last day of carnival in 1836. As does Balzac, Trollope invokes the trope of a horticulturist's conservatory. Here, though, the correspondence is more real than imagined.

The spectacle was then assuredly one of the most singular, as well as prettiest, in the world. . . . Instead of diamonds [the women were] bedight with the loveliest blossoms of spring. I never saw toilets so delicately elegant. Having reached the end of the carnival, that great arena for a contest of modes, I am decidedly of opinion that in exquisite perfection of dress the women of Vienna outdo Paris, as much as Paris outdoes London. On this occasion many ladies wore wreaths of genuine hyacinth and myrtle in their hair, arranged by their milliners with such skill, that by aid of light wires they defied waltzing itself to displace them. Others had their fair brows bound with immortal amaranth; while all the rest, trusting, not in vain, to the skill of a French fleurist, were adorned with such a profusion of what looked like living and breathing blossoms, that I could almost have persuaded myself the lantern-like ball-room was a conservatory, and this beautiful method of showing off plants, the result of some extremely ingenious, new, and imperial contrivance. It was not the lovely heads alone that bloomed in such saucy defiance of the season; the arms too were encircled with flowery wreaths, the bosoms were encircled with flowery wreaths, flowery wreaths floated round and about the light draperies in unnumbered graceful vagaries: so that each noble beauty looked like the queen of May. . . . The colours chosen for the dresses were of the freshest, but most delicate tints, – lemon, lilac, primrose, and pale green, all rendered fainter and more delicate still by the gossamer robes of tulle or gauze worn over them. . . . Strauss and "his merry men" all effectually kept their fingers from freezing by the unceasing spirit of their performance. . . . [T]he ball-room continued to be the chief attraction, and certainly furnished a spectacle that might be long looked at without weariness. (Trollope 1838, 2:255–58)

While Balzac only mentions the presence of men at the end of his description, as a rhetorical foil highlighting the beauty of the women, men, as equal partners in the waltz, are entirely absent from Trollope's account. As these quotes clearly illustrate, people attended balls not only to dance but also to watch dancers dance; and the focus of the spectator rested on the waltzing women, who provided the viewer a swirling concert of colors, perfumes, textures, and feminine forms all wedded to music that both reflected and motivated the dancers' beauty.

Perhaps the most famous nineteenth-century literary portrait of the waltz is contained in Gustave Flaubert's novel *Sentimental Education*, published in 1869. Flaubert's account of a ball attended by Frédéric, the main character, artfully balances the aesthetic forces of perpetual repetition and variety. He also captures the kaleidoscopic effect of viewing the dancers from a fixed point on the perimeter of the dancing space.

A waltz was striking up. At this the women sitting on the sofas along the walls all rose to their feet, one by one, with great alacrity, and their skirts and shawls and head-dresses all began to swirl around.

They swirled past Frédéric so closely that he could see the tiny beads of sweat on their foreheads; and this giddy spinning motion quickened and

FIGURE 3.4. Robert Cruickshank, *A ball in progress at the Argylle Rooms*, 1825. *Reproduced by permission of Taylor & Francis Books UK.*

fell into a constant rhythm; he was gripped by a kind of intoxication, and all these equally dazzling women gyrating in front of his eyes, each with her own special fascination, brought other thoughts surging into his mind. (Flaubert [1869] 1989, 131–32)

Flaubert goes on to describe in vivid detail the individual costume and distinctive sensual beauty of six different women who swirl before him, each eliciting a different erotic fantasy. Such lyrical contemplations suspend the flow of narrative time, creating a chain of imaginary gestalts, each unified and complete within itself. Also, as in the Trollope excerpt, there is no mention of dancing men; a reader not familiar with the waltz might assume there were no men dancing at all! Indeed, while one can easily interject the presence of dancing partners in Trollope's account, Flaubert wrests the waltzing women away from their partners and removes them into the inner sanctum of his erotic imagination. The use of women as either unknowing or exhibitionistic objects of sexual stimulation through sight is a prominent theme in the literature and iconography of the waltz. In a description of waltzing in his novel *Serge Panine*, the French writer Georges Ohnet refers to such prurient eyes as "the vulgar gaze" (1882, 271); feminist theorists today commonly refer to those eyes as the "male gaze."[15] Robert Cruickshank's 1825 illustration of waltzing in a London ballroom is presented in Figure 3.4. On the far left side of the print a group of men ogle the exposed breasts of a female waltzer, and even her dancing partner stoops down to admire. In this case the woman appears to invite knowingly the male gaze not only through her low-cut gown but also by her arching posture.

The spectacle of the waltz, whether directly experienced or imagined through music, literature, or illustrations, provided the nineteenth-century viewer satisfying visual pleasure. There were many possible motivations for gazing into the private spheres of waltzing couples: the novelty of the spectacle, the sensual beauty of the spectacle, the spectacle as a source of male erotic fantasy, or the spectacle as a source of moral and social condemnation.[16] What they all have in common is that the primary object of the gaze is the woman. It is important to point out that no other ballroom dance of the period receives this type of literary attention in which the presence of the male partner is either marginalized or completely removed. In comparison to other dances, the waltz is an ideal vehicle for the visual imagination not only because of the close physical embrace of the man and woman, one in which the woman surrenders physical control to the male, but also because of the variety of feminine visions and the manner in which they are presented: the viewer is entertained to an unending cavalcade of swirling, beautifully dressed women adorned with jewelry, perfume, powder, and flowers. And, unless spectators were positioned in a gallery overlooking the dance floor, they would not be able to track a single couple. Their gazes constantly shifted from one woman to the next.

We are now in a position to construct a set of generalizations about ballroom waltzing during the first half of the nineteenth century from the vantage of the spectator.

- Watching waltzers waltz was an important form of entertainment at balls.
- The experience of watching waltzers was voyeuristic in nature: spectators, standing off to the side, sought visual pleasure by peering into the private, self-contained spheres of the waltzing couples.
- The focus of the spectator was on the sensual beauty of the woman. Within the conventions of nineteenth-century European society, women's appearances were constructed to stimulate and hold the gaze of the spectator.

· The step pattern of the *valse à trois temps* is highly repetitive, marked by continuous clockwise circling motions that require two bars to complete.

· In the face of the consistent motion of the dance, the spectator was entertained by a constantly shifting showcase of feminine variety.

    Forms of variety included:

    styles, colors, and materials of ball gowns

    ball gown accessories (flowers, fans, jewelry, hair fixtures, etc.)

    physical attributes of the women

    manners of waltzing (speed, style, ability)[17]

    smells (perfumes, powders, flowers all combined with personal scents)

    personal dynamics of each couple (married, unmarried, mutual affection, completely uninterested in each other, etc.)

Underlying these generalizations is an interacting cluster of four aesthetic categories: (1) repetitive continuity, (2) self-containment, (3) feminine beauty, and (4) variety. In the section that follows, I attempt to show how these aesthetic categories are also integral to the early Viennese waltz music of Lanner and Strauss Sr. This common ground of correspondences allows one to shuttle easily between the conceptual domains of spectacle and music, whereby the music offers a sonic analogue of the dance, and the dance offers a visual analogue of the music. Furthermore, we are now in a position to show how the emergence of a popular music language is rooted in dance-music relations of the Viennese ballroom.

THE VIENNESE WALTZ AS A "MUSICAL VISION"

The Austrian music scholar Max Graf writes: "If there exists a form of music that is a direct expression of sensuality, it is the Viennese Waltz" (1945, 49). Victor Zuckerkandl speaks of the waltzes of Lanner and Strauss Sr. as "true musical visions."[18] Balzac inverts the dance-music relationship by giving music the dominant role: "The whir of the [dancers] harmoniously accompanied the music." Each of these authors, and many others, perceived some sort of analogical relation between the ballroom dance floor and the music. Building upon this premise, I argue that Viennese waltz composers such as Lanner and Strauss Sr. translated aesthetic qualities drawn from visual experience into appropriate musical corollaries. The corollaries I propose are only approximate and should not be considered completely isomorphic (in any literal or fixed sense), but neither are they fully artificial and arbitrary. Rather, there will be some constant and consistent relation between the two domains that allows the listener to go from one to the other.[19] As Peter Kivy explains, "what must be preserved is analogy of structure" in which "a musical map or model is . . . established, which reflects in its structure some of the parts or elements of an object, phenomenon, or state of affairs, and some of the relations in which these parts or elements stand" (1984, 74–75). In other words, such cross-media interactions are defined by some type of perceived intersection; the two domains are not related directly (A = B) but rather by virtue of some structure, process, or attribute that they both embody or share. According to Lawrence Marks, once such "an analogy is made between A and B, a whole gamut of associated meanings also becomes available. Not only is B like A in a certain way, but any and all of A's properties now become fair game to be absorbed into B" (1978, 252–53). Building upon Kivy, Marks, and George Lakoff and Mark Johnson (1980), among others, Nicholas Cook views cross-media interactions as essentially metaphoric, involving "a reciprocal transfer of attributes that gives rise to meaning constructed, not just reproduced" (1998, 97). By "constructed" Cook means that, because of their inherent differences, the metaphoric interaction of two media will create additional meaning unavailable to each individually. Establishing the spectacle as an important element in the ballroom waltz suggests the possibility of transferring aspects of the spectacle onto the music (and vice versa), but only if there is an "enabling similarity," to use Cook's term (1998, 70), between the two domains.[20] For Lawrence Zbikowski, such enabling similarities allow music to serve as a "sonic analogue" of some other dynamic process of human experience, such as emotion or the movement of a body through space: "One of the places sonic analogues are most evident is in music for dance" (2008, 286).

In this chapter, however, I am not so much considering correspondences between music and the physical gestures of a waltzing couple (i.e., how it felt to dance the waltz); instead, my focus is on identifying enabling similarities between the music and the spectacle of the entire group of waltzing couples as viewed from a fixed position on the ballroom dance floor. While each of the correspondences I discuss are by themselves robust enough to establish some sort of connection between the music of the waltz and the spectacle of the waltz, they are also general enough that they can be found, to varying degrees, in other dance genres. It is the combination, constancy, and degree of all these sonic analogues working in consort – and their cumulative effect – that

Attributes of the Waltz as Seen (Visual Spectacle)		Aesthetic Categories (Enabling Similarities)		Attributes of the Waltz as Heard (Music)
Continuously repeated dance steps	←→	*Repetitive Continuity* AAAA...	←→	Continuous accompaniment pattern (um-pah-pah)
Socially self-contained couples	←→	*Self-Containment* Ⓐ	←→	Musically self-contained themes
Variety of waltzing women	←→	*Variety* ABCD...	←→	Variety of thematic material
Beauty of the waltzing woman: well-formed, attracts attention, memorable, pleasurable to look at	←→	*Feminine Beauty*	←→	Lyrical themes: tight-knit, rhythmically vibrant, memorable, pleasurable to listen to

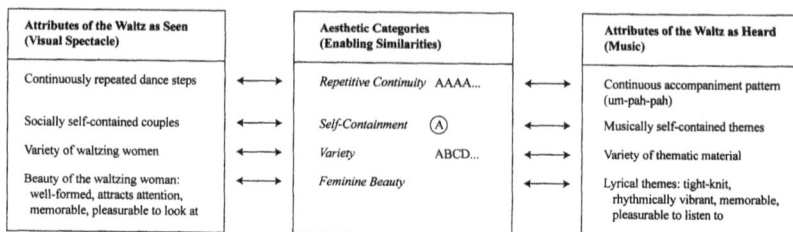

DIAGRAM 3.3. Cross-media relations between the dance and the music.

allows the listener to engage in the music as a musical representation of the visual experience of watching waltzers waltz, that is, as a "true musical vision."

Diagram 3.3 schematizes the cross-media relations between the waltz as seen (spectacle) and the waltz as heard (music). The enabling similarities between the domains are the aesthetic categories of repetitive continuity, self-containment, variety, and feminine beauty. As shown in the diagram, the categories of repetitive continuity, self-containment, and variety can be represented by the image schemata AAAA . . . , Ⓐ, and ABCD . . . , respectively. The notion of feminine beauty is far more complex. It involves a shared collection of culturally constructed attributes that writers and illustrators drew upon in their representations of waltzing women, the most important of which are as follows: an object of feminine beauty is tight-knit (which is to say, well formed), attracts attention, is memorable, and is pleasurable to experience.[21]

Repetitive Continuity: AAAA . . .

As discussed earlier, the *valse à trois temps* is marked by the continuous repetition of a single turning dance step, six beats in length, throughout the entire course of the dance. While performing small clockwise circles, the dancers circumscribe larger counterclockwise circles around the perimeter of the dancing space. According to the dancing master Henri Cellarius, the "principal disadvantage" of the *valse à trois temps* is this "incessant movement of rotation, which the waltzers are obliged to describe" (1840, 29). This "slight monotony," Cellarius believed (1840, 29), contributed to the partial abandonment of the *valse à trois temps* (around 1840) in favor of the *valse à deux temps*, which allowed dancers to move freely in any direction they chose. While Cellarius speaks from the perspective of the dancer, visually, too, the *valse à trois temps* is marked by a consistency of movement without any choreographic divisions. From the vantage of the spectator, the dancers coalesce into a large rotating mass engaged in steps of "endless self-renewal" in "stylized infinity" (Fantel 1971, 151). In some contemporary prints, one can even see the "eye of the storm" – the empty space in the middle of the cyclonic swirl of rotating dancers.[22]

The waltz's accompanimental "drone" analogizes the dynamic processes of the spectacle of the dancers on several levels.[23] On a local level, quarter-note accentuations of the oom-pah-pah accompaniment match the dancers' footsteps with the downbeat bass notes marking the swinging turn of the dance. Given the waltz's moderately fast tempo, slow harmonic rhythm, and two-bar motivic organization, the primary metrical level of the waltz, however, is not the notated quarter note ($\frac{3}{4}$) but rather the dotted half note ($\frac{6}{4}$), in which notated bars are heard as alternating strong and weak hyperbeats within a duple pattern. These $\frac{6}{4}$ hypermeasures match the duration of the individual rotations of the waltzing couple. In looking at larger musical units, a standard eight-bar theme is comprised of four $\frac{6}{4}$ hypermeasures, which correspond to four complete revolutions of the dancers; the eight-bar themes are typically repeated to form sixteen-bar sections in which eight hypermeasures correspond to eight dance revolutions; and the sixteen-bar units typically comprise one part of a complete thirty-two-bar waltz in which sixteen hypermeasures correspond to sixteen dance revolutions.[24] Thus, at a larger level, the rhythmic and metrical consistency, continuity, and cyclicity of the accompaniment pattern match not only the bodily motions of the individual couples but also the combined movements of all the dancers on the ballroom floor.

Interestingly, starting around 1830, Lanner begins experimenting with hypermetric shifts that disrupt the repetitive continuity of the music. One common source of hypermetric shifts is one-bar melodic anacruses. To illustrate, Example 3.1 presents a segment from the fourth waltz of Lanner's "Die Werber," op. 103. The brackets above the music indicate the grouping organization; the arabic numbers in between the staves indicate the two-bar hypermeter. Notice that the hypermeter, which is supported by the terraced dynamics and changes in the accompaniment pattern every two bars, is perfectly in phase with the grouping organization. In bar 142, however, the upper two voices enter without the accompaniment with a three-beat anacrusis marked with a ritardando. This anacrusis together with the resumption of the tempo and the reentrance of the accompaniment in bar 143 create a metrical shift that results in the succession of two weak hyperbeats. The new hyper-

EXAMPLE 3.1. The fourth waltz from Lanner's "Die Werber," op. 103.

metric pattern is clearly supported by the harmonic rhythm. As shown by
the brackets, however, the four-bar grouping organization of the new theme
beginning in bar 142 is now out of phase with the hypermeter by one bar.
An in-phase phrase rhythm is abruptly resumed in bar 158, resulting in the
succession of two hyperdownbeats, a metrical hiccup, so to speak. Also of
rhythmic interest in this passage are the melodic hemiolas, which create a
conflicting beat pattern against the accompaniment. I shall discuss hemiolas
as a characteristic of the Viennese waltz in more detail later in the chapter.

    These hypermetrical disruptions are not motivated by the waltz's chore-
ography. Indeed, as shown in Example 3.1, the shifted two-bar hypermeter is
out of phase not only with the melody but also with the two-bar rotations of
the dancers – hyperdownbeats now punctuate the middles of their rotations
rather than the beginnings. Apparently, waltzers were able to dance through
these passages without losing their footing. That such disruptions become
common only after Lanner had established himself as a successful waltz composer and that they occur throughout the remainder of his works suggest that
he recognized some musical virtue in their use, the most apparent of which is

contrast of phrase rhythm. If Lanner's and Strauss's waltz music was ever to aspire beyond that of a pretty metronome for the dancers, it had to break free from an overly predictable phrase rhythm that results from an unmitigated reliance on eight-bar phrase lengths coordinated with a two-bar hypermeter initiated on the first bar of every phrase. Derek B. Scott cites the significance of this process whereby Lanner and Strauss Sr. increasingly introduced elements into their music that were not directly tethered to the choreographic requirements of the dancers. Drawing on the work of Howard Becker (1982), Scott suggests that waltz music composed before 1830 falls into the category of a "craft world" as opposed to an "art world." However, "it is not unusual," as Scott observes, "to find that a craft world changes into an art world. This happens when values extraneous to the functional purpose become important. When Strauss Sr. began to be concerned with the aesthetics of waltz composition, he was moving from craft to art" (2008, 94).

Metrical shifts brought about by one-bar anacruses are most often accompanied by a contrast in melodic style. Anacrustic themes are characterized by cantabile melodies (often supported by another voice in parallel thirds or sixths), soft dynamics, and a *dolce* or *delicatissimo* expression marking; in other words, they are strongly feminine. These soft, flowing melodies are typically flanked by themes more assertive in nature, as is the case in Example 3.1. The feminine theme's solo entrance, which would typically be performed slightly under tempo, temporarily arrests the flow of metrical time. The resulting metrical disruption not only highlights the entrance of the theme, thereby drawing attention to itself, but also provides the listener a conceptual space in which to savor the unfolding of its sensual beauty.

Hypermetrical disruptions of a different sort are commonly found at the beginnings of codas or somewhere within the opening section of the coda; and here, I believe, there are strong correlations between the music and the visual experience of the spectator, though not necessarily, as we shall see, between the music and the dance. From the earliest to the latest, the openings of Lanner's and Strauss's codas are marked by tonal disjunction, metrical disjunction, and sharp contrasts in texture, orchestration, dynamics, rhythm, and melodic material. The typical features are as follows: the oom-pah-pah accompaniment texture is replaced by thick repeated block chords that highlight the metrical level of the quarter note; the melodic material is nonlyrical and fragmentary, often drawing on fanfare motives; there is a noisy move to the dominant, often accompanied with a long crescendo; and, lastly, after the dominant is reached, the music either eventually resolves to a tonic, breaks

EXAMPLE 3.2. The opening of the coda from Lanner's "Fortsetzung der Katherinen Tänze," op. 41.

off into silence, or dissipates into a solo or unison texture that leads to the entrance of a stable theme. And it is at this climactic juncture that hypermetrical disruptions or ambiguities are commonly found.[25]

All of these elements combine to form powerful, assertive music that draws attention away from the dance floor to the music itself. To illustrate, the opening of the coda from Lanner's waltz "Fortsetzung der Katherinen Tänze," op. 41, is provided in Example 3.2. The previous waltz (not shown) ends in A♭ major. The opening of the coda reasserts the overall tonic key of E♭ major and, through a descending chromatic tetrachord, forcefully drives to a prolonged dominant. In bar 208 the dominant resolves to a hypermetrically accented tonic, the first such hypermetrically accented cadence in the piece. After two beats of silence, the music resumes with a reprise of the melody from the second part of waltz no. 6. The reestablishment of a symmetrical 4 + 4 melodic grouping structure together with a stable oompah-pah accompaniment and the return of a melody previously heard as in phase with the hypermeter all suggest hearing bar 209 as a hyperdownbeat, thereby resulting in the direct succession of two hyperdownbeats (bars 208 and 209).

There are at least two possible explanations as to why Lanner and Strauss Sr. would want to disrupt the repetitive continuity at this point in the piece; neither explanation is mutually exclusive. The first is drawn from the perspective of the dancers: the beginning of the coda was aurally marked so that dancers would know that closure was imminent. While dancers are free to enter and leave the dancing space at their own discretion, the official end of the waltz as danced is not determined by the choreography of the waltz but rather by when the music ends. If dancers wished to remain on the dance floor for the entire duration of the waltz, they needed to be cued when musical closure was close at hand in order not to be taken by surprise. The announcement of the coda thus signals the beginning of a time period during which the gentlemen could carefully escort their dancing partners back to their seats before the beginning of the next dance. Such responsibility was not to be taken lightly. Cellarius cautions the gentleman that he "should take care never to relinquish his lady until he feels that she has entirely recovered herself. The effect of the rotary motion, even after stopping, is sometimes so great, that he would risk his partner's losing her equilibrium by detaching himself from her too suddenly" (1840, 43–44).

Such musical disruptions had little correlation to what the gallery was watching on the ballroom dance floor, except for the fact that soon after the beginning of the coda one might begin to see more and more couples gradually take leave of the ballroom dance floor. The important point here is that there is nothing in the dancers' choreography that correlates to or motivates these musical disruptions. In such instances, as is the case also with metrical disruptions resulting from anacrustic melodies, the music takes prominence, not only asserting a controlling presence apart from the dance but also creating a perceptual rift between the spectacle and the music. The music of such passages is not so much about the dance; instead, it is *music about music*. Moreover, these rifts violate a cardinal rule of functional dance music in that it "should not be in the forefront, obscuring the dance or distracting the audience from the movement of the dancers" (Krumhansl and Schenck 1997, 65). This conventional sentiment can be found as early as 1746 in Charles Batteux's treatise *Les beaux-arts réduits à un même principe*. Batteux observes that "dance music must not be distractingly brilliant. It should merely hold out a helping hand in order to bar with greater precision the character and movement of the dance" ([1746] 1981, 51).

As for the spectators, their eyes would most naturally be diverted to the ones responsible for the disruption: the dance orchestra and especially the conductor, who in most cases was also the author of the disruption. Paralleling the development of these musical techniques is a remarkable shift in the iconography of dance orchestras from the eighteenth century to the beginning of the nineteenth century. In eighteenth-century depictions, musicians, if included at all, were rarely given visual prominence. And when they are shown, one seldom sees orchestral leaders. Almost without exception, however, beginning in the early nineteenth century, depictions of ballroom dancing not only include the dance orchestra in a visually prominent position but also include an orchestra leader standing and holding a violin. And in many cases, the visual presence of the leader is accentuated by his position relative to the viewer: instead of facing the musicians, he faces outward with his violin bow held high above his head.

This iconographic shift reflects the rise of the conductor/composer as a popular public figure and a shift in the dance-music hierarchy whereby dance music is as important or more important than the dance itself. As Hector Berlioz recounts in his memoir, "sometimes, when one of the new waltzes which [Strauss Sr.] writes for every society ball makes a special hit, the dancers stop to applaud and the ladies go over to his rostrum and throw him their bouquets" (1969, 377). And at least as early as the 1820s, dance music introduced in the Viennese ballroom was also performed during the summer months in public parks and in restaurants year round without dancing.

Self-Containment: (A)

The visual experience of watching self-contained couples, socially and choreographically complete in themselves, is represented by melodies that are motivically stable and exhibit clearly defined beginnings, middles, and endings. Amazingly, the ends of the vast majority of Viennese waltz themes are articulated by authentic cadences; half cadences are rare. Moreover, thematic development is near absent, and ABA-type repetition schemes are seldom used, at least in the early waltzes of Lanner and Strauss Sr. Unless it is restated in the coda, once a theme is heard, it is forever gone. This self-contained, nondevelopmental approach to thematic material is, of course, antithetical to the compositional aesthetics of art music, which places a high value on thematic economy, thematic unity, and thematic development. The absence of thematic repetition and development, especially, rankled many critics. Eduard Hanslick, for example, laments that "the narrow compact of the waltz does not permit the slightest development of melody; as soon as it has come to a close it disappears without a trace, making way for the second, the third, the fourth, until all five themes have been played. . . . [T]his is inartistic wastefulness which must exhaust even the most talented."[26]

Viennese waltz themes are thus thematically and tonally closed, offering self-sufficient melodies that do not point outside of themselves. Rather than being involved in a process of becoming, waltz melodies exist full bloom in the present and, as such, project suspended temporal states. In other words, they are gestalts whose parts, while not stated simultaneously, express a single, unified whole. Raymond Monelle (2000, 90–114) uses the term "lyrical time" for such temporal units and describes them as evocative, descriptive, and picturesque. A complete Viennese waltz may be heard as a succession of suspended temporal units or images that in and of themselves do not suggest any conventional Classical narrative order of cause and effect. This new temporality is perhaps the most revolutionary aspect of Viennese waltzes and a dominant feature of the emerging language of popular music.

While the accompaniment pattern provides the music a sense of cyclicity through and across the succession of thematic images, Lanner and Strauss Sr. also relied on other musical means to provide the listener a sense of forward momentum and continuity: auxiliary progressions and middleground tonal trajectories. I shall discuss these compositional techniques later in the chapter.

Feminine Beauty

The primary evocative object of Viennese waltz melodies is the same as that of the spectator – the waltzing woman. The sensual beauty of the woman is captured by melodies that are tight-knit, rhythmically vibrant, memorable, and pleasing to listen to.

"Tight-knit," a term introduced by Erwin Ratz (1973) and subsequently developed by William Caplin in his study of form in Classical music, refers to a melodic organization "characterized by harmonic-tonal stability, cadential confirmation, unity of melodic-motivic material, efficiency of functional expression, and symmetrical phrase groupings" (1998, 17). In their well-formedness and by their twofold repetitions through repeat marks, Viennese waltz melodies are strongly presentational in function, which is to say that they are exhibitionist in character. In pointing only to themselves without motivic reference to previous or ensuing themes, waltz melodies are presented to listeners as the sole objects of their attention. Furthermore, the transparency of texture, symmetry of grouping, efficiency of functions, and wholeness of organization allow Viennese waltz melodies to be readily grasped and, therefore, memorable.

These attractive, well-dressed melodies, which glide so effortlessly atop the steady drone of the accompaniment, often form rhythmically conflicting patterns against the prevailing $\frac{3}{4}$ meter. Not only do these rhythmic dissonances draw attention to the melody, they also result in a clear perceptual distinction between the melody and the accompaniment. In this way the effort and physicality of the (female) dancer's footwork, as modeled by the oom-pah-pah accompaniment, is separated from the lyrical contemplation of her beauty.

Berlioz confesses that when he visited Vienna in 1845 he would spend "whole nights watching these incomparable waltzers whirling around in great clouds" (1969, 377). Not only was he enchanted by the spectacle, but he was also transfixed by Strauss's rhythmic genius. Some eight years earlier, Berlioz wrote an article entitled "Strauss: His Orchestra, His Waltzes – the Future of Rhythm" in which he locates one source of the waltz's femininity in the cross-rhythms found between the melody and accompaniment: "The pieces they play – these charming waltzes in which the melody seems to delight in teasing and tormenting the measure in a thousand ways – contain some fairly exacting problems, and the ease and aplomb with which they are handled only adds an irresistible charm to the rhythmic coquetting."[27]

Melodies that form hemiolic patterns against the prevailing $\frac{3}{4}$ meter of the accompaniment are the most common type of metrical dissonance that Berlioz identifies.[28] As previously mentioned, in terms of our perception, however, the accompaniment is more easily heard hypermetrically in $\frac{6}{4}$ rather than in the notated $\frac{3}{4}$. Playing against the accompaniment's $\frac{6}{4}$, the melodies project their own $\frac{3}{2}$ grouping patterns. Example 3.3 provides some examples. As seen in the first three melodies, a common maneuver employed by Lanner and Strauss Sr. is the progression from metrical dissonance to metrical consonance within an eight-bar phrase or within a four-bar subphrase. Occasionally, as in the fourth melody, the melody's hemiola is preserved through the entire phrase. It is remarkable how much rhythmic variety Lanner and Strauss Sr. were able to achieve within such a tight compositional framework. As Berlioz marveled, Strauss Sr. "made use of every beat in the bar" for some rhythmic effect.[29] The same can be said of Lanner, as the third melody attests. In its first three bars, every beat initiates a different grouping pattern: the oom-pah-pah accompaniment begins on beat 1; a repeating four-note pattern begins in the melody on beat 2; and accents occur on every other beat beginning on beat 3. Because the melody has two different two-beat accentual patterns, there are two possible hemiolic interpretations. If one privileges

Strauss, Op. 32, bars 169–76

Lanner, Op. 52, bars 76–83

Lanner, Op. 92, bars 46–53

Lanner, Op. 95, bars 53–60

EXAMPLE 3.3. Examples of metrical dissonance in the waltzes of Lanner and Strauss Sr.

the repeating four-note pattern, then a $\frac{3}{2}$ pattern may be heard, with the first complete measure beginning on the downbeat of the second bar. The arrival of the *f* in the fourth bar and the harmonic rhythm both lend support to this reading. The E in the fifth bar as well as the A in the last bar would function as syncopations. If, however, one privileges the evenly placed dynamic accents, then a different $\frac{3}{2}$ pattern may be heard beginning on the downbeat of the first measure.

Because of their tight-knit organization, rhythmic vitality, and lyrical nature, Viennese waltz melodies are pleasurable to listen to, and they incite pleasurable behavior.[30] Moreover, the pleasure afforded by waltz music is immediate and requires no mental effort of the sort needed to appreciate and enjoy the formal processes and musical grammar of a Beethoven string quartet, for example. As quoted earlier, La Garde-Chambonas observes that as soon as the orchestra begins playing waltz music, "the features relax, the eyes become animated, and a thrill of delight runs through the company" (1902, 40). In his autobiography, Richard Wagner recounts the behavior effects of Strauss's music in Vienna during the summer of 1832 at the Sträusselsäle when he was but nineteen years old: "I shall never forget the enthusiasm, bordering on derangement, generated in that extraordinary figure Johann Strauss whenever he played. . . . [A]nd veritable whinnies of pleasure from the audience, indubitably attributable more to his music than to the drinks they had enjoyed, whipped up the ecstasies of this magician of the violin to heights that nearly frightened me" (1983, 63). Critics cited the music's ability to lure listeners and dancers into mental states of magical delight, frenzy, and intoxication, whereby they were apt to lose their better judgment and fall into some lascivious behavior. In a travel report written in 1833 for the Leipzig periodical *Zeitung für die elegante Welt*, Heinrich Laube provides a firsthand account of an evening at the Sperl dance hall under the direction of Strauss Sr. According to Laube, Strauss's new music "stirs the young blood like the bite of a tarantula." Once under his spell, Laube continues, Strauss "exorcises the wicked devils from our bodies and he does it with waltzes, which is modern exorcism, and he . . . captures our senses in a sweet trance. . . . A dangerous power has been given into the hands of this dark man; he may call it his good fortune that to music one may think all kinds of thoughts, that no censorship can have anything to do with waltzes, that music stimulates our emotions directly, and not through the channel of thought."[31]

Thus, similar to Flaubert's account of Frédéric watching waltzers waltz, waltz music in these accounts both unconsciously triggers pleasurable emotions and sensations and activates a mental space in which to construct and contemplate thoughts and images – real or imaginary – drawn from the domain of the ballroom. In the contemporary literature one finds a broad range of expressive interpretations of waltz music, from the most innocent, naive expressions of love and images of feminine beauty to the most lascivious sexual desires. In the majority of reports, the pleasures that come from the music are of the sort associated with pleasures that come from women; when performed without dancing, the music thus acts as a type of surrogate for the woman. The combination of music and dance creates an amplified, multimedial image of the woman whereby, as we have previously seen in the quotes by Flaubert and Trollope, the presence of the man is diminished almost to the point of extinction.

The unmitigated pleasures afforded by waltz music, however, also served as a distraction from the harsh realities of Viennese political and social life, where any intellectual activity was held suspect and officially discouraged. According to Hanslick, waltz music provided listeners a blissful contentment that rendered them "less capable of intellectual effort" (1950, 21). "If I were a despot," quips the Viennese poet Georg Adolph Glasbrenner, "I would award a ton of gold to Strauss and Lanner to lull the heads of my subjects and halt all public discussions."[32] According to Maximilian Leopold Langenschwarz, waltzing "clouded the brain, aroused sexual appetites, and quashed any thought of revolution."[33] Indeed, Prince Clemens von Metternich, the principal author of Vienna's strict censorship policies, himself admits, "with Strauss and the Apollo [dance hall] you keep the demagogues quiet."[34]

Variety: ABCD . . .

Of all the aesthetic categories, variety is the central premise of the Viennese waltz, both as a spectacle and as a musical genre. The variety displayed on the ballroom dance floor is captured by an astounding variety in thematic material, whereby a parade of waltzing women is matched by a parade of beautiful melodies. And this is perhaps the most striking feature of Viennese waltzes: the profusion of themes. No other dance or instrumental genre comes close to matching the quantity and variety of themes found in Viennese waltzes. Diagram 3.4 illustrates the standard thematic layout of Viennese waltzes from around 1830: an introduction followed by six waltzes and anchored by a lengthy coda.[35] The individual waltzes are typically in simple binary form (A:‖:B) with each section closed by an authentic cadence. It is not unusual for the second half of a waltz to be in a different key than the first half. Thus, instead of hearing a succession of six independent waltzes, a listener is more apt to hear an open-ended succession of twelve or more contrasting, self-contained lyrical themes framed by an introduction and coda. And it was not unusual for codas to introduce new themes as well. While the 1820s and 1830s saw a gradual reduction in the number of themes waltz compositions contained, there were occasional outbursts of thematic extravagance. Lanner's

Viennese waltz as notated

	waltz 1	waltz 2	waltz 3	waltz 4	waltz 5	waltz 6	
intro	a :||: b	c :||: d	e :||: f	g :||: h	i :||: j	k :||: l	coda

Viennese waltz as heard

	1	2	3	4	5	6	7	8	9	10	11	12	
intro	a	b	c	d	e	f	g	h	i	j	k	l	coda

DIAGRAM 3.4. Standard thematic layout of a Viennese waltz 1830–35.

"The Waltz Flood or Twenty Years in Twenty Minutes," op. 129, for example, contains over one hundred themes.[36]

The succession of waltz themes, each self-contained, lyrical, and pleasurable to listen to, may be experienced as a chain of temporal gestalts, each eliciting from the listener a broad range of emotional, sensual, and visual associations. As I have argued, a primary source or anchor for the production of meaning in the Viennese waltz in the first half of the nineteenth century is the conceptual domain of the ballroom. The enabling similarities between the dance and the music provided listeners an interpretive framework from which they could construct their own individual expressive readings. The succession of themes can thereby be thought of as prompting in the listener a "slide show" of imagined events, expressive states, or objects drawn from the ballroom. And, as I have argued, the most captivating image is the waltzing woman. Thus, it is no surprise that so many waltzes are dedicated to women or have titles with feminine associations.

To further illustrate generic features of Viennese waltzes, Diagram 3.5 provides form charts of two waltzes by Lanner. As is typical, they are cast in the major mode. Lanner and Strauss Sr. prefer the keys of D major, A major, and E major since they are the most resonant keys for the violin. All themes are eight bars long unless indicated otherwise.[37] Most of the individual waltzes are in simple binary form, which allows for long stretches of open-ended thematic variety. In "Paradies Soirée Walzer," for example, all sixteen themes are heard in succession (abcdefghijklmnop); only at the end is there an element of thematic return, and then only of three themes (m, n, and c).

"Redout Carneval Tänze," op. 42 (1830)

abcdefghijklmnopqr (18)

Waltz 1	Waltz 2	Waltz 3	Waltz 4	Waltz 5	Waltz 6

‖: a :‖: b :‖ ‖: c c :‖: d d :‖ ‖: e f :‖: g g :‖ ‖: h h :‖: i :‖: h h :‖ ‖: j j :‖: k l :‖: m m :‖ ‖: n :‖: o :‖ coda (pqr)

(16) (135)

TT XT   TT TT XT XT   TT XT XT XT   TT TT XD TT TT   XT XT XT XT XT XT   TT XT

D major: I   IV   I   vi   V   I

"Paradies Soirée Walzer," op. 52 (1830)

abcdefghijklmnop (16)

Waltz 1	Waltz 2	Waltz 3	Waltz 4	Waltz 5	Waltz 6	Waltz 7 (waltz-trio-waltz)

(16)
intro ‖: a a :‖: b b :‖ ‖: c c c :‖: d :‖ ‖: e :‖: f :‖ ‖: g :‖: h :‖ ‖: i :‖: j j :‖ ‖: k :‖: l :‖ ‖: m m :‖: n n :‖ o ‖: p :‖: m m :‖: n n :‖ coda (ak)

(70)

XT XT TT TT   XT XT TT   TT TT   XT XT   XD XT XT   XT TT   TT TT TT TT TD XT TT TT TT TT

C major: I   IV   bVI   V-I   IV   V-I   IV   I

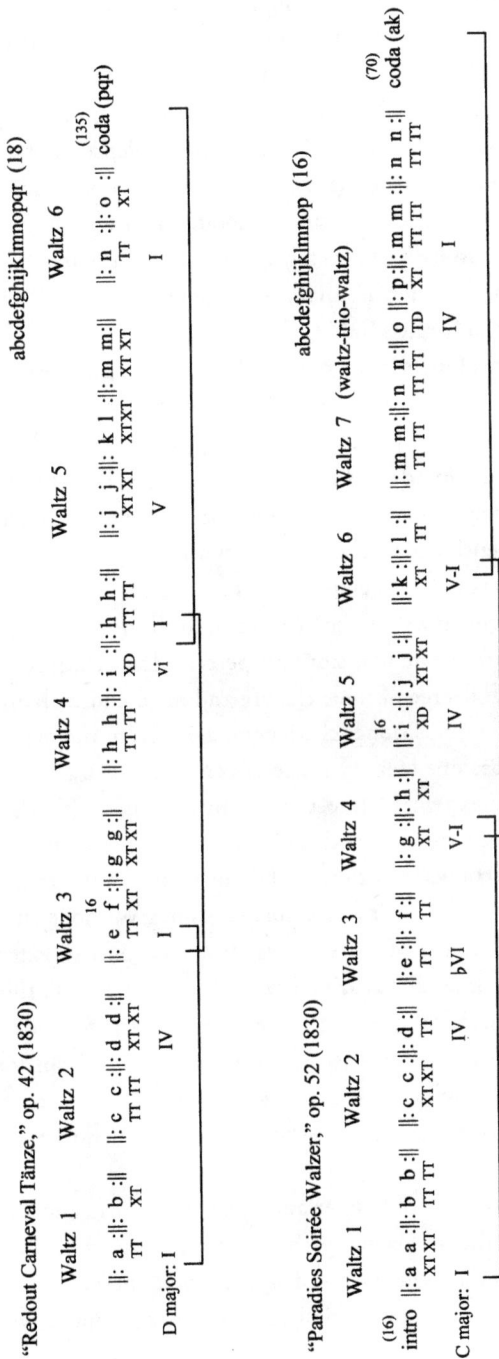

DIAGRAM 3-5. Form charts of two waltzes by Joseph Lanner.

Given beneath the thematic design of each waltz are two letters that indicate the opening and closing harmonies of the individual themes. Themes begin either with a tonic (T) or a nontonic (X) harmony, most typically a dominant, and end with a tonic (T) or dominant (D) harmony. When a theme ends with T, T will be part of an authentic cadence (root position V–I progression); when a theme ends with D, D will be a half cadence. This is admittedly a rather crude shorthand method for depicting harmonic aspects of the music, but, despite its extremely limited focus, it is able to reveal some interesting harmonic tendencies that are characteristic of the Viennese waltz music of Lanner and Strauss Sr.

For example, as I mentioned previously, the waltz themes of Lanner and Strauss Sr. are strongly characterized by an unusually high degree of tonal closure. As can be seen in the diagram, nearly every theme (forty-six out of forty-nine) is tonally closed with an authentic cadence. If part of a paired thematic statement, the end of the first statement is most often articulated with an imperfect authentic cadence, the second with a perfect authentic cadence. The strong tonal articulation contributes to a theme's sense of self-containment, which in turn allows it to be mapped onto the domain of the dance, in which each couple (or woman) is similarly perceived as an independent entity.

With the high degree of tonic closure and open-ended thematic design come two related compositional challenges: aside from the ongoing accompaniment, how does one create a sense of continuity and momentum from one theme to the next when almost every theme closes with a stable tonic? And how does one create large-scale unity and coherence without recourse to thematic repetition or without the use of thematically and/or tonally unstable sections in alternation with more stable sections? Without such unifying devices, Adolph Bernard Marx observes that "the content, extent, and arrangement [of a waltz cycle] is arbitrary and, for that reason, the unity less energetic" ([1856] 1997, 77). Certainly, the introduction and coda provide an overall framework ensuring a sense of global initiation and closure, but what about the succession of themes in between? Were Lanner and Strauss Sr. operating from a compositional aesthetic in which such matters were not important?

Even if many waltzes of Lanner and Strauss Sr. are in effect patchworks of individual waltz themes sewn together without a compelling formal or thematic logic guiding their sequence and organization, there are others where it appears that Strauss Sr., and especially Lanner, were grappling with issues of continuity and large-scale coherence. These attempts to gain greater control over their musical materials perhaps may be read as evidence of a natural development in their compositional abilities. It is also possible, however, that Lanner and Strauss Sr. felt a certain level of anxiety over the ephemeral and indulgent qualities of their waltz themes, their static temporalities, and their erotic powers. And one must also consider that their music was increasingly being performed without dancing, as concert music for the sole pleasure of listening, and what is effective on the dance floor may not work on the concert stage. Whatever the motivation, the result of their appropriation of teleological compositional techniques from art music is that the musical representation of feminine beauty becomes subdued and subsumed within overarching tonal processes.

On a small scale, one remarkable feature that provides tonal continuity is thematic entrances that begin off tonic, which Heinrich Schenker identifies as "auxiliary progressions." Such in medias res beginnings give waltz themes a sense of motion at their very beginnings, as if they were already moving before they entered our field of perception. Auxiliary progressions are indeed a signal feature of the Viennese waltz. In the two waltzes represented in Diagram 3.5, well over half of the themes begin off tonic; this percentage is representative of most Viennese waltzes composed from the early 1830s onward.

On a larger scale, continuity and coherence result from tonal trajectories that combine three or more waltz themes within a single large-scale progression. The progressions are typically realized through a series of modulations in which changes in key are aligned with new thematic entrances. Simple three-chord progressions, such as I–V–I and I–IV–I, are standard fare for the early waltzes of Lanner and Strauss Sr. For example, Lanner's "Redout Carneval Tänze" (Diagram 3.5a) is comprised of three such overlapping progressions: I–IV–I–vi–I–V–I. Notice that themes a, b, and c are all in the tonic, D major. Theme d, the second theme of Waltz 2, is entirely set in the key of G major, the subdominant of D major. The pairing of themes c and d together as Waltz 2 is thus arbitrary; there is no musical reason to suggest hearing them together as a formal syntactical unit. Rather, one is more apt to hear themes a, b, and c as one unit and theme d as a self-standing unit. Indeed, Lanner supports this interpretation not only by tonal contrast but also by a marked change in melodic style: whereas themes a, b, and c are energetic and rhythmically active, theme d, marked *dolce*, is more relaxed and in a cantabile melodic style.

EXAMPLE 3.4. Two bass-line sketches of Lanner's "Die Werber," op. 103.

Already by the early 1830s, Lanner begins experimenting with more sophisticated tonal designs, as can be seen in his "Paradies Soirée Walzer"
(Diagram 3.5b). The first eight themes of "Paradies" are united within a single
overarching progression, I–IV–♭VI–V–I. Notice how the subdominant *Stufe*
enters in the second half of Waltz 2. The V–I auxiliary progression that begins theme g of Waltz 4 assumes structural significance in that it completes
the middleground progression initiated in Waltz 1. The waltz continues with
two more overlapping progressions, I–IV–V–I–IV–I.

Example 3.4 presents two bass-line sketches of "Die Werber," a work
Mendelssohn (1972, 134) deemed worthy of careful study. The thematic design
is presented above the bass line in level *a*; a deeper middleground reading is
presented in level *b*. A rotation of eleven different waltz themes is heard in
direct succession (abcdefghijk); it is only in the coda, which itself introduces
three new themes (l, m, and n), that previously heard material reappears (c
and k). This thematic extravagance is tempered by three large tonal progressions (see level *b*), none of which is aligned with the boundary points of
the individual waltzes. The opening progression (I–III♯–vi–ii⁶–V–I), which
is based on descending fifths, encompasses the introduction and first two
waltz themes (a and b). The opening waltz not only begins off tonic but also
off key in F♯ minor. Moreover, the particular pitch sequence of the bass is an
enlarged motivic repetition of the principal motive (*y*) of the introduction. The
annotated score given in Example 3.5a shows the appearances of this motive
in the opening fourteen bars of the introduction. The high degree of motivic
integration between different levels of tonal structure is quite unusual for
Lanner (and Strauss Sr.), and perhaps this is a feature that caught the attention of Mendelssohn's ear. Also unusual is the use of the same motive within
different waltzes. Example 3.5b shows one particularly clever manipulation
of the motive resulting in a tonal double entendre. In bar 118, coming off the
heels of a perfect authentic cadence in the key of E major, the motive is heard
as an arpeggiation of an E-major triad with C♯ functioning as an incomplete

EXAMPLE 3.5A. Motivic repetition in the opening fourteen bars
of Lanner's "Die Werber," op. 103.

EXAMPLE 3.5B. Tonal reinterpretation of the motive in Lanner's
"Die Werber," op. 103.

EXAMPLE 3.5C. Voice-leading sketch of a passage
from Lanner's "Die Werber," op. 103.

upper neighbor to the B that follows. The first ending, however, completely changes the tonal context from which the motive will again appear; it tonicizes the key of C♯ minor, the relative minor of E major. Following an assertive dominant of C♯ minor, the return of the motive is now heard as an arpeggiated C♯-minor triad. As shown in Example 3.5c, underlying this passage is a large-scale motivic repetition of the same motive that, in a manner similar to the large-scale motivic repetition shown in Example 3.4 (level *b*), straddles sectional boundaries of the form.

Given the prominence of this motive up to this point in the work, it is interesting to observe that Lanner drops all reference to it in the music that follows – it is never heard again, not even in the coda. Certainly, this does not follow the standard narrative strategy of motivic development as found in art music of the same period, where it is the proper business of codas to recall important motives. Thus, from the perspective of art music, its absence in the second half of this work is puzzling. However, fully integrated techniques of motivic development were not necessary for the Viennese waltz to be effective, given the social purposes it was intended to fulfill. One must also keep in mind that motivic integration from the beginning of a work to its end runs contrary to the notion of open-ended (feminine) variety, which, as I have argued, is one of the dominant aesthetics of the Viennese waltz. Thus, this work exhibits a creative tension brought about by the incongruity of composition techniques drawn from two musical worlds: popular dance music and art music.

Returning to Example 3.4 (level *b*), the second large progression, I–V/V–V–I, creates an underlying momentum that unites the next five themes (cdefg) within a single tonal trajectory. The third large tonal progression again begins with a descending-fifths motion that goes well beyond the previous two progressions, leading eventually to the subtonic, G major. Note that the descending fifths were initiated in the second progression, thereby resulting in a tonal process that stretches across six waltz themes (efghij). Placing the point of furthest remove – G major, the goal of the descending-fifths motion – roughly three-quarters of the way through the piece and directly before a recapitulatory coda gives this work a well-formed dynamic curve common to many instrumental works of the concert stage. The coda begins with an E-minor chord, first heard as the submediant of G major. Shortly thereafter, G♯ is reintroduced, transforming the E-minor chord into the dominant of A major. The rather lengthy coda (109 bars), which introduces several new themes, remains in the tonic key. The final passage of the coda (bar 290 to the end) is pure musical showmanship designed to capture the listener's ear. The passage begins with a *fortissimo* unison outburst that climbs chromatically to a dominant. After a three-bar anacrusis, Lanner then initiates a "fade-out." Not only does the melodic line gradually descend three octaves, but the dynamics also drop every eight bars from *p* to *pp* to *ppp*. Once *ppp* is reached, the oom-pah-pah ceases, and in its place sounds a sustained pedal A over which is twice repeated a plaintive progression I–iv–vii°⁷–I. The *ppp* passage continues with a four-bar diminuendo that fades into four beats of silence. The music has thus relinquished all ties to the dancers on the dance floor. Lanner suddenly breaks the spell with two crashing *ff* tonic chords, which conclude the piece. Lanner could only have conceived and performed such a passage if he were reasonably confident that it would be effective in a large, crowded ballroom – such as the Grosser Redoutensaal, where he was musical director of Imperial Court balls beginning in 1829. A vital part of this passage's effectiveness depends upon the ball participants turning their attention away from the dance and to the music.

While the high degree of motivic integration exhibited in this waltz is rather unusual for Viennese waltzes of this time, the use of overarching tonal progressions to provide continuity and coherence across wide spans of music had become a standard fixture of Viennese waltzes by the early 1830s. This compositional development in the genre of the Viennese waltz was an important if not an essential step in establishing the waltz music of Lanner and Strauss Sr. as music to be enjoyed for its own sake, outside the confines of the dance hall.

CONCLUSION

"The vision is universal: turning, whirling, the music of Johann Strauss, elegantly attired women in long sweeping skirts, romance. These are some of the notions commonly associated with the *waltz*." So begins Elizabeth Aldrich's discussion of the waltz in her essay "Social Dancing in Schubert's World" (1997, 131). It is interesting to note the close correspondence between Aldrich's description and contemporary accounts: the vision is centered on the whirling women, beautiful in appearance; there is no mention of the male partner (although a man is implied by the word "romance"); and she notes the importance of music as an essential component to the multimedia vision. In an earlier essay (Aldrich 1990, 30), however, she correctly observes that the waltz was *not* intentionally designed and performed for the enjoyment of a viewing audience; nonetheless, the scopophilic pleasures that the spectacle afforded the viewer were so great that the activity of watching waltzers waltz quickly became a favorite pastime at balls. Furthermore, the musical attributes of the Viennese waltz were so well defined and, more important, the music and vision were so indelibly linked – each being a reflection of the other – that waltz music by itself spontaneously activated the vision of ballroom waltzers in the creative imagination of the listener. This is why, as we shall see in chapter 5, nineteenth-century commentators on Chopin's waltz music all interpreted it within the context of the ballroom. The same cannot be said for his mazurkas and polonaises.

I would suggest that the Viennese waltz's enduring popularity and universality, first as a dance and then as a musical genre and style topic, do not rest entirely upon this vision but are due in large part to the enabling similarities between the dance and the music. As I have shown, the aesthetic categories of repetitive continuity, self-containment, feminine beauty, and variety are essential both to the dance and the music. Thus, dance and music not only reflect but also, by their inherent differences, enhance each other's aesthetic qualities, thereby creating a greater whole. This high degree of correspondence, together with moments of noncongruity, provides the listener a richer interpretive field and a greater depth of meaning than is found in other dance types of the nineteenth-century ballroom, such as the cotillion, quadrille, gallop, or, later in the century, the polka.[38] It is not until the sultry tango that we have another dance type with such strong analogical relations between the spectacle of the dance and the music that accompanies it.

4th

Dance and the Music of Chopin: Historical Background

[Chopin] would turn into a lusty musician and start thundering out mazurkas, waltzes and polkas until, tired of playing and eager to join in the dancing himself, he would cede the keyboard to a humbler replacement.

KAZIMIERZ WÓJCICKI

No other Romantic composer of art music was more devoted to the composition of dance music than Fryderyk Chopin (1810–49). From the irregular rhythms of the mazurka to the pulsating drive of the waltz, nearly half of Chopin's works are dances, and a large portion of the remaining works incorporate dance elements within them. Despite the prominence of popular dance music in Chopin's compositions and within his social world, musicologists and theorists have been somewhat reluctant to view his music in light of the urban social dance practices upon which they are based.[1] The devaluation of popular music, the feminine association of the salon, the ideology of autonomy, and, in the case of the mazurka, the "myth of the folk" have all diverted attention from the feet of the well-heeled dancer.[2]

In the three remaining chapters, I offer fresh analytical insights into the waltzes of Chopin by viewing them in light of early nineteenth-century urban dance practices as found in Europe and, more specifically, in Warsaw, the city where Chopin lived during his youth. As in the earlier chapters, an underlying premise guiding this study is that to better understand the musical structure and expressive meaning in Chopin's dance music, it is crucial to understand the bodily rhythms and social contexts of the dances upon which they are based.

I first present an overview of social dancing in Warsaw from roughly 1800 to 1830 and discuss the reception of the waltz in Warsaw during this time. I then examine Chopin's involvement with social dancing, both as a dancer and as a dance musician.

SOCIAL DANCING IN WARSAW

Despite political unrest, Warsaw, the city where Chopin grew up and spent his first twenty years, was a robust cosmopolitan center in the midst of a cultural renaissance and economic boom (Goldberg 2008, 4–5). Importantly for Chopin, Warsaw was well connected to the social and artistic trends of Vienna and Paris, and, as in other European capitals, ballroom dancing was deeply woven into the warp and woof of its social fabric. Foreign dancing masters, largely French, kept Warsaw's cultural elite abreast of Europe's most current dances, dance steps, and dance etiquette. Two of the most popular ballroom Polish dances were the mazurka and the polonaise. Although both of these dances have their roots in regional folk dances, by Chopin's time they had been transformed into stylized urban dances for the upper classes.

In his two books devoted to statistical, historical, and social descriptions of Warsaw (1827, 1831), the historian Łukasz Gołębiowski (1773–1849) provides the first detailed account of social dancing in Warsaw during the second half of the eighteenth century and into the first quarter of the nineteenth century. Gołębiowski ([1827] 1979, 222) reports that *redutas* (small dance parties held in rented halls or palaces) were given at least three times a week from October to Lent. Certain entrepreneurs became well known for the splendor and opulence of their *redutas*, which also included – in addition to dancing – eating, drinking, and gambling. Gołębiowski ([1827] 1979, 222) observes that at one such dance party more than ten thousand złotys changed hands, a considerable amount even by today's standards.

Balls, a general designation for a dancing occasion larger and more formal than *redutas,* were the most common form of dance entertainment in Warsaw. It seems that almost any occasion warranted a ball. There were charity balls, friendly balls, children's balls, balls for old people, birthday balls, almond balls, professional assembly balls, saint's day balls, balls for foreign dignitaries, balls for the commemoration of historical events, military balls, political balls, and special balls organized for the lower classes. Masquerade balls, first introduced by King August II (1670–1733) in the first half of the eighteenth century, were a particular favorite of the upper classes. According to Gołębiowski ([1827] 1979, 223), their popularity was due to an enticing combination of music, dancing, theater, gambling, and the thrill of appearing incognito. Exorbitant amounts of money were spent on lavish costumes. An entertainment writer for the *Kurier warszawski,* Warsaw's daily newspaper, describes the various costumes worn at a masquerade held at the National Theater on 1 January 1830: "Of masks, we can mention a wise *Pilgrim* and an old *German,* who with his constant movement entertained all. Also there was a *Man from Crakow* coupled with a *Greek Woman,* a *Spaniard* with a *Warsaw Woman,* a joyful *Squire,* a very polite *Hunchback,* and a *Shepherd Girl* in dark trousers, etc." (1 January 1830, 2).[3]

In the 1820s, when Chopin became active in Warsaw's social life, public balls were regularly held in four halls: the Merchant's Resursa, the New Resursa, the Variety Theater, and the National Theater, which, apart from the main theater, also had a hall specifically designed for dancing. The main halls of the Variety and National Theaters could easily accommodate large numbers of dancers, since there were no permanent chairs and their main floors were flat, not pitched, as is customary in modern halls.[4] Many palaces such as the Royal Palace, Łazienki Palace, and the Branicki Palace also contained their own dance halls. During the summer months there were dancing entertainments in the parks and gardens in and around Warsaw (e.g., at the Saxon Gardens and Tamka) (Gołębiowski [1827] 1979, 225). Gołębiowski also tells of dancing at casinos, picnics, and concerts ([1827] 1979, 222).

The main venue for social dancing in Warsaw, besides the public and private dance halls, were salons, the private entertaining rooms of the middle and upper classes. According to Goldberg, "Warsaw had over 40 significant salons, just as splendid and socially refined as their counterparts in Paris, and direct evidence of Chopin's musical presence can be established in most of them" (1997, v). Although Chopin received a comprehensive formal musical education at the Warsaw Conservatory under the direction of Józef Elsner

(1769–1854), it was in the salons where he perfected his ability to improvise, both freely and for the pleasure of the dancers.[5]

The most intense period of dancing in a given year occurred during carnival season, which was celebrated in Warsaw from Epiphany to the beginning of Ash Wednesday. Warsaw, which was predominantly Roman Catholic, celebrated carnival with no less zeal than Vienna or Paris.[6] Indeed, a significant part of Warsaw's economy was built around carnival season. Warsaw's newspapers were filled with advertisements and notices for the latest costumes or for costume ornaments, such as flowers, ribbons, feathers, and exotic fabrics, for the rental of dance halls, for musicians to provide the dance music, for caterers who would provide choice food and beverages, and for various perfumes, which were doused on the dance floor not only to mask unpleasant odors but also to keep the dust down.

The newspapers also carried notices for dancing parties held in apartments or rented halls (*redutas*). During carnival it was not uncommon for Warsaw to have ten to fifteen dancing parties in one night, these in addition to dancing in the four main theaters and in private salons. For a small entrance fee (no charge for ladies), one could have access to an entire night of alleged good music, adequate dancing space and lighting, and hospitable service, including food and beverages. Many writers of such notices exercised creativity in appealing to the public to attend their dancing parties. One such notice reads:

> While in attendance . . . at a noble house where quite a number of people were present, I heard one of my friends telling the ladies about an evening dancing party that was to take place that same day in a house called the Gdańsk Cellar; as the name of this house was unknown to most of the guests . . . and as the expression "party at the Gdańsk cellar" was enjoyed by the young ladies, they, guided by their curiosity, sent me immediately to that place in order that, when I returned, they would have even more fun. Obeying their orders, I went. But when faced with well-furnished rooms, music the same as played in the Resursa, buffets full of delightful food and drink . . . I almost forgot the purpose of my trip; and choosing a beautiful dancing partner, I began a mazurka, and then came other dances. With full delight I enjoyed the party until daybreak. . . . The next day I clarified the confusion of my curious ladies, explaining to them how much enjoyment could be had by one wrongly understood word [cellar]. I am, what is more, publishing this account in order that the good master of this house, looking after the best of company as well as to their comfort will not suffer financial

losses when, on the demand of his friends, he will give a party again next
Saturday. . . . He undertakes this effort in order to support an unfortunate
family. (*Kurier warszawski*, 13 January 1830, 53)

Largely because of the strong patronage of Poland's last king, King Stanisław
August Poniatowski (ruled 1764–95), French ballet was visibly present in
Warsaw at the end of the eighteenth century into the beginning of the nineteenth century. In 1776 a ballet school was founded on the estate of Count
Antoni Tyzenhauz in Grodno (about two hundred miles northeast of War-
saw). In 1784 Tyzenhauz hired the most influential dancer in the early history
of Warsaw's ballet, François Gabriel Le Doux (1755–1823), a former dancer
with the Paris Opéra and student of Gaëtan Vestris (Ciepliński 1983, 27).
The ballet school offered not only a curriculum designed to prepare dancers
for a professional career but also instruction for amateurs. After the death of
Tyzenhauz in 1785 the ballet company came under the aegis of King Staniław
August, who moved Le Doux and company to Warsaw and renamed it His
Majesty's National Dancers. During its existence, His Majesty's National
Dancers premiered approximately one hundred ballets, including works of
Charles Le Picq and Jean-Georges Noverre (Pudełek 1998, 5:215). Le Doux
remained active as a choreographer and ballet master until 1805, during which
time he founded several more ballet schools. The obituary for Le Doux that
was published in the *Kurier warszawski* mentions that toward the end of his
career he was especially active in teaching dance to the children of Warsaw
(3 February 1823, 20).

Polish ballet and court dancing in the first quarter of the nineteenth
century continued to be dominated by French dancers, choreographers, and
ballet masters, including Louis Duport, Louis Thierry, Maurice Pion, the
Volange family, and Alexander Debrey.[7] Gradually, however, the emergence
of a specifically Polish ballet complete with Polish topics, costumes, music,
and dances made it possible for native Polish dancers, choreographers, and
composers to assert a greater influence.[8]

During the eighteenth century, social and theatrical dances were closely
related; the same techniques used onstage were used on the ballroom floor;
and it was common for dancing masters, such as Le Doux, to teach both professional ballet and social ballroom dancing. During the opening decades of
the nineteenth century, however, ballet increasingly became more virtuosic,
and the technical division between theatrical and ballroom dance increased
to a point where each discipline began to develop its own technique and

protocol.[9] Increasingly, ballet masters no longer taught ballroom dancing, and as a result a new breed of dancing masters emerged. An 1829 statistical report for the city of Warsaw lists ten dancing masters who specialized in the instruction of ballroom dances (*Przewodnik warszawski 1829*, 47). Such dancing masters typically began to advertise lessons in September in preparation for the upcoming carnival season. For example, in 1830, between 5 September and 28 October, seven dancing masters ran notices in the *Kurier warszawski* advertising dance instruction.[10] One of the most active among them, Jakub Zieliński, held weekly classes and parties during carnival in his Warsaw apartment. A notice of Zieliński's that was published in the *Kurier warszawski* reads: "J. Zieliński, dance master of social dancing, announces that on the 3rd of January, i.e. Sunday, in his apartment . . . he will give a *Dance Party* called *Casino*, and that he will give similar parties on every carnival Sunday. Persons that are unknown to me, if they wish to make their presence known to me, which would be my honor, are kindly asked to inform me beforehand. At the same place one can rent various ballroom costumes" (1 January 1830, 2).

Instruction in ballroom dancing was also part of the curricula in Warsaw's public schools and military training schools.[11] One cadet complained: "One of the faults of our education was that we were used by the upper classes. We played at comedies and learned to dance. We were taken to balls at all the best houses."[12] An important outcome of such training was that, upon graduation from military school, these polished military cadets disseminated Polish dance practices across western and eastern Europe, especially during the Napoleonic military campaigns, when Polish soldiers served in the Polish Legion, France's largest foreign contingent. The Polish composer and historian Michał Kleofas Ogiński (1765–1833) writes: "After the formation of the Duchy of Warszawa, the Polish soldiers who served with Napoleon first introduced the mazur at Parisian Balls. It was danced in the highest circles by 1809–10. It was the rage and common throughout this most elegant of capitals not only due to the merits of the dance itself but also because it was popularized by the best-loved unit of Napoleon: the officers of the Polish lancers – the Emperor's Guards."[13]

The economic sector that most benefited from Warsaw's passion for dancing was the music-publishing industry, which thrived on the publication of dance music.[14] As Gołębiowski sadly observes: "Should future generations want to judge the present state of music in Poland based on printed

FIGURE 4.1. Title page from a waltz composed by Aleksander Świeszewski
(Cracow, Jagiellonian Library, Tom. 1420).

musical works, how demeaning would their opinion of us be if they found
only waltzes, mazurkas, gallops, polonaises, and those composed mostly by
amateurs."[15]

Typically, newly written dance compositions were first performed by
dance orchestras at public balls. Afterward, one had to wait only a short
time before the hits of the dance floor became available as sheet music for the
piano. Such works were often marketed as musical souvenirs that allowed
the performer (typically female) to recapture memories, in music, of some
enchanted evening. Much information can be gleaned from the title pages
of these publications. Figures 4.1 and 4.2 show the title pages of two dance
compositions. The first is from a waltz by Aleksander Świeszewski published
in Warsaw in 1830 by Józef Kośmiński. In a letter written while he was living
in Vienna in 1830, Chopin (1963, 129) refers to Świeszewski and his brother as
the Lanner and Strauss Sr. of Warsaw. The title page reads:

FIGURE 4.2. Title page from a polonez composed by Karol Kurpiński (Kraków, Jagiellonian Library, Tom. 1185).

> Waltz
> composed by
> A. Świeszewski
> transcribed from the Orchestra
> for the
> Piano-Forte
> for four hands
> played for Soirées at the Resursa
> can be found at A. Brzezina, C. Magnus,
> F. Klukowski and at many other
> Music Shops
> in Warsaw

As was typical of Warsaw dance publications of the first quarter of the nineteenth century, the text is in French, which was the language of Warsaw's high culture. One foreign traveler observed that while visiting Warsaw in 1818 it was his experience that in good society only French was spoken and that Polish was spoken only to children and domestics (Smith 1827, 148–49).[16]

As national sentiment increased during the 1820s, however, dance publications increasingly appeared in Polish. The fashions of the waltzing couple are French. The long, loose-fitting dress of the woman, *sans* corset and ornamented with ribbons, accentuates her whirling movements. The two waltzers return our gaze as if to invite us into their dance.

The second example (Figure 4.2) is a title page from a polonaise by Karol Kurpiński (1785–1857), an influential Polish composer of opera and music director of Warsaw's National Opera Company from 1810 to 1840. The title page, now in Polish, provides a full context for the ball at which it (presumably) was first performed:

Polonez
Composed on the eighteenth day of December in the year 1828
as an annual Celebration of the exalted Name Day of
His Most Gracious Majesty Emperor of Russia and King of Poland
NICOLAUS I
Performed on this very day by the Great Orchestra
of the Regiment of Grenadiers of the Polish Guard
and
arranged for Pianoforte
by
K. KURPIŃSKI
Kapellmeister of the Court of the Kingdom of Poland
Publishing House of A. Brzezina, Warsaw

While the czar was not present in Warsaw for his name day celebration, he did arrive several months later on 17 May to be crowned king of Poland. It is likely that Kurpiński's polonaise was quickly published and marketed with the upcoming coronation in mind.[17]

In conclusion, the importance of dance in Warsaw during Chopin's youth cannot be overestimated: it was a vibrant and ubiquitous activity deeply woven into the social and economic fabric of Warsaw's society. As Gołębiowski observes, social dance was an "innate and indispensable need of the people" ([1831] 1983, 304). Warsaw's population in 1827 was approximately 123,000, of which 16,000 were of noble descent (*szlachta*).[18] This group was increased by the ranks of the innumerable intelligentsia and bourgeoisie (artists, merchants, administrators, teachers, etc.) who could not claim noble birth but most certainly participated in Warsaw's dance events. When one considers that during carnival, dancing was present in Warsaw's private salons and palaces, in dozens of rented halls, and in four large theaters, it is not unreasonable to assume that the only people who were not in attendance at a dance event during any given week of carnival were those who were physically unable to attend. And through cultural and political ties to France and the presence of French dancing masters, ballroom dancing in Warsaw was strongly influenced by French tastes.

The Waltz in Warsaw

The historian Kazimierz Władysław Wójcicki (1807–79) reports that the waltz was first introduced to Poland during the Prussian occupation (1794–1806) (1877, 155). Given the early popularity of the waltz in Berlin, Wójcicki is probably right. Just two years before the beginning of the occupation, a Berlin journal reported that "waltzes and nothing but waltzes are now so much the fashion that at dances nothing else is seen; one need only be able to dance the waltz and everything is all right."[19] The following year the waltz made its entrance to Berlin's high society. Princess Louise Hohenzollern, the niece of Fryderyk II and future wife of Prince Anton Radziwiłł, recalls that, at a ball held at the Prussian Royal Court, "the King admired their waltzing. This dance had hitherto been forbidden at Court. . . . However, as the dance was much in vogue in the Imperial dominions, the King now sanctioned it" (Radziwiłł 1912, 111–12). Although the king greatly enjoyed the whirling spectacle, the queen mother was not impressed: "The Queen was duly shocked at this indecency, and to see her daughters-in-law introduce a dance she disapproved of. She reiterated her prohibition to her daughters and averted her eyes to avoid seeing her daughters-in-law waltzing" (Radziwiłł 1912, 112).

When Prussia took control of Warsaw in 1794, only Germans were placed in governmental positions (Radziwiłł 1912, 155). The influx of Prussian families, many of great wealth and influence, resulted in a visible presence of Prussian culture, including their favorite dances. Polish society did not immediately embrace the waltz, however. As Wojciech Tomaszewski's research on Warsaw's music-publishing industry reveals, in the opening years of the nineteenth century, the polonaise was by far the Poles' favorite dance, constituting an amazing 96 percent of the published dance works for piano (1992b, 167). During the years 1815 to 1825, however, the waltz gradually overtook the polonaise in popularity. And after 1820 the waltz enjoyed a surge of popularity as Warsaw became yet another European city to fall victim to the throes of the "waltz craze." The publishing market was flooded with waltzes, a great many written by amateurs and, consequently, a great many of low artistic quality. Indeed, composing waltzes became fashionable among the cultural elite as a type of parlor game. One publication by Józef Damse (1829) even went so far as to make the following fantastic claim: "A million waltzes or a way to compose a million waltzes even for those who know nothing about music."[20]

The extreme popularity of the waltz and its saturation into Warsaw's social life allowed it to be used as a normative background from which to measure the bizarre, unusual, and extraordinary. For example, within the span of only two months the *Kurier warszawski* ran the following stories: in a show of strength a Polish strongman dances to the waltz from *Der Freischütz* with two Turkish men standing on his shoulders (3 January 1830, 10); a beautiful Spanish woman, born without arms and legs, knits stockings and with her nose plucks out a waltz on the piano (3 January 1830, 12); at a ball in Madrid a woman waltzes flawlessly even though she was blind from birth (5 January 1830, 19); in Istanbul, Turkish women are prohibited at public gatherings, so at balls Turkish men waltz with Christian women (7 January 1830, 10); and at a Parisian ball for the elderly a seventy-year-old woman cannot find a waltz partner because all the men are too drunk to dance (22 February 1830, 255).

Warsaw Waltz Music

A survey of piano waltzes published in Warsaw between 1816 and 1830 reveals a rich and diverse production of works, ranging from low-quality vanity publications of the upper class to sophisticated works of professional composers and performers.[21] One finds piano transcriptions of orchestral ballroom waltzes, virtuosic piano waltzes, simple piano waltzes intended as dance accompaniment in the salon, programmatic waltzes,[22] and waltz arrangements of concert music, not only of popular operas – *Il barbiere di Siviglia* and *La gazza ladra* by Rossini were particular favorites – but also of instrumental music. Even Chopin could not escape such tribute. His friend and classmate from the Warsaw Conservatory, Antoni Orłowski, set the opening theme from the last movement of his Concerto in F Minor, op. 21, as a waltz (Tom. 1370).

Prior to 1830 Viennese waltz composers seem to have exerted little influence on Warsaw dance composers.[23] The most notable difference between Warsaw waltzes and Viennese waltzes is that Warsaw waltzes contain far less thematic content and variety than Viennese waltzes. While Lanner and Strauss Sr. were developing the Viennese waltz cycle, professional dance com-

Waltz 1	Trio	Waltz 1 (*da capo*)
12 (8 + 4)		12 (8 + 4)
‖: intro a a :‖: b a :‖	‖: c c :‖: d d :‖: c c :‖	‖: intro a a :‖: b a :‖
TT TT TD XD TT	TD TT XT TD TD TT	TT TT TD XD TT
G major: I	IV	I

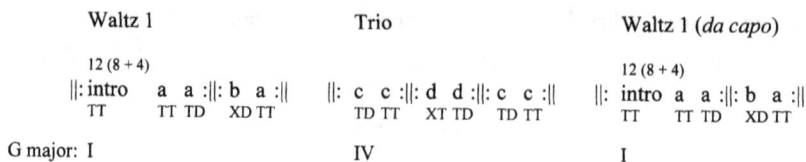

DIAGRAM 4.1. Form chart of a waltz by Józef Stefani.

posers in Warsaw during Chopin's youth favored the ternary *da capo* form
(waltz-trio-waltz), which was also the standard musical form of Warsaw mazurkas and polonaises. Introductions and codas are rarely found. Thus, while
Viennese waltzes may contain twelve or more distinct themes, Warsaw waltzes
typically offer no more than three or four themes. Other significant differences
that distinguish Warsaw waltzes from Viennese waltzes are Warsaw composers' preference for rounded binary form (A⫶║BA) for individual waltzes, as opposed to the simple binary form of Viennese waltzes (A⫶║B), and much greater
variety in cadential patterns, including half cadences.

Generic features that Warsaw waltzes share with Viennese waltzes are
(1) a preference for the major mode, (2) the frequent use of an oom-pah-pah
accompaniment pattern, (3) eight-bar phrase lengths organized in two-bar
segments, and (4) the rhythmic pattern quarter note/two eighth notes/quar-
ter note. A common rhythmic pattern peculiar to Warsaw waltzes (and mazurkas) is triplet eighth notes/two eighth notes/two eighth notes.

While there are exceptions, Warsaw waltzes as a whole lack the melodic
ingenuity and variety, tonal sophistication, and rhythmic flexibility of those by
Lanner and Strauss Sr. The most prolific among the ballroom dance composers in Warsaw during the 1820s were Józef Damse and Józef Stefani (Stefani
was a conservatory classmate of Chopin).[24] Diagram 4.1 provides a form chart
of a piano transcription by Stefani of an orchestral waltz he wrote for a ball
held at the Merchant's Resursa during the carnival season of 1830 (Tom. 1409).
Stefani follows the standard three-part *da capo* form. Individually, the first
waltz is organized as a rounded binary form with an introduction and the
trio as a small ternary form set within the key of the subdominant. Notice
that nearly half of the themes end with a half cadence. This is a rather high
percentage even for Warsaw waltz composers, who employ half cadences with
greater frequency than Viennese waltz composers. In general, however, the
more experienced the composer (and especially those who studied under the

direction of Józef Elsner at the Warsaw Conservatory), the greater the range and variety of his cadential formulas.[25] As we have seen, Lanner and Strauss Sr., despite their considerable experience and compositional abilities, limited themselves almost exclusively to authentic cadences.

CHOPIN AS A DANCER

Chopin's contact with authentic peasant dance music and the purported influence that it exerted on his music – especially his mazurkas – has been greatly exaggerated (Milewski 1999, 134–35). The type of dance Chopin had most contact with while living in Warsaw was not the dance of the peasants but rather the urban ballroom dances of the upper classes.

Dance was considered an essential part of the education of the cultural elite, and all children who were physically able took dance lessons. Instruction in dance not only included knowledge of current ballroom dances but also encompassed such basic physical activities as sitting down and standing up, walking across a room, stepping in and out of a carriage, and, most important, gestures of greeting and departure. The manner in which one moved signaled one's socioeconomic position and allowed the upper classes to identify with one another and exclude those who had neither the money nor the time to learn such social codes. By all contemporary accounts, Chopin was a gentleman who moved comfortably in high aristocratic circles: he had great personal charm, exquisite manners, and an extremely refined sense of noble ease. Such attributes of attitude and bodily motion do not come naturally but are learned at a very young age.

As a child Chopin would have had the opportunity to learn etiquette and dance at children's afternoon tea parties and costume balls given by his benefactors, Countess Zofia Zamoyska, Princess Izabela Czartoryska, and Countess Aleksandra Potocka (Koźmian 1867, 1:72–73).[26] Such events were common throughout Warsaw in the homes of the upper class, especially during carnival season. By his fifteenth year Chopin appears to have acquired a fair amount of skill – or at least confidence – as a dancer. At an impromptu dancing party in Szafarnia, Chopin took it upon himself to lead the opening dance, a waltz, with a young cousin of the host.[27] Customarily, only the very best dancers were permitted this privilege.

Chopin's letters clearly indicate that he eagerly and actively took part in Warsaw's ball scene, especially during carnival. But while Chopin notes his attendance at various balls and soirées, he only mentions dancing if something unusual or unexpected occurred during the dance. This suggests that dancing was such a common activity for Chopin that it was not noteworthy in its own right. For example, in 1825 he committed to verse a night of wild dancing where he spent half the time playing for the dancers and the rest of the time dancing. Toward the end of the evening, while dancing a mazurka, he slipped and sprained his ankle.[28] In a letter from November 1829, he brags about an evening party where a beautiful woman asked him to be her partner in a mazurka, and, moreover, she had only just refused to dance with a Polish general (Chopin 1954–60, 1:141–42). And while dancing the mazurka at a soirée in December 1830, one of his friends took to the floor pretending to be some sort of sheep (Chopin 1963, 72).

Although Chopin rarely commented on performing for dancers, his friends and acquaintances did. By all accounts he was not only a consummate dance musician but also an enthusiastic one. Józefa Wodzińska recounts that Chopin enjoyed entertaining his younger friends either by playing pranks on the piano or by playing waltzes, polkas, gallops, and mazurkas for them to dance to.[29] Occasionally after improvising, according to another report, Chopin "would turn into a lusty musician and start thundering out mazurkas, waltzes and polkas until, tired of playing and eager to join in the dancing himself, he would cede the keyboard to a humbler replacement" (Wójcicki 1974, 2:545). It is not entirely clear from the sources cited above whether Chopin improvised the dance music or used preexisting dance music. It is conceivable, however, that, given Chopin's extraordinary ability as an improviser, many of Chopin's Warsaw waltzes and mazurkas originated on the dance floor as dance improvisations and were only later committed to paper. Two of Chopin's earliest mazurkas, for example, were reported to have been first improvised in the salon of Samuel Linde and later, at the suggestion of Oskar Kolberg, committed to paper (Samson 1996, 43).

Although accounts of his dancing activity decline after Chopin left Warsaw, partly because of his progressing illness, they do continue. The latest account I have found dates from November 1847, when Chopin played for dancers at a soirée given by the Czartoryskis in Paris (M. Tomaszewski 1990, 228).

Chopin kept abreast of what was being played in the ballrooms of Warsaw and who was doing the playing. In a letter to his close friend Jan Białobłocki, written in November 1825, Chopin compares the work of his sister to the general fare: "Louise has written an excellent mazurka such as Warsaw has

Figure 4.3. A waltz composed by Aleksander Rembieliński
(Kraków, Jagiellonian Library, Tom. 1079).

not danced to in a long time. It is her *non plus ultra,* and really it is a unique *non plus ultra* of its kind – bouncing, charming; in short – ideal for dancing and, without flattery, of a rare quality. When you come I will play it for you" (1963, 4).

In another letter to Białobłocki written in June 1826, Chopin modestly writes: "Do let me know whether you received the music. As a matter of fact, instead of my own poor efforts, I sent you some of Rembieliński's waltzes. They ought to please you and, if one or two of them seem at first too difficult, just begin to move your stiff fingers . . . and you will see that they are worthy of you – that is, as handsome as you yourself" (1963, 6). Aleksander Rembieliński was an amateur pianist whose fluid and relaxed technique Chopin greatly admired.[30] Figure 4.3 shows one of only three extant waltzes that Rembieliński composed. Published in 1828, it was dedicated to Princess Radziwiłł, wife of Prince Antoni Radziwiłł. In its virtuosic pianism, rhythmic subtleties, and melodic and tonal organization, one can perhaps understand Chopin's attraction to Rembieliński's work. In the opening three bars, the repeating three-note arpeggiation of the melody creates a 3 + 3 eighth-note grouping against the oom-pah-pah quarter-note accompaniment.[31] Rembieliński rhythmically

EXAMPLE 4.1. Bass-line sketch of Rembieliński's waltz.

varies the arpeggiated motive upon its return in bar 9. The rhythmic variation creates a melodic connection between the highest notes of the arpeggiation, G and F. In bars 13–14 Rembieliński restates the G–F motive in a new rhythmic configuration. The successive development of an opening motive belies a compositional sophistication quite uncharacteristic of most Warsaw dance publications.

Rembieliński's fluid melodies avoid the standard four-bar segmentation typical of Warsaw dances of the time. In the opening of the first waltz, the large arching contour, which explores the extreme high register of the piano, and the lack of any tonal articulation in bar 4 unify the eight measures as a single gesture. In the second reprise, the melody's $\frac{3}{2}$ hemiola in bars 12–13 rhythmically veils the varied return of bars 9–10 in bars 13–14. (The motivic parallelism suggests that reprise is conceptually based upon a 4 + 4 model.)

Also noteworthy is Rembieliński's maverick tonal design. The standard tonal organization of Warsaw waltzes was extremely conservative: simple diatonic progressions without modulation. Here each of the four reprises establishes a different key: the first, E♭ major, the second, B♭ major, the third, D major, and the fourth, A major. Taken as a whole in a conventional *da capo* layout (e.g., waltz 1–waltz 2–waltz 1), Rembieliński provides large-scale continuity by joining the waltzes in the statement of a large tonal progression: I–III–IV–V–I (see Example 4.1).[32] Notice that the opening waltz does not begin squarely in the tonic key of B♭ major; it first establishes E♭ major, the subdominant of B♭, which then progresses to V–I in the second reprise. This tonal procedure of beginning a piece off tonic with an auxiliary progression is a trademark technique of Chopin (and Lanner and Strauss Sr.).

As a final observation in establishing Chopin's role as a dance musician, it should not be overlooked that Chopin, throughout his life, was not averse to performing music as an accompaniment to other activities. He often accompanied singers and instrumentalists; he apparently was quite good at mimicking other pianists for comic relief; and, according to some sources, which are not completely reliable, in his younger years he was fond of playing musical games and improvising music to spoken stories (Karasowski 1970, 29–30).[33] The latter gains support from his pivotal role in the creation of the marionette theater years later at Nohant. According to George Sand, Chopin "improvised at the piano while the young people performed different scenes together with comical dance. . . . As soon as Chopin noticed a performer, he immediately, and with incredible skill, adapted to his role the content and form of the music."[34]

The foregoing evidence suggests that Chopin's conception of dance music grew directly out of his experience with urban ballroom dancing both as a dancer and as a dance musician. Both Franz Liszt and Robert Schumann also identified the source of Chopin's inspiration for his waltz music within the attitudes and bodily motions of the dancers on the ballroom dance floor.[35] In his biography of Chopin, Liszt writes:

> Through the mediation of [Princess Czetweryńska] he had the honor of being presented at the home of Princess de Lowicz, and here he was brought together with Countess Zamoyska, Princess Radziwill, Princess Thérèsa Jablonowska, enchantresses all. . . . It was [Chopin's] lot, while still young, to play the piano for their dancing. At these parties . . . he was able to discover, many times perhaps, the secrets of excited and tender hearts fleetingly disclosed in whirling rounds. . . . Did no group, like frolicking nymphs, to wheedle some waltz of dizzying speed, shower him with smiles which taught him to merge with their merriment? ([1851] 1963, 136–37)[36]

Thus, it follows that an important source of inspiration for Chopin's dance music may be found in the gestures and social practices of the dance itself. In chapter 5 I show that Chopin was not only receptive to the needs of the dancers but also able to translate their bodily motions into an artistic musical vision. Or, to put it in Liszt's terms, at an early age Chopin learned how to "merge with the merriment" of the dancers.

The Musical Visions
of Chopin

❧

> Perhaps he was inspired to new creations while he gazed, great artist that he
> is, among the dancers whom he has just roused by playing.

ROBERT SCHUMANN

In this chapter I work from the premise that Chopin was receptive to the
wishes of a body in motion. In so doing, I attempt to demonstrate how Chopin
translates physical motions into musical gestures and uses these musical gestures as compositional source material of a sort whose potential is developed
on different levels of musical organization, from the smallest to the largest.
Another issue that I begin to develop during the course of this chapter and
that I continue in the following chapter is the nature of the musical differences
between the waltzes Chopin chose to publish during his lifetime and those
he intentionally left unpublished. Table 5.1 provides a list of all of Chopin's
known waltzes.[1] Eight were published by Chopin. Nine of the waltzes were
in completed form, but Chopin intentionally left them unpublished. Eleven
more are known to have existed but are now lost. Within each category, the
table groups the waltzes according to their chronology. I argue that those
Chopin left unpublished are in most cases not somehow incomplete or inferior
in quality or conception but constitute a separate category of waltzes that were
conceived by compositional motivations quite different from those he chose to

TABLE 5.1. CHOPIN'S WALTZES (KK = KOBYLANSKA, KATALOG)

			COMPOSED	PUBLISHED
Published by Chopin				
op. 18	E♭	*Grande valse brillante*	1831–32	1834
op. 34, no. 1	A♭	*Grande valse brillante*	1835	1838
op. 34, no. 2	a	*Grande valse brillante*	1838	1838
op. 34, no. 3	F	*Grande valse brillante*	1838	1838
op. 42	A♭	*Grande valse*	1840	1840
op. 64, no. 1	D♭	*Valse*	1847	1847
op. 64, no. 2	c♯	*Valse*	1847	1847
op. 64, no. 3	A♭	*Valse*	1847	1847
Left Unpublished by Chopin				
WARSAW WALTZES				
KK 1209–11	A♭	*Valse*	c. 1826–30	1902
op. 69, no. 2	b	*Valse (dolente)*	1829	1855
op. 70, no. 3	D♭	*Valse (dolce e legato)*	1829	1855
KK 1207–1208	E	*Valse*	1829 or 1830	1861
KK 1213–14	e	*Valse*	1830	1868
PARIS WALTZES				
op. 70, no. 1	G♭	*Valse*	1832	1855
op. 69, no. 1	A♭	*Valse*	1835	1855
op. 70, no. 2	f	*Valse*	1842	1855
KK 1238–39	a	*Valse*	1847	1955
Lost				
KK 1266	a	description only	1824	
KK 1248	C	incipit only	1824	
KK 1249	C	incipit only	1826	
KK 1250/1268	Ab	incipit only	1827	
KK 1252	d	incipit only	1828	
KK 1251/1267/1270	A♭	incipit only	1829	
KK 1253/1267/1270	E♭	incipit only	1829	
KK 1295		description only		
KK 1308		description only	1832	
KK 1316		description only	1845	
KK 1245	B	description only	1848	

publish. Although there are exceptions, Chopin's published waltzes are more virtuosic, extroverted, and conceived on a larger scale than those he chose not to publish, which are more lyrical and private in character.

CIRCLES

The *valse à trois temps* is often described as a dance of circles: small clockwise circles embedded within larger counterclockwise ones.[2] Viewers on the perimeter of the dance space were entertained by a whirling spectacle of couples "eternally turning in dizzying circles along a wider circumferential path, self contained and oblivious planets" (Allanbrook 1983, 65).[3] As a geometric design, however, a circle involves a relatively even movement around a fixed point. Sevin Yaraman (2002, 18–19) and Lawrence Zbikowski (2008, 287) have rightly noted that on the dance floor, since there is no fixed point, the smaller clockwise motions of the dancers resemble a spiral more than a circle. The notion of a circle, however, is so deeply embedded in the discourse of the waltz that I will continue to use it here.

According to the composer and theorist Adolph Bernhard Marx (1795–1866), waltz composers must "at the very least . . . bring into prominence this basic motive of motion [the circle]. . . . Each bar, or better, each two-bar segment, must correspond to the dance motive, marking . . . the swinging turn of the dance" (1837–38, 2:55, my translation).[4] As an example of what he considers a "genuine waltz motive," Marx cites the waltz from act 1, scene 3, of Carl Maria von Weber's *Der Freischütz* (first performance, Berlin, 18 June 1821), which is provided in Example 5.1. The Warsaw premiere of *Der Freischütz*, which Chopin eagerly awaited, took place on 4 July 1826. By that time, however, Chopin was most likely already familiar with much of the music; dance arrangements began to appear in Warsaw as early as 1822, and the *Freischütz* waltz was a particular favorite. Marx explains the analogic relation between Weber's waltz and the dance: "[Weber's] rustic dance satisfies itself with the pure unaltered raw material, the motive of three steps, without forming clearer musical segments for the complete movement of twice three steps, which befits a more complete and nobler conception of the dance" (1837–38, 2:55).

As can be seen, the basic motive of Weber's waltz is a melodic arch. In its circular design, a melodic arch is particularly apt as a musical vision of the rotating dancers: its beginning and ending points are the same, or nearly the

EXAMPLE 5.1. The waltz from Carl Maria von Weber's opera
Der Freischütz, act 1, scene 3.

same, and its pitches move at a relatively even rate around a fixed axis. After
the oom-pah-pah accompaniment, melodic arches are perhaps the next most
important characteristic of waltzes, especially Chopin's waltzes. It was most
likely this feature that prompted Lord Byron to take aim at the waltz in his
poem "Waltz: An Apostrophic Hymn" and describe it as "a damned see-saw
up and down sort of tune" ([1813] 1907, 156). Certainly, Weber's little waltz fits
this description.

The arching motive used in the introduction to Chopin's posthumously
published Waltz in E Minor, given in Example 5.2, opens with what Marx
would surely call a genuine waltz motive. As shown in Example 5.3, the first
complete bar is a tonal inversion of Weber's motive. In the music that follows,
Chopin injects this motive into the flesh and bones of the work. By the term
"motive" I do not mean to imply a similarity relation based on a specific voice-
leading technique or characteristic scale degrees but rather a basic shape or
contour with a well-defined beginning, middle, and end.

The waltz proper begins in bar 9. Instead of using a more standard oom-
pah-pah accompaniment, where the second and third beats are identical, the
left hand registrally peaks on the second beat and then arpeggiates down to
the beginning of the next bar. Returning to the introduction, the downbeats

EXAMPLE 5.2. Chopin's Waltz in E Minor, KK 1213–14, bars 1–16.

EXAMPLE 5.3. A comparison of Weber's
waltz motive to the waltz motive from
Chopin's Waltz in E Minor, KK 1213–14.

of the first three bars imply an apparent ascending stepwise line D♯–E F♯–G
A♯–B. The line is "apparent" because the chromatic tones function as nonhar-
monic, accented neighbor tones that decorate an ascending tonic arpeggiation (E–G–B). The downbeats of the arching bass line in bars 9–14 present
a varied repetition of this same line, thereby underscoring the relationship
between the bass line and the introduction's dance motive. And in this case
all of the pitches of the line are harmonically supported and thus form a co-
herent linear progression. And, finally, the dance motive of the introduction

EXAMPLE 5.4. Chopin's Waltz in E Minor, KK 1213–14, bars 25–40.

is also used in the melody. The opening upward sweep of the first half of the arching motive reappears in slightly varied form as the basis of the melody in bars 10–11.

A new melody begins in bar 25, as shown in Example 5.4. Here Chopin incorporates the arching motive into a sequence of figurated 7–6 suspensions. In the eight-bar melody that follows (bars 33–40), Chopin expands the dance motive into a "more complete and nobler" two-bar statement while at the same time preserving the voice-leading organization of the previous eight-bar phrase (although without the suspensions). The expanded motive now perfectly matches the complete rotation of the dancers. Turning our attention to the left hand, in bars 25–32 the arching bass line is rhythmically contracted to fit within the bar, thereby corresponding in duration to the melody's one-bar arches. In bars 33–40, the arch of the bass line is expanded back to its original duration. Although it is expanded in relation to bars 25–32, it does not match the durational expansion of the melody's arch: for every one arch of the melody, the bass completes two of its own.

The basic shape of the dance motive – an arch, typically ascending – is also present at the level of the eight-bar phrase. Musical climaxes in western

* = structural highpoint

EXAMPLE 5.5. Chopin's Prelude in A Major, op. 28, no. 7.

European art music typically occur toward the end of a musical segment, be it a phrase, a section, or the entire work.[5] The climax is usually achieved, in part, through an ascent to a registral high point. The opening eight-bar phrase from the first movement of Beethoven's Piano Sonata in F Minor, op. 2, no. 1, is often used as a paradigmatic example of this type of organization. Example 5.5 presents an illustration from a well-known work by Chopin.[6] What we find in Chopin's waltzes, to a degree unknown in his other genres, are phrases organized as large, balanced arches in which the registral high point occurs roughly midway through the phrase. Returning to the E-minor waltz, the overall contour of the eight-bar phrase beginning in bar 9 is organized as a large arch. Although there is no single high point, the upward ascent of the first four bars, which is propelled by the varied fragment of the introduction's dance motive, is balanced by the downward-sweeping gestures of the second four-bar segment. Underneath, the stepwise ascent of the bass provides continuity across the 4 + 4 melodic division and places its registral climax more conventionally toward the end of the phrase.

The eight-bar phrase beginning in bar 57, given in Example 5.6, is also organized as a large balanced arch. Here there is a clear registral high point at the end of the first four-bar segment. The second four-bar segment provides a graceful descent to the end of the phrase. Similar balanced arches can also be found in op. 18, op. 34, no. 3, op. 42, op. 64, nos. 1 and 3, and op. 70, no. 3. It is significant, although perhaps not surprising, that with the exceptions

EXAMPLE 5.6. Chopin's Waltz in E Minor, KK 1213–14, bars 57–72.

of the E-minor waltz and op. 70, no. 3, such expansions of the dance motive to an entire eight-bar phrase or period only occur in the waltzes he chose to publish, which were conceived on a larger scale than the waltzes he chose not to publish.

In the E-minor waltz, the dance motive is used in varied forms, in different parts of the texture, and at different temporal levels.[7] The most condensed form of a melodic arch is a neighboring motion.[8] Despite their narrow range and apparent simplicity, neighboring motions are a potent source and generator of musical content on many levels of tonal structure. They are also a signal feature of Chopin's waltzes. Returning to Example 5.2, the successive rising statements of the introduction's one-bar dance motive are fused together by lower-neighbor notes on the downbeats of each bar. In bars 9–10, $\hat{5}$ is elaborated with a lower-neighbor motion, just as it was in bar 3. In the following bar, a complex of neighbor notes revolving around B delays the fragmented return of the dance motive. More specifically, B is prolonged by a double-neighbor figure in which the upper neighbor, C♯, on the downbeat of bar 11, is itself elaborated with its own upper neighbor.

EXAMPLE 5.7. Chopin's Waltz in A Minor, op. 34, no. 2, bars 1–36.

EXAMPLE 5.8. Voice-leading sketch of Chopin's Waltz in
A Minor, op. 32, no. 2, bars 1–16.

The opening of Chopin's Waltz in A Minor, op. 34, no. 2, is given in Example 5.7. Stephen Hiller (1811–85), a pianist and Chopin's friend, reports that when he told Chopin that he liked the A-minor waltz best of all of Chopin's waltzes, Chopin replied: "I am glad you do; it is also my favourite."[9] With its minor mode, slow tempo, prominent use of the low register, and smooth serpentine melodies, it is one of his most introspective and languid waltzes, a *valse mélancolique*.[10] It also is a sophisticated study in neighbor notes.

The opening sixteen-bar parallel period (8 + 8) is comprised almost solely of neighboring figures. As shown in Example 5.8, during the first four bars the texture breathes in and out with steadily undulating one-bar neighbor motions. Furthermore, each note of the low tenor melody is itself elaborated with its own neighboring motion, thereby creating circles within circles. In bar 5 the neighboring motion accelerates into a trill. The increase of energy generated by the trill, together with the culminating D♯ chromatic lower neighbor, catapults the melody temporarily into a higher register, where it circumscribes $\hat{2}$ with upper and lower neighbors.

The next section, bars 17–36, is also organized as a parallel period. Its consequent phrase, though, is expanded from eight to twelve bars. As Example 5.9 illustrates, there are remarkable parallelisms between the opening two periods. The contents of both are largely generated by neighbor notes, and, more specifically, the twice-repeated neighbor motion $\hat{5}$–$\hat{6}$–$\hat{5}$ plays a prominent role in both.

EXAMPLE 5.9. Voice-leading sketch of Chopin's Waltz in A Minor, op. 32, no. 2, bars 17–36.

The antecedent phrase beginning in bar 17 issues from an E, but it is two octaves higher than the opening melody. This high E initiates a middleground neighboring motion that is partially concealed by three register transfers. In bar 20, F is transferred down one octave, where it is held over as a suspension, which resolves on the third beat of bar 21. In bar 22, F is regained in the soprano voice but is immediately transferred to the bass voice through voice exchange, which places the neighboring F back in its original register (see bars 1–3). Also noteworthy are the alto's neighboring motions in bars 17–20, which prolong Î through a double-neighbor motion, A–G♯–B–A. Chopin further elaborates this neighbor complex by providing the opening A and the penultimate B with their own upper neighbors, which resolve as suspension figures.

In the consequent, Chopin unleashes a cascade of figurations that both elaborate and expand the neighboring motions of the antecedent phrase. The phrase expansion occurs in two parts. The voice exchange between F and D that begins in bar 30 is extended by one bar through the insertion of a second-inversion passing chord in bar 31. The expanded voice exchange transfers the F from the soprano voice to the bass voice in bar 32, and it resolves to E in bar 33, just as it did in the antecedent. Under the E, however, a G♯ (itself a lower neighbor to the A of bar 25) now appears. The unstable inversion of the V⁷, together with a varied and transposed restatement of bars 29–32, propel the music forward to a perfect authentic cadence in bar 36. It is important to note that the phrase expansion does not disrupt the two-bar hypermeter

EXAMPLE 5.10. Chopin's Waltz in F Major, op. 34, no. 3, bars 1–20.

but rather results in a symmetrical 4 + 4 group. The music is thus entirely regular and danceable.

Perhaps the best-known waltzes in which neighbor notes take root in the musical terrain are the Waltz in F Major, op. 34, no. 3, and the Waltz in D♭ Major, op. 64, no. 1. Example 5.10 provides the opening to op. 34, no. 3. After an eight-bar "call to the dance floor," bar 9 begins a stepwise chromatic ascent to the beginning of the waltz proper (bar 17). The ascent, which accelerates as it nears its goal, is elaborated with double-neighbor figures. The only pitch in the ascent not to receive a neighbor-note embellishment is $\hat{3}$, the goal and climax of the introduction. And in the music that immediately follows, Chopin is careful not to exceed the A. Instead, by means of neighboring $^6_4$ chords, Chopin leaves it to an inner voice of the accompaniment to provide the A with its own upper neighbor, B♭. The melodic motion $\hat{3}$–$\hat{4}$–$\hat{3}$ (A–B♭–A), here buried within the texture, eventually emerges in this waltz as an important structural motive.

The opening of Chopin's Waltz in D♭ Major, op. 64, no. 1, is provided in Example 5.11. The waltz begins with a whirlwind of neighboring figures rotating around A♭, $\hat{5}$. As shown in Example 5.12, the principal neighboring motion is $\hat{5}$–$\hat{6}$–$\hat{5}$, which accelerates in bars 3 ff. (The neighboring tone $\hat{6}$ is also embellished with its own incomplete neighbor, C.) The culminating arrival

EXAMPLE 5.11. Chopin's Waltz in D♭ Major, op. 64, no. 1, bars 1–20.

EXAMPLE 5.12. Voice-leading sketch of Chopin's Waltz in
D♭ Major, op. 64, no. 1, bars 1–12.

of the B♭ on the downbeat of bar 9, an octave higher, creates a larger-level
neighboring motion, unifying the entire passage. Also note that the entire
phrase is a modified balanced arch. A heightening of energy and register in
the first half of the phrase, which is augmented with a four-bar prefix, is balanced with a twice-repeated two-bar descent and decrescendo in the second
half. And, finally, the accompaniment spins out arches on two durational
levels. First, the oom-pah-pah creates an overlapping quarter-note pattern
of low-high-high, and, second, the bass notes on the downbeats create a

dotted-half-note durational pattern of low-high-low. Frederick Niecks, an early biographer of Chopin, reports that the spinning motions of George Sand's dog trying to catch its tail served as the creative inspiration for this work (1902, 2:142). Although the story is apocryphal, the image of a perpetually circling motion is apt.

"LIFTOFF"

For dancers, the most active part of the two-bar rotation, in terms of motion and energy exerted, comes on beats 1 and 4. Going into beats 1 and 4, dancers rise from a sink – that is, they move from the heel to the toe and then remain on the toe until the end of the bar. Also, the dancers' steps on beats 1 and 4 use the largest stride covering the most distance and thus require the fastest leg motion in order not to lose time with the music. And, finally, whoever is twirling needs to create enough momentum in order to continue the twirl into the second and third beats. Accordingly, Marx advises the composer musically to mark the beginning of the bar with a "melody that springs energetically away from the first note. . . . In [Weber's] piece, auxiliary tones are placed before the purely chordal ones in order to bring out the beginning of the [dancer's] first step; every other melodic, harmonic, or rhythmic accentuation serves the same end" (1837–38, 2:55–56).

Marx translates physical motion into musical motion through the use of dissonance as found in auxiliary tones – what we would normally call appoggiaturas. As musical entities, appoggiaturas provide a sense of motion in that they require resolution, a need to "move" to another, more stable pitch. In contrast to the short, eighth-note appoggiaturas found in Weber's waltz and in the introduction to Chopin's Waltz in E Minor, KK 1213–14, Chopin most often uses appoggiaturas of a dotted-quarter-note or half-note duration. The longer duration results in a musical correspondence between the appoggiatura and the three-beat twirl, which requires of the dancer only one true step.

As mentioned in chapter 3, the three-beat twirl is first performed by the man in the first bar and then echoed by the woman in the second bar of the six-beat rotation (refer to Diagram 3.2). Interestingly, Chopin most often uses the longer appoggiatura for the second bar of a six-beat rotation, thereby drawing attention to the woman's twirl. It is my opinion that this correspondence is not fortuitous but rather a direct result of Chopin's firsthand knowledge of the dance as danced. Chopin, in many of his waltzes, perhaps turns his gaze on the waltzing woman.

EXAMPLE 5.13. Chopin's Waltz in E Major, KK 1207–1208, bars 1–24.

Example 5.13 provides an illustration from the opening of Chopin's Waltz in E Major, KK 1207–1208. The waltz begins with a short introduction, organized in two four-bar segments. In the first segment, a *sonnerie* calls the dancers to the dance floor; the second segment announces the principal rhythmic motive of the work, the motive of the female waltzer. A stepwise ascent leads to a half-note dissonant C♯ on the downbeat of bar 6. Although a dissonant neighbor rather than an appoggiatura (see bar 10 for the latter figure), the effect is still the same – it requires resolution (movement) to the consonant B. In performance, the unstressed resolution of the dissonance provides a sense of relaxation and repose. Similarly, in the dance this is when the movement of the twirl comes to an end and the dancer relaxes into a sink in preparation for the rise to the toes in the following bar. In bars 7–8 Chopin twice repeats the second bar of the motive, thereby creating waves of pulsating neighboring motions that suggest the twirling motions of both dancers. Neighboring figures are a prominent feature throughout this waltz.

The waltz proper begins in bar 9. The section of the waltz provided in the example is organized as a parallel period (8 + 8). At the head of each phrase the motive of the female waltzer appears in its purest form, followed by varied repetitions of this new, two-bar motive. The woman's initial three steps are perfectly matched by three quarter notes and her twirl by the two-beat appoggiatura, which resolves on the last beat of the bar.

There is, in fact, a general tendency in Chopin's waltzes to highlight, through a variety of means, the bar of the woman's twirl. In bars 5–6, for example, the crescendo, melodic contour, dynamic accents, and rhythmic acceleration leading to an agogic accent all serve to accentuate the beginning of the second bar. I know of no other composer of waltz music during this era who matches Chopin in this respect. It is interesting to note that, by highlighting the woman's twirl, Chopin provides a musical lift to the very movement that carries with it the most risk. For it is at this point, while turning on a tight axis, that the woman would experience the greatest sense of spinning and, with it, a dangerous combination of euphoria and vertigo. The possibility of a woman losing control of her mind and bodily functions appears to have held a special fascination for male critics of the waltz. Writing in 1836, Donald Walker observes: "Vertigo is one of the great inconveniences of the waltz; and the character of this dance, its rapid turnings, the clasping of the dancers, their excited contact, and the too quick and too long continued succession of lively and agreeable emotions, produce sometimes, in women of a very irritable constitution, syncopes, spasms and other accidents which should induce them to renounce it."[11] From a cautionary rather than critical stance, the dancing master Henri Cellarius advises the gentleman: "Take care never to relinquish his lady until he feels that she has entirely recovered herself. The effect of the rotatory motion, even after stopping, is sometimes so great, that he would risk his partner's losing her equilibrium by detaching himself from her too suddenly" (1840, 44–45).[12]

1 + 3

One of the more unusual ways Chopin emphasizes the bar of the woman's twirl is by segmenting a four-bar melody asymmetrically into two parts: 1 + 3.[13] Because the three-bar segment is longer in duration than the one-bar segment, it is more strongly accentuated in the listener's mind. The second half of the introduction (bars 5–8) of Chopin's E-major waltz, shown in Example 5.13, exhibits this grouping proportion. Another example of this

EXAMPLE 5.14. Chopin's Waltz in B Minor, op. 69, no. 2, bars 31–40.

EXAMPLE 5.15. Voice-leading sketch of Chopin's Waltz in
B Minor, op. 69, no. 2, bars 32–40.

technique can be found in Chopin's Waltz in B Minor, op. 69, no. 2, shown
in Example 5.14. The pickup into bar 33 begins a contrasting section. While
the melody retains the same rhythmic pattern throughout (dotted quarter
note followed by three eighth notes), the voice-leading organization suggests
a grouping division between the first and second bars. As the voice-leading
sketch in Example 5.15 illustrates, the arpeggiation from the A up to the F♯,
which is embellished by an appoggiatura, brings the melody into a new register. The F♯ then initiates a descending third progression. Below the upper
voice, the A continues as a common tone until bar 40, where it moves to an A♯,
the leading tone of B minor.[14] The beginning of bar 34, the bar of the woman's
twirl, is also highlighted by the crescendo/decrescendo markings, which, in
combination with the registral high point, mark the downbeat of the second
bar as the structural high point of the phrase.

The opening of Chopin's Waltz in G♭ Major, op. 70, no. 1, shown in Example 5.16, provides another example in which the voice leading is very similar
to the waltz previously discussed. The asymmetrical grouping is more clearly
established in this example by the initiation of a different motivic design in
bar 2 that is then repeated in bars 3–4. Notice also in this passage the profu-

EXAMPLE 5.16. Chopin's Waltz in G♭ Major, op. 70, no. 1, bars 1–4.

EXAMPLE 5.17. Chopin's Waltz in G♭ Major, op. 70, no. 1, bars 33–37.

sion of neighboring motions. The opening melody of the B section, as shown in Example 5.17, also exhibits a 1 + 3 melodic organization.

It is important to note that the musical characteristics that I have cited as corollaries to the waltz as danced are not exclusive to the waltz; they can be found in other dances and nondance genres.[15] In fact, the only essential characteristic feature of a waltz, if it is to be perceived unambiguously as a waltz, is a perpetual oom-pah-pah accompaniment. As composers have proven many times, often with dreadful results, any tune, in any meter and style, can be retooled as a waltz.[16] What is significant in Chopin's waltzes is (1) the high degree in which these characteristics occur in comparison to other genres; (2) their appropriateness as sonic analogues for the physical motions contained in the dance; and (3) their prominence in the opening sections of Chopin's waltzes, where they are crucial means of establishing the genre of the work. When these secondary characteristics (melodic arches, neighboring motions, appoggiaturas, and grace notes) are used in combination with the oom-pah-pah accompaniment, they serve to refine and amplify an artistic vision of the waltz.

CHOPIN'S UNPUBLISHED WALTZES

As we have seen, early commentators on Chopin's music often interpreted his waltzes within the context of the ballroom. In a review of Chopin's op. 34 waltzes, Robert Schumann, an early champion of Chopin's music, makes this connection: "His three waltzes [op. 34] will delight above all – so different in

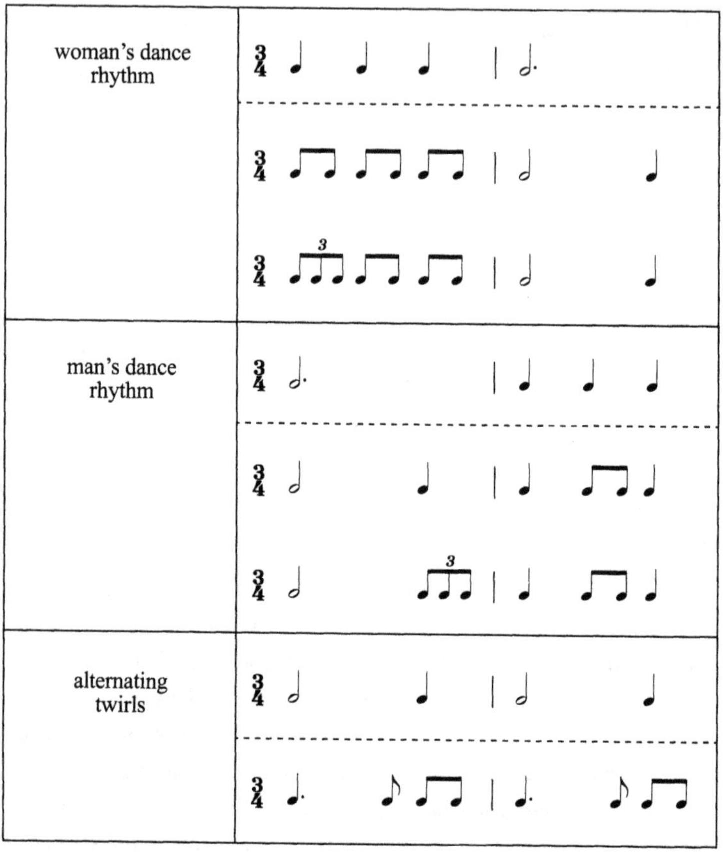

FIGURE 5.1. Rhythmic representation of gender in Chopin's waltzes.

type are they from the ordinary ones, and of a kind as could occur only to Chopin – perhaps he was inspired to new creations while he gazed, great artist that he is, among the dancers whom he has just roused by playing. So throbbing a life flows in them that they seem to have been actually improvised in the ballroom" (1952, 139). In a somewhat similar vein, I have argued that Chopin's waltzes are, on one level, based directly on the physical motions of the dance and, on another, an artistic portrait, an idealized vision, of the dance. As an artistic vision, it is conceivable that Chopin, at times, turned his gaze upon the dancing woman. Certainly, in the public reception of the waltz, as I have shown in chapter 3, it was the woman who attracted the most attention, and the feminine associations of the visual spectacle carried over into the music of the waltz. Composers of waltz music could thus choose to accentuate and develop the idea of femininity or choose to develop another realm such as virtuosity, humor, or melancholy. I have already suggested that, through a variety of means, in many of his waltzes Chopin strategically highlights the bar of the woman's twirl and captures its dynamic energy. As a working hypothesis, then, since the man and the woman do not perform the same steps simultaneously, it is entirely possible for a composer to focus on the rhythmic pattern of one or the other and thereby musically portray gender. The diagram presented in Figure 5.1 refines this hypothesis. The rhythms above the dotted lines correspond to the basic dance rhythms. Given below the dotted lines are common variants as found in Chopin's waltzes.

A close examination of Chopin's waltzes, however, reveals that the woman's rhythmic pattern is not a prominent feature of the waltzes Chopin chose to publish. It appears only in op. 18, and there it is in a formally subordinate section (bars 165–80). On the other hand, in the nine extant waltzes he withheld from publication, it appears prominently in all but two. One of these two, the Waltz in A♭ Major, KK 1209–11, is in a category by itself – more of a *Ländler* than a waltz. The other is the enigmatic Waltz in A Minor, KK 1238–39, which Chopin composed toward the end of his life. This evidence suggests that the majority of Chopin's unpublished waltzes are unified in their coded depiction of femininity.

Two of Chopin's unpublished waltzes were inspired by women he loved (or at least was deeply infatuated with): the Waltz in A♭ Major, op. 69, no. 1, and the Waltz in D♭ Major, op. 70, no. 3. Op. 69, no. 1, the opening of which is shown in Example 5.18, was written in Dresden in the fall of 1835 during his courtship with Maria Wodzińska. Maria's younger sister, writing many years later, recalls that, during one evening of music making, Maria requested Chopin to improvise a waltz for her. On the day of his departure, he presented her with an autograph of the waltz as a souvenir of their time together. Maria, in a letter written shortly after his departure, recalls to Chopin that the waltz "was the last thing we received and heard played by you."[17]

To a degree greater than any other waltz Chopin composed, this dance overflows with the rhythmic motive of the twirling female waltzer. While Chopin artfully varies the faster rhythm of the first bar of the woman's dance figure, the twirl rhythm of the second bar is repeated like a mantra throughout the opening section (bars 1–32). In sharp contrast, the B section (bars 65–92), shown in Example 5.19, explores the rhythm of the male waltzer and perhaps of Chopin himself.

EXAMPLE 5.18. Chopin's Waltz in A♭ Major, op. 69, no. 1, bars 1–16.

Note that a contrast in rhythm is evident not only between the two sections but also in the affective quality of the musical motion. A description that uses gendered metaphors might describe the B section as masculine because of its more vigorous leaps, its energetic off-beat accents, and the self-assertive and goal-oriented drive of the ascending sequence in bars 81–88 that pushes toward a loud climax, a climax that, by halting the musical flow, commands attention. The A section, on the other hand, is more tender and lyrical in expression, and more attention is given to the intricate detail of the musical surface.[18] Also, the descending chromatic bass controls and regulates the movement of the spontaneously ornamented melody.[19] In this interpretation, the depiction of gender in this waltz thereby assumes a form-generative role in a ternary ABA form.

In a letter written on 3 October 1829 to his close friend Tytus Woycie-chowski, Chopin confides that both his Waltz in D♭ Major and the slow movement from his Piano Concerto in F Minor, op. 21, were inspired by his feelings

EXAMPLE 5.19. Chopin's Waltz in A♭ Major, op. 69, no. 1, bars 65–92.

toward the young and beautiful singer Konstancja Gładkowska, Chopin's "ideal." With regard to the waltz, Chopin tells his friend: "Notice the place marked with a cross. No one but you knows of this" (1963, 34). Although we cannot know for certain where Chopin placed his X, since the manuscript is lost, the most striking passage in the waltz is the opening eight-bar phrase of the B section, which is pictured in Example 5.20. The entire waltz, in a ternary ABA form, is a duet, the only waltz by Chopin conceived as such. In the opening A section, the soprano and alto move together in constant eighth-note motion. The tenor voice takes over in the B section, supported by the soprano in parallel sixths. Except for the opening G♭, a functional bass

EXAMPLE 5.20. Chopin's Waltz in D♭ Major, op. 70, no. 3, bars 29–48.

is absent. Chopin instructs Woyciechowski that the low voice "must stand out as far as the upper E flat in the fifth bar [bar 37]. There's no need to write about it – you will feel it" (1963, 34). Overall, the phrase in bars 33–41 is a large balanced arch initiated by the rising tenor melody, which is answered by the descending soprano voice (accompanied by the tenor).

In the two-bar motive that opens the passage, Chopin uses several techniques commonly found in his unpublished waltzes, all of which bring emphasis to the beginning of the second bar: the crescendo marking, the dynamic and agogic accents, the asymmetrical grouping organization 1 + 3, and, finally, the rhythm of the waltzing woman.

Interestingly, the motive of the female dancer, and perhaps of Konstancja, appears as the principal motive of the third movement of the Concerto in F Minor, op. 21, the opening of which is shown in Example 5.21. Example 5.22 provides a rhythmic simplification of the concerto motive and the waltz motive. As mentioned above, both were conceived during the same period, the fall of 1829. By 3 October 1829 Chopin had completed the waltz and the slow

EXAMPLE 5.21. The opening of the last movement of Chopin's Concerto in F Minor, op. 21, bars 1–7.

EXAMPLE 5.22. Rhythmic simplification of the principal motives from the last movement of the Concerto in F Minor, op. 21, and the trio from the Waltz in D♭ Major, op. 70, no. 3.

movement of the concerto. Chopin apparently had difficulty completing the last movement. On 20 October he tells Woyciechowski that he is "not quite satisfied" with the last movement, and by mid-November it was still not finished (Chopin 1963, 36). The concerto premiered in Warsaw on 17 March 1830 at the National Theatre.

Contrary to what is commonly suggested, I believe the controlling genre of the opening section of the last movement of this concerto to be a waltz rather than a mazurka.[20] In fact, in the opening section, where it is most important to reference the controlling genre, there is little to suggest the presence of a mazurka.[21] There are no dotted rhythms, no triple figures, no drones, no accents on the second or third beats (instead, downbeats are emphasized), raised $\hat{4}$ does not play a prominent role, and the melodic motion is predominantly stepwise, with few melodic leaps within the melodic segments. Perhaps the most compelling evidence, aside from the motivic parallelism with the D♭-major waltz, is the piano accompaniment. It is a modified oom-pah-pah in which the second and third beats arpeggiate the one-bar harmonic rhythm. Within Chopin's titled dance music, this type of oom-pah-pah accompaniment only occurs in waltzes; moreover, it is most prominent in two waltzes written within the same time period (KK 1207–1208 and KK 1213–14). Chopin creates two-bar arches in the accompaniment by using downward arpeggiations on the second and third beats in the first bar and upward arpeggiations in the following bar; the bass line follows this pattern of arpeggiations. The opening four-bar phrase is a balanced arch against which the cellos play a simplified inversion of the piano's arch. And in bars 5–8 the rhythm of the twirling female dancer twice appears in the soloist's left hand.

Further evidence comes from the fact that in arranging themes from the concerto into a collection of waltzes and mazurkas (published separately by Brzezina, April 1830; Tom. 1370 and 1365), Chopin's friend and classmate from the Warsaw Conservatory, Antoni Orłowski, set the opening theme of the last movement as a waltz and not a mazurka. On three separate occasions, Chopin makes reference in letters to Orłowski's arrangements; in none does he say Orłowski mistook the genre.[22]

As Halina Goldberg observes, it is the second theme of the movement, with its strong emphasis on second beats, Lydian fourths, and an arpeggiated melody constructed out of small motivic cells, that speaks the language of the mazurka. And Orłowski's published arrangement of it as a mazurka preserves its generic identity. Building upon my previously published observations about the waltz features of the first theme (McKee 2004, 153–55), Goldberg interprets this movement as "an interplay of the waltz and mazur genres" (2008, 69). Very briefly, the movement is organized as an ABA form with two interconnecting transitional episodes. As I have suggested, the material of the opening A section is based on the waltz, and the episode that follows develops this material as it modulates to A♭ major. In expressive contrast, the B section presents four mazurka tunes, which are developed in the subsequent episode. While the final section opens with a reprise of the waltz theme, it soon gives way to a playful mixture and development of mazurka and waltz elements.[23] In the final section of the coda, Chopin wisely concludes his ballroom narrative by allowing the mazurka to have the last word (the concerto was premiered in Warsaw for a Polish audience at a time when Polish nationalism was particularly strong).

CONCLUSION

Whether Chopin was in the salon or the ballroom, on the dance floor or at the piano providing music for the dancers, social dancing was an important part of his life. In this chapter I have attempted to demonstrate how Chopin's firsthand experience of the waltz as danced served as a broad and rich source of compositional inspiration. In various ways, he translated the rhythms and bodily motions of the dancers into appropriate musical corollaries. The perpetual whirling of the dancers is reflected by a prevalence of neighbor-note figures and arching contours in different parts of the texture as well as at different levels of the structure. I have also suggested that in the waltzes he withheld from publication, his creative gaze rested upon the waltzing woman, whereby he translates the dynamic motion and rhythm of her three steps and twirl into musical sound. In her bucolic novel *Les maîtres sonneurs* (*The Master Pipers*), George Sand, after describing how difficult it is to dance to the tunes of a musical oaf, rhapsodizes about a musician who truly understands the nature of the dance: "He gave us the finest dances in the world . . . so attractive and easy to dance to that we seemed to fly through the air" (1994, 75). I would suggest that Chopin was such a musician as Sand describes and that in listening to, performing, and studying his waltzes, mazurkas, and polonaises, it is best to keep the dancers in mind.

6th

Chopin's Approach to Waltz Form

❧

I have picked up nothing that is essentially Viennese. For example, I can't dance a waltz properly—that speaks for itself! My piano has heard nothing but mazurkas.

FRYDERYK CHOPIN

In this chapter I consider Chopin's approach to large-scale form (thematic design and tonal organization) in his published and unpublished waltzes. I begin by examining the normative formal procedures of the waltzes Chopin composed while he was living in Warsaw, all of which were unpublished. I then consider the radical shift in Chopin's approach to waltz form found in two waltzes he composed in the early 1830s (KK 1213–14 and op. 18) and explore the possible Viennese influence that may have motivated this compositional shift. I conclude with an overview of the seven remaining published waltzes (op. 34, nos. 1–3, op. 42, and op. 64, nos. 1–3).

THE WARSAW WALTZES

Five waltzes survive from Chopin's Warsaw years (see Table 5.1). All follow a three-part design (ABA) typical for Warsaw waltz composers of that time. Diagram 6.1 provides form charts of the first four of these waltzes. (I discuss the fifth Warsaw waltz later.) As can be seen, in comparison to Viennese

Waltz in A♭ Major, KK 1209–11 (c. 1826–30)   abc
Artlessly simple

    Waltz 1   Waltz 2   Waltz 1 (*da capo*)

                                4 4

‖: a a :‖‖: b :‖ a a   ‖: c c :‖   ‖: a a :‖
 XT XD   XT   XT XT   XT XT   XT XD

    I   vi   I   IV   I

    I   IV   I

Waltz in B Minor, op. 69, no. 2 (1829)   abc
Lyrical/Melancholy

    Waltz 1   Waltz 2   Waltz 1

a a a a b b a a b b a a   c c c c   a a b b a a
TD TT TD TT XD XD TD TT XD XD TD TT   TD TD TD TD   TD TT XD XD TD TT

i   I   i

Waltz in D♭ Major, op. 70, no. 3 (1829)   abcd
Lyrical/Melancholy

    Waltz 1   Waltz 2   Waltz 1 (*da capo*)
4 4 4 4   4 4   4 4 4 4
a a a a b b   ‖: c c :‖‖:d d :‖ c c   a a a a b b
TD TT TD TT XT XT   TD TT XT XT TD TT TD TT TD TT XT XT

    I   IV   I

Waltz in E Major, KK 1207–8 (1829 or 1830)   abc
Lyrical/Melancholy

       Waltz 1   Waltz 2   Waltz 1 (written out, but not modified)
        9 7   4   9 7
intro a a b b a a   c c   intro a a b b a a
      TD TT TT XT TD TT   XD XT   TD TT TT XT TD TT

        I   iii   I   IV   I   I   iii   I

        I   IV   I

DIAGRAM 6.1. Form charts of the first four of Chopin's Warsaw waltzes.

practice, Chopin's Warsaw waltzes are limited in their thematic contents: each contains only three to four distinct themes. The trio sections, notated as second waltzes in the diagram, are in the key of either the subdominant or the parallel major, resulting in the large-scale tonal designs I–IV–I and i–I–i. As John Rink observes, such "closed, symmetrical harmonic foundations" (1992, 88) are typical of Chopin's early works, especially of his smaller genres. Aside from the abbreviated returns of the opening sections in KK 1209–11 and op. 69, no. 2, Chopin takes a literal approach to the return of the opening section: the material is replicated note for note without variation. In this regard, it is noteworthy that he does not alter the final cadence in such a way as to give it greater rhetorical emphasis, nor does he provide codas, which, in both cases, would provide a greater sense of global closure. Overall, these early waltzes are paratactic in design: an ordered succession of tonally closed sections that lack any strong sense of structural momentum from one part to the next.

Chopin's Waltz in A♭ Major, KK 1209–11, is artlessly simple in nature. Scholars are not in agreement as to its date of composition, but, based on stylistic evidence alone, it would appear to be the earliest surviving waltz by Chopin, possibly composed in 1826 or 1827.[1] It is the only waltz Chopin notates in $\frac{3}{8}$ meter; the harmonic vocabulary is extremely limited; and its proportions are unusually brief. The trio, for example, is only eight bars long (without repeats). Additionally, its melodies are subdivided into one-bar segments instead of a more typical two-bar length, which would correspond to the two-bar rotation of the dancers. Adolph Bernhard Marx identifies such waltzes with one-bar groupings as "rustic" and "primitive," more suited for twirling peasants; as noted in chapter 5, as an example he cites the waltz tune from Weber's *Der Freischütz* (Marx 1837–38, 2:55). If it is true that Chopin did compose this waltz in 1830, as some claim (Chomiński and Turło 1990), then he did so using a different conceptual framework whereby he intentionally wrote unsophisticated music. Perhaps it was conceived as a *Ländler*, or perhaps it was intended for a dancing occasion of a rustic nature. Whatever its date and purpose, it stands apart stylistically from his other Warsaw waltzes.

Filled with bittersweet melodies, the next three Warsaw waltzes (op. 69, no. 2, op. 70, no. 3, and KK 1207–1208) are more typical of Chopin's unpublished waltzes composed in Warsaw and of those he left unpublished throughout his life. An expression of melancholy is achieved through the use of the minor mode (or mixture), moderate tempi, and lyrical melodies.[2] A fourth *valse mélancolique* in D minor, KK 1252, was written by Chopin in 1828 but only survives as an incipit with the title "Valse la partenza." Chopin appears to have had particular affinity for such doleful waltzes, for they are uncommon in waltzes published by other composers in Warsaw or Vienna during the 1820s. Out of the 116 Warsaw waltzes I examined, only three could be classified as "melancholy waltzes": a waltz in F minor by Maria Szymanowska-Wołowska (1821, Tom. 275), a waltz in F minor by Stanisław Grabowski titled "Valse mélancolique" (1821, Tom. 282), and a waltz in F major by Ludwik Nidecki (c. 1822–30, Tom. 458).[3] Within the Viennese repertoire, all the waltzes of Lanner and Strauss Sr.–without exception–are set overall within major keys. The minor mode is only occasionally used for individual waltz themes; and while mixture is not uncommon in the codas, the major mode always prevails by the end. Indeed, waltz scholar Max Schönherr doubts that a truly sad Viennese waltz actually exists, as if to say that it would go against the very core of the Viennese spirit, which is characterized by an unflappable sense of gaiety in the face of harsh political and social realities (1976, 104).[4]

Cadences and Phrase Connections

As the form charts provided in Diagram 6.1 show, an important feature of Chopin's approach to waltz form in his Warsaw waltzes is cadential variety. His Warsaw waltzes employ the full range of cadences (half cadences, imperfect authentic cadences, and perfect authentic cadences) and are organized by Classical principles of tonal hierarchy as elaborated by the treatises of Heinrich Koch and later by Anton Reicha. As mentioned earlier, Chopin would have learned these principles from Józef Elsner, his composition teacher at the Warsaw Conservatory, whose pedagogy and compositional approach were strongly rooted in the Austro-German Classical tradition (Goldberg 2008, 115–33). It is important to keep in mind that this Classical approach to phrase organization is antithetical to the approach taken by Lanner and Strauss Sr. Nearly every waltz theme of Lanner and Strauss Sr. is articulated with a V–I authentic cadence. Dominant punctuations are rare. As discussed in chapter 3, the extremely high degree of tonic closure correlates to the visual aesthetic category of self-containment. Quite at the opposite end of the spectrum, Chopin revels in tonally open-ended themes. For example, 50 percent of the themes from his three lyrical Warsaw waltzes (op. 69, no. 2, op. 70, no. 3, and KK 1207–1208) close with half cadences. And, not surprisingly, parallel periods in which the opening antecedent phrase is articulated with a half cadence are Chopin's favorite type of period organization.

   A compositional feature related to the high number of half cadences in Chopin's Warsaw waltzes is Chopin's subtle play of phrase boundaries, in which he often provides an apparent or real cadential dominant (and, on occasion, a cadential tonic) with some sense of continuing tonal and rhythmic motion into the beginning of the next phrase. Edward T. Cone (1968, 80) was one of the first to cite the blurring of phrase boundaries as a signal feature of

Chopin's approach to phrase rhythm. William Rothstein calls Chopin "one of the greatest masters of the phrase overlap, and he uses the technique as one of his principal means of achieving continuity in phrase rhythm, especially in his shorter pieces" (1989, 226). The "two most striking features of Chopin's style," adds Carl Schachter, are "his tendency to accept four-bar groupings as a given and his unending inventive strategies for creating free rhythmic patterns that work counter to these large periodicities" (1989, 189). Cone (1968, 80) asserts, and I agree, that Chopin's basic grammar of the four-bar unit is based on the phrase rhythms of the ballroom dance.

Diagram 6.1 indicates blurred phrase boundaries with a small underline mark connecting the cadential harmony of one phrase to the beginning harmony of the next. Reflecting its simple, unsophisticated nature, the Waltz in A♭ Major contains no overlapping motions. By contrast, the next three of the Warsaw waltzes, especially the Waltz in B Minor and the Waltz in E Major, are rife with ongoing rhythmic and tonal motions that result in some sort of overlap between the end of one phrase and the beginning of the next.

Example 6.1 provides one illustration from Chopin's Waltz in B Minor, op. 69, no. 2, composed in 1829. The waltz opens with a sixteen-bar parallel period comprised of an antecedent phrase and a consequent phrase. The antecedent phrase arrives on the expected cadential dominant in bar 8. Several factors, however, undercut the rhetorical force of this dominant and its function as a half cadence: (1) rhythmically, there is no caesura—the melody's eighth-note motion in bar 8 runs uninterrupted into the opening bar of the consequent phrase, eventually landing on the A♯ of bar 10; (2) the left hand tolls repeated pedal Bs on the downbeats through the cadential progression into the tonic return of bar 9; and, perhaps most important, (3) Chopin alters the first note of the consequent's melody from an F♯ to a D. This seemingly slight alteration allows the completion of a linear descent from the F♯ at the beginning of the antecedent to the D at the beginning of the consequent. Notice also how the descent pushes past the D in bar 9 to the A♯ on the downbeat of bar 10 (in Example 6.1 I have notated this foreground fourth descent with slurs). The unifying force of the middleground descent from F♯ to D, together with the static bass line and the rhythmic continuity of the melody, call into question the articulative clarity of the phrase boundary in bars 8 and 9. Rubbing against our expectations of a symmetrical 8 + 8 parallel period (interpretation #1) is the possibility of hearing the antecedent's melody end on the downbeat of bar 9. In this reading, there are at least two

EXAMPLE 6.1. Chopin's Waltz in B Minor, op. 69, no. 2, bars 1–16.

ways to interpret and perform the melodic boundaries between the antecedent and the consequent. One may hear an overlap in which the D of bar 9 elides as both the end of the antecedent and the beginning of the consequent (interpretation #2); or one may hear the melody of the consequent begin with the second eighth note in bar 9 as an anacrustic figure that falls to the downbeat of bar 10 (interpretation #3).[5] Indeed, the melodic design, bass line, and harmonic rhythm of this passage suggest the possibility of hearing the opening bar of the antecedent and consequent as weak hyperbeats that lead to hyperdownbeats in bars 2 and 10. Supporting this reading is the performance practice of beginning bar 1 slightly under tempo and speeding up to tempo by the downbeat of bar 2.[6]

Sergei Rachmaninoff in his 1919 recording (RCA 1131785) and Alfred Cortot in his 1943 recording (EMI 7673592) offer a far more radical solution to the question of where the consequent ends and the antecedent begins (interpretation #4). By completely sidestepping any emphasis on the downbeat of bar 9, Rachmaninoff and Cortot unite the falling melodic line of bars 8 and 9 into a single, undivided gesture leading to the A♯ in bar 10. This results in an extended overlap: the antecedent ends with the A♯ in bar 10, but the consequent begins three bars earlier with the high C♯. Chopin confirms the viability of this reading later in the piece when the opening theme returns.

EXAMPLE 6.2. Chopin's Waltz in B Minor, op. 69, no. 2, bars 44–60.

As shown in the excerpt given in Example 6.2, upon its return the opening descent of the melody is utterly subsumed within a larger anacrusis that drives purposefully to the A♯ in bar 50. Chopin's phrasing slur indicates to the performer not to make any articulative breaks within the chromatic descent; and while within the first descent (bars 47–50) there is a return to the original contour of the theme that could potentially signal a beginning boundary, the second anacrusis (bars 56–58) descends chromatically to the A♯ without any change of contour.

My goal here is not to arrive at a preferred reading of these complex passages but rather to demonstrate a basic feature of Chopin's approach to phrase rhythm in his Warsaw waltzes—a feature that sets him apart from Viennese practice: the masterful veiling of phrase boundaries, which, in its inherent ambiguity, allows for a range of performative approaches and listening interpretations. With Viennese waltzes there is never any doubt as to where one phrase ends and the next phrase begins. Ambiguity in the realm of phrase organization was not part of the Viennese ballroom compositional mindset.

We are now in a better position to draw some stylistic distinctions between Chopin's Warsaw waltzes and the Viennese waltzes of Lanner and Strauss Sr. Table 6.1 provides a summary. A list of musical categories is given in the first column. The next two columns either indicate their prevalence or specify a stylistic type with a category. The second column represents Chopin's Warsaw waltzes, and the third column represents the Viennese waltzes of Lanner and Strauss Sr. As can be seen, the Warsaw waltzes of Chopin and the Viennese waltzes of Lanner and Strauss Sr. are musically worlds apart. Chopin employs the full range of cadential types, whereas Lanner and Strauss

TABLE 6.1. SUMMARY OF STYLISTIC DISTINCTIONS BETWEEN
THE WARSAW WALTZES OF CHOPIN AND THE VIENNESE WALTZES
OF LANNER AND STRAUSS SR.

	CHOPIN'S WARSAW WALTZES[a]	LANNER'S AND STRAUSS SR.'S VIENNESE WALTZES[b]
half cadences	50 percent of all phrases	6 percent of all phrases
phrase overlap	common	not used
overall form	three-part *da capo* (ABA)	medley (ABCD . . .)
number of themes	3–4	average of 16
form of each waltz	rounded binary (a :‖ ba)	predominantly simple binary (a :‖ b)
introduction and coda	not used	standard practice
crisis point at or near the beginning of the coda	not used	standard practice
melodic style	pianistic and vocal	violinistic and vocal
melodic hemiola	not used	common
nontonic phrase openings	29 percent of all phrases	48 percent of all phrases

[a] Op. 69, no. 2, op. 70, no. 3, and KK 1207–1208 (1829–30)
[b] Published between 1829 and 1832.

Sr. confine themselves almost exclusively to authentic cadences. Chopin often uses the technique of phrase overlap; Lanner and Strauss Sr. do not. Chopin favors *da capo* ternary form (waltz 1–waltz 2–waltz 1) rather than the Viennese medley format, which for Chopin results in far less thematic quantity and variety. Chopin prefers rounded binary form for each individual waltz over the Viennese preference for simple binary form. Lanner and Strauss Sr. regularly use introductions and codas and employ crisis points near the beginning of codas, thereby drawing attention to the process of global closure; Chopin does not employ introductions and codas or emphasize the final cadence in any way. Chopin's textures are pianistic, while the majority of the waltz themes of Lanner and Strauss Sr. are conceived for the violin. Melodic hemiolas are a common feature of the themes of Lanner and Strauss Sr.; Chopin never uses them, nor does he use auxiliary progressions to the degree Lanner and Strauss Sr. do. And, finally, Chopin's Warsaw waltzes are generally slower and more lyrical, and they lean toward the expression of melancholy.

The Viennese aesthetics of thematic self-containment and variety in the succession of themes simply were not part of Chopin's compositional mindset. And although both Schumann and Liszt locate Chopin's creative inspiration for his waltzes on the ballroom dance floor, his creative focus, at least for his Warsaw waltzes, appears not to be fixed on the panoply of dancers but rather, as I have suggested earlier, on the attitudes and bodily motions of a single waltzing couple and, more specifically, on the female waltzer. Furthermore, Chopin's musical grammar is firmly rooted in Classical conventions, as is his approach to form, which is modeled on the *da capo* designs of the minuet and polonaise. What we see in Lanner and Strauss Sr. is the emergence and development of a vernacular musical language quite distinct in certain regards from the language and aesthetics of art music. Importantly, this distinction is not a result of deliberate vulgarity within existing conventions, as was the case with Mozart's and Beethoven's *Deutsche* or with Weber's waltz from *Der Freischütz*. Rather, the emergence of a distinct popular style, as I argued in chapter 3, was motivated by a different set of aesthetic assumptions drawn from the visual and bodily experiences of the ballroom dance floor and from the music's primary function as social entertainment.

Finally, it is important to recognize that the style of Chopin's lyrical or melancholy waltzes—a style he returned to throughout his life—was well formed before he left Warsaw. Considering the vast stylistic differences between Chopin's Warsaw waltz practice and that of Lanner and Strauss Sr. and that Chopin was to a large extent insulated from Viennese waltz practice, one can consider his early approach to waltz composition as constituting what could be called his Warsaw or Polish waltz style. And while Chopin's Warsaw waltz practice is in large part distinct from that of his Polish contemporaries, his lyrical waltzes have much in common with his lyrical mazurkas (e.g., op. 7, no. 2 and op. 17, no. 4). Indeed, Edwin Stadnicki (1962, 112–46), Jim Samson (1985, 120), and Halina Goldberg (2008, 66–69) have observed that in Warsaw dance publications the mazurka and the waltz "showed a certain degree of generic interchangeability" (Goldberg 2008, 66).

CHOPIN IN VIENNA

I turn now to consider Chopin's exposure to the music of Lanner and Strauss Sr. Chopin visited Vienna on two occasions. He embarked on his first trip after graduating from the Warsaw Conservatory in the summer of 1829. While musically this was a highly successful trip, he stayed in Vienna for less than three weeks. And while it is likely that he visited one of the restaurants, parks, or beer gardens where Lanner and Strauss Sr. regularly performed, he does not mention it in the surviving letters.[7] It was during his second trip to Vienna that we have evidence of Chopin's direct engagement with the dance music of Lanner and Strauss Sr. He arrived in Vienna on 23 November 1830 and stayed until midsummer of the following year. Thus, he was in Vienna for the entire carnival season, 6 January (Epiphany) to 16 February (Ash Wednesday), during which time it was not uncommon for Vienna to average over one hundred balls per week. In less than a month after he arrived, Chopin had already become familiar with Viennese nightlife.[8] In a letter to his family dated 22 December 1830, he writes: "Best known among the many Viennese entertainments are those evenings in the beer-halls where Strauss or Lanner (who correspond to the Świeszewskis in Warsaw) play waltzes during supper. After each waltz the applause is terrific: but if they play . . . a pot-pourri of opera-tunes, songs and dances, the audience is so delighted that they can scarcely contain themselves. It just shows you how corrupted the taste of the Viennese public is" (1963, 72).

It is clear from this and other early letters from Vienna that, although he was deeply troubled over the November Uprising and his inability to recapture the musical glories of his first trip to Vienna, Chopin actively took part in Viennese social life. And while no letters survive from the first half of February, the climax of carnival season that year, one can assume that, at least to some degree, Chopin continued to take part in Viennese social life. The activity that defined the Viennese carnival more than any other was the waltz. One observer in 1830 referred to waltzing as a "Viennese obsession."[9] Chopin, in another letter from 26 January, complains that every barrel-organ in the city churns out the waltzes of Strauss and, in the same letter, laments to his composition teacher, Józef Elsner, that "only waltzes get printed" (1963, 137). Just a few years later, Frances Trollope, the English travel writer, remarked that during the Viennese carnival "the whole population seems as much actuated by one common and universal feeling, as if an irresistible spell had fallen on the empire, enforcing them all to waltz. . . . And I never observe half-a-dozen men and women together, without expecting to see them set off, and spin into a waltz" (1838, 176). Thus, wherever Chopin turned, be it to the boulevards, the restaurants, the publishing houses, the beer halls, the salons of private homes, or the ballrooms, he could not escape the lilting strains of the Viennese waltz.

Chopin's Viennese Waltzes

There are two waltzes composed by Chopin in the early 1830s that bear the unmistakable stamp of Lanner and Strauss Sr.: the Waltz in E Minor, KK 1213–14, which was left unpublished, and the Waltz in E♭ Major, op. 18, Chopin's first published waltz. The E-minor waltz is thought to have been composed in 1830, possibly in May. If that is correct, it would have been conceived after Chopin's first trip to Vienna. Most scholars believe that op. 18 was begun in 1831, either during the last months of his second stay in Vienna or after he arrived in Paris.[10] In comparison to his previous waltzes, these two works are marked by a radically different approach to phrase structure, thematic content, and, especially in the case of op. 18, formal design.

Cadences and Phrase Connections

Diagram 6.2 provides a form chart of the E-minor waltz, and Diagram 6.3 provides a form chart of the E♭-major waltz aligned with a middleground voice-leading sketch. For the first time, Chopin flanks his waltzes with both an introduction and a coda. But more telling of Viennese influence is that Chopin, in a move completely out of character with his musical sensibilities, grounds nearly every phrase with an authentic cadence (forty out of forty-one phrases). The exception occurs in the E♭-major waltz, where the final statement of the opening theme ends with a dominant (bars 236–37). Even here, though, the phrase does not truly end with a half cadence but rather with what can be referred to as an "incomplete" perfect authentic cadence.[11] Example 6.3 compares the final statement of the theme with its first appearance. As can be seen, the restatement of the theme is fractured in the middle by two bars of silence, after which the second half of the phrase resumes. But after the second half reaches the dominant of the expected perfect authentic cadence, the music again breaks off into silence, leaving it to the listener to supply the final tonic. As I discussed in chapter 3, such crisis points, which disrupt the rhythmic continuity of the music at or near the entrance of the coda, are a signature technique of Lanner and Strauss Sr. These disruptions stirred listeners and dancers out of their lyrical reveries—or whatever else was occupying them—and drew their attention back to the music and, ultimately, to the performer/conductor. Lanner and especially Strauss Sr. were known for their consummate showmanship, and an important part of being a good

Waltz 1	Waltz 2	Waltz 1

intro a a ‖: b b a a :‖   ‖: c c :‖: d c c :‖   a a   coda
XT XT   XT XT XT XT   XT XT   TT XT XT   XT XT

i   I   iii V–I   i

With "15!" and "13" above Waltz 1 (right).

DIAGRAM 6.2. Form chart of Chopin's Waltz in E Minor, KK 1213–14.

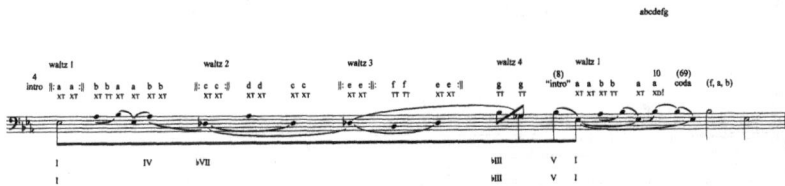

DIAGRAM 6.3. Form chart of Chopin's Waltz in E♭ Major, op. 18.

EXAMPLE 6.3. Comparison of two phrases in Chopin's op. 18 (bars 5–12, 229–39).

entertainer is knowing how to maintain and manipulate the attention of the audience; crisis points are one musical technique that seemingly require the intercession of the performer/conductor to rescue the music from rhythmic peril, put it back on track, and thereby shine a dramatic spotlight on the heroic deeds of the conductor.

EXAMPLE 6.4. (*above and facing*) Chopin's Waltz in E Minor,
KK 1213–14, bars 97–131.

In a passage immediately preceding the coda, Chopin's E-minor waltz,
KK 1213–14, also veers dangerously out of control. As shown in Example 6.4,
theme a returns in bar 97. The second statement of theme a, which begins in
bar 105, is expanded from eight bars to fifteen bars.[12] A crisis point is reached
in bar 108, where in place of a tonic chord, which had occurred on every
prior appearance of this theme, Chopin substitutes a fully diminished seventh
chord. To make matters worse, despite the considerable rhetorical emphasis

given to this rogue chord, it carries no harmonic function; instead, it serves as a voice-leading chord to connect bar 108 to bar 109 by half-step and common-tone motion. Chopin then launches into an expanded cadential progression in which the melody spirals wildly into another fully diminished seventh chord in bar 113. Against a rising arpeggiated bass line, the melody falls three octaves into a perfect authentic cadence. The phrase expansion not only increases musical tension but also allows the final cadential bar of the phrase (bar 119) to arrive on a metrically strong bar, all of which increases the sense of global closure. Except for this waltz, metrically accented cadences and crisis points are found only in Chopin's published waltzes.[13]

Returning to Chopin's use of authentic cadences in his two "Viennese waltzes," if we consider op. 69, no. 2, op. 70, no. 3, and KK 1207–1208 as representative of Chopin's Warsaw waltz practice, we find that 50 percent of the phrases contained in those waltzes are punctuated by half cadences. In stark contrast, all forty-one phrases of KK 1213–14 and op. 18 are punctuated by authentic cadences (i.e., if we consider the broken cadence of op. 18 as a variant of an authentic cadence). Furthermore, all phrase boundaries in KK 1213–14 and op. 18 are clearly articulated; there are no instances of phrase overlap. To offset the potential heavy-footed stability and lack of structural momentum that could easily result from a steady succession of authentic cadences, Chopin relies on nontonic phrase openings to a greater extent than he did in his Warsaw waltzes. In KK 1213–14 all but one phrase begins off tonic. Theme d (bars 73–80) is the only one that opens with a tonic. While the entire theme is set in the key of G♯ minor and begins and ends with a tonic G♯-minor triad, within the larger tonal context of waltz 2 G♯ minor functions as the mediant of E major within the middleground progression I–iii–V–I. Furthermore, while the previous phrase does end with a tonic, resulting in the direct succession of two tonics, they are different tonics–E major and G♯ minor.

In op. 18, twenty-two out of twenty-eight phrases begin with auxiliary progressions; and the opening tonic harmonies of four of the six remaining phrases (themes f and g) are newly established tonics. Theme f begins with a tonic in B♭ minor, which is heard as the submediant within the locally governing key of D♭ major. Theme g also begins with a new tonic, G♭ major, in first inversion, which functions as ♭III within the overall key of E♭ major. Thus, in these particular cases the tonic that opens the phrase is not the same tonic that ended the previous phrase. It is remarkable, I believe, that in the entire piece there are only four instances where the same tonic is used at the end of one phrase and the beginning of the next. The compositional principle at work here is that whether through nontonic phrase openings or through the use of "new" tonics, Chopin generally avoids using the same harmony at the boundary points of phrases.

In comparing Chopin's KK 1213–14 and op. 18 with his Warsaw waltzes, his complete avoidance of half cadences (from 50 percent to 0 percent), his complete avoidance of phrase overlaps (from 33 percent to 0 percent), and the increased use of nontonic phrase openings (an increase from 29 percent to 78 percent) strongly suggest a self-conscience shift in compositional practice. I believe the motivating force behind this right-angle turn was Chopin's first-hand experience with Viennese waltz music. If we accept the premise that the waltzes of Lanner and Strauss Sr. served as models for Chopin, then KK 1213–14 and op. 18 may be read as compositional experiments. Not only does Chopin incorporate characteristic features of the Viennese waltz, he intentionally limits himself to them to a degree greater than is actually found in the Viennese waltz.

MELODIC STYLE

The distinctive dialect of the Viennese waltz can be heard within Chopin's op. 18 in the domain of melody. While KK 1213–14 bears hallmark features of the Viennese waltz, its melodic material is infused with a virtuosic pianism peculiar to Chopin. The melodic content of op. 18, on the other hand, gushes with the sensual language of the Viennese ballroom orchestra. Not only is there an abundance of thematic material (roughly twice as many themes as found in his Warsaw waltzes), but the melodic style is also strikingly similar to the melodies of Lanner and Strauss Sr. Here it is important to point out the violinistic nature of op. 18; although he refers to op. 18 as *Grande valse brillante*, he refrains from using a virtuosic piano style. Excluding the coda, there are no sweeping scalar passages, no arabesque flourishes, nor are there any perpetual eighth-note melodies as found in the themes of his other *brillante* waltzes. Furthermore, every melody falls within the comfortable range of an experienced violinist–the highest note is G^5, requiring fifth position on the violin, and the lowest note is C^4, which falls on the G string.[14] All of his other *brillante* waltzes explore either much higher registers or, as in the case of op. 34, no. 2, a lower register well beyond the physical limits of the violin. The only somewhat unviolinistic–and therefore un-Viennese–aspect of op. 18 is its key. Lanner and Strauss Sr. favored the keys of G major, D major, and A major, for these are the most resonant keys on the violin; seldom did they employ flat keys.

Both Lanner and Strauss Sr. were gifted violinists and led their orchestras with their violins. As a consequence, the majority of their melodies were conceived on and scored for the violin. As Mosco Carner observes:

> [The] violin character is the hall-mark of the Viennese waltz. Many a waltz of Lanner and Strauss originated in simple violin improvisations which were later elaborated and scored for full orchestra. Hence the abundance of characteristic violin effects such as . . . double-stopping, euphonious sixths and "sobbing" thirds . . . , wide leaps over the strings from the E to the G strings, tunes to be played on the fourth string, and all the effects produced by different bowings–legato, staccato, spiccato, saltando, *sul ponticello*–and short, crisp up-bows, notably at the opening of a waltz. . . . Naturally, effects on other instruments were not neglected, woodwind and brass being often given interesting details; but on the whole it was the brilliant and sympathetic treatment of the violins that lent the orchestra of Lanner and Strauss its characteristic stamp. (1948, 43–44)

Example 6.5 illustrates similarities between the melodies of Chopin's op. 18 and selected waltz melodies of Lanner and Strauss Sr. that were composed, published, and performed in Vienna during the late 1820s and early 1830s. In his study of Viennese waltz melodies, which focuses primarily on the waltzes of Lanner and Strauss Sr., Max Schönherr (1976) provides a list of ninety-nine melodic types. In Example 6.5 I have indicated the correspondence to Schönherr's categories in parentheses when appropriate. While it is quite possible that Chopin may have heard some of the Viennese waltz melodies

Theme a. Post horn rhythm melodies (*Posthorn*)

Chopin, Op. 18, bars 5–25

Lanner, Op. 30, waltz no. 1

Theme b. Repeated-note spiccato melodies

Chopin, Op. 18, bars 21–25

Lanner, Op. 42, waltz no. 3

Theme c. Melodies doubled in thirds or sixths

Chopin, Op. 18, bars 69–76

Lanner, Op. 48, waltz no. 3

EXAMPLE 6.5. (*above and facing*) Similarities between the melodies of Chopin's op. 18 and the melodies of Lanner and Strauss Sr.

provided in Example 6.5, it is not my intent to suggest any specific composition as an influence. I only wish to demonstrate general stylistic affinities between op. 18 and the waltz melodies of Lanner and Strauss Sr. Indeed, all of the melodies of op. 18 are strongly characteristic of Viennese waltzes, and for each of Chopin's melodies given in Example 6.5, many more Viennese counterparts could be provided. Importantly, except for the first (a) and last category (g) given (post horn melodies and cantabile melodies), these melodic types are not found in Chopin's Warsaw waltzes, nor are they typical of the Warsaw waltzes composed and published by Chopin's contemporaries.

Theme d. Melodies that contain hemiolas (Hemiole)

Chopin, Op. 18, bars 85–90

Strauss, Op. 32, waltz no. 4

Theme e. Melodies with a standard Viennese waltz rhythm

Chopin, Op. 18, bars 117–24

Lanner, Op. 34, waltz no. 6

Theme f. Melodies embellished with grace notes ("Lach"-Walzer)

Chopin, Op. 18, bars 133–38

Strauss I, Op. 23, waltz no. 3

Theme g. Cantabile melodies ("Liebes"-Walzer)

Chopin, Op. 18, bars 165–70

Lanner, Op. 33, waltz no. 2

The opening theme of op. 18 is based on a rhythm typical of post horn calls (quarter note/two eighth notes/quarter note) and is a ubiquitous feature of Viennese waltzes, especially commonplace in introductions, in first themes, and at the openings of codas–places where clarion calls to action would be appropriate. There are two categories of post horn melodies: (1) melodies that use both rhythmic and melodic gestures associated with post horn melodies (often these melodies are scored for the post horn or trumpet) and (2) melodies that use the post horn rhythmic motive but melodically are not conceived as post horn melodies.[15] The melody from the opening theme of Chopin's op. 18 falls into the second category. Variations of the post horn rhythm are first sounded in the introduction as a call to the dance floor. Chopin then uses it not only as the principal rhythmic material of the first theme but also as a unifying device throughout the piece.

While the first theme alludes to the sound of a post horn, the second theme falls squarely within the sonic world of the violin. Chopin's theme b corresponds to Lanner's and Strauss Sr.'s spiccato violin melodies, which are characterized by repeated notes within a continuous eighth-note motion.[16] While the staccato marks would have sufficed to indicate that the performer use an off-the-string stroke, Lanner also includes the term "spiccato." Spiccato is a violin technique in which the bow bounces evenly and lightly off the string; it is typically used in a fast tempo for running eighth notes (or sixteenth notes). To capture the effect of this string technique, Chopin similarly places staccato marks over his repeated notes and uses the term "leggieramente" (with lightness).

The doubling of the melody in thirds or sixths, as found in Chopin's theme c, is a texture used by Lanner and Strauss Sr. within a wide range of melodic styles. Notice how Chopin uses the rhythmic motive of the first waltz, the post horn rhythm, as a motivic counterpart to the cantabile thirds.

Lanner's and Strauss Sr.'s influence within the domain of rhythm upon the first generation of Romantic composers who were coming of age during the late 1820s and early 1830s, including Chopin, Schumann, Mendelssohn, Wagner, and Berlioz, cannot be overestimated. According to Berlioz, Strauss Sr.'s place in the history of music–and by association Lanner's as well–is secured by his novel experiments in rhythmic dissonance (Barzun 1969, 339). As discussed in chapter 3, melodies that form hemiolic patterns against the accompaniment are the most characteristically "Viennese" type of rhythmic (and metrical) dissonance. As I suggested, the accompaniment is more easily heard and felt in $\frac{6}{4}$ rather than in the notated $\frac{3}{4}$. Playing against the accompaniment's $\frac{6}{4}$, the melodies often project their own $\frac{3}{2}$ metrical patterns. While one can consider the metrical and grouping organization of the melody as a hemiola, there are two characteristics that distinguish Lanner's and Strauss Sr.'s approach to hemiola from that of previous composers. First, Lanner and Strauss Sr. employ hemiola as a strong presentational element of melodies, often initiated at the very beginning of a melody, while earlier composers tend to use hemiolas as markers of cadential activity, typically occurring in the two bars immediately preceding the final bar of a phrase. Second, the projected $\frac{3}{2}$ meter of Viennese hemiolic melodies is clearly distinguished from the steady $\frac{6}{4}$ oom-pah-pah accompanimental drone, resulting in two metrically independent strands in the texture (polymeter); such clear textural segmentation is rare in cadential hemiolas of earlier music, where typically the entire texture (or at least a good part of it) supports the metrical shift to $\frac{3}{2}$.[17] While Lanner's and Strauss Sr.'s earliest publications date from 1826, they only began experimenting with hemiolic melodies on a consistent basis in waltzes published beginning in 1830.[18] The Strauss excerpt provided in Example 6.5d illustrates a typical case in which the music progresses from metrical dissonance to metrical consonance within the confines of an eight-bar theme. Chopin employs a similar tactic in theme d of op. 18.

The rhythm of theme e is another characteristic rhythm of Viennese waltzes, but it is not associated with any particular instrument, as is the post horn rhythm of theme a. The characteristic features are quarter notes on beats 1 and 3 and a quarter or eighth rest on beat 2. Schönherr (1976, 70) observes that in such cases performers would emphasize the accompaniment on beat 2. This type of melodic rhythm occurs within a variety of melodic styles, from *dolce* cantabile melodies (Strauss Sr.'s op. 65, waltz no. 1) to more rhythmically vibrant ones (Chopin's op. 18).

Theme g of op. 18 falls into Schönherr's category of *"Lach"-Walzer*, or laughing waltz melodies (1976, 79–80). They are characterized by the consistent use of grace notes within a predominantly quarter-note melody. Schönherr refers to these as laughing melodies not only because they resemble the rhythmic and intonational vocal gestures of laughter but also because of their occasional associations to waltz titles that contain references to gaiety or laughter as well as to songs that actually contain syllables of laughter and that later were arranged as instrumental waltzes.

The last theme of op. 18 is what Schönherr would most likely call a *"Liebes"-Walzer*, or love waltz melody. This melodic type is characterized by flowing, legato melodies performed at a soft dynamic level and often marked with the expression indication *dolce*. Rhythmically, there are two varieties: a bar of running eighth notes followed by a half note and quarter note, and a dotted half note tied over to a bar of running eighth notes. By far the more common of the two variants is the first, which, as noted in chapter 5, correlates to the rhythm and dynamic motions of the female waltzer.

Except for the first and last of the melodic categories given (post horn melodies and cantabile melodies), these melodic types are not found in Chopin's Warsaw waltzes, nor are they typical of the Warsaw waltzes composed and published by Chopin's contemporaries. Furthermore, the melodic type represented by Chopin's theme b (spiccato melody) is the only clear instance of this category that I am aware of in all of Chopin's music; and the characteristic Viennese rhythm of theme e and the laughing melodic type of theme f are only used in one other subsequent work: the Waltz in F Major, op. 34, no. 3. The rarity of these melodic types within Chopin's music, especially when one considers that he not only continued to compose waltzes but also incorporated the waltz as a topic within nonwaltz genres, suggests that Chopin's melodic invention was not naturally inclined toward these melodic types—that they were in some sense foreign to his compositional sensibilities. This in turn supports the notion of op. 18 as a test piece in which Chopin intentionally limited himself to and experimented with what he heard as characteristic features of the Viennese waltz. He would go on to discard those features that did not resonate with his own compositional style and aesthetics.

MEDLEY FORMAT

Out of all of Chopin's waltzes, published and unpublished, op. 18 contains the most themes (seven) and most closely matches the medley design of the Viennese waltz of the early 1830s. Indeed, op. 18 is Chopin's first waltz to break free of the *da capo* ternary form used in his Warsaw waltzes. It opens with a short introduction (a call to the dance floor), proceeds with a parade of five waltzes, and ends with a lengthy coda—the longest waltz coda he ever wrote. And, as I have shown, Chopin's op. 18 is a veritable catalog of Viennese melodic types. Thus, in its formal design, cadential articulations, and profusion of beautiful melodies, op. 18 embodies the Viennese aesthetic categories of self-containment, feminine beauty, and variety.

Evidence of Chopin's awareness of these attributes as representative of Viennese waltz practice is suggested in a letter to his family quoted earlier (1963, 72). In this letter Chopin compares Lanner and Strauss Sr. to the

"Valse pour le pianoforte composée et dediée à son excellence Mademoiselle la
Comtesse Leocadie Suchodolska par Alexandre Swieszewski, executée aux
Soirées de l'ancienne Ressource, arrangée d'apres l'orchestre pour le piano"
(Warsaw, 1829, Tom. 1269)

abcdefg

```
       4     16                16   16             fine
||: intro   a :||: b    c :|||: d    e :||: f    g :||
            XT      XT   XT      XD   TT      XD   XT


   D major:  I        V         I           IV
```

"Valse composée par A. Swieszewski arrangée d'après l'orchestre pour le pianoforte, executée aux soirées de la Ressource on le trouve chez A. Brzezina &
Magnus, Fr. Kluowski et dans plusieurs autres depots de musique" (Warsaw,
1830, Tom. 1420)

abcdefg

```
      𝄉                     16   16   16   16       16      dal segno [no fine given]
   intro  ||: a    a :|||: b    c :||  d    d    e    d  ||: f :|||: g    g :||
             TD   TT       XT   XT     TD   TD   XD   TT      TT      XT   XT

   D major:   I        V     I     V         I                   IV
```

DIAGRAM 6.4. Form charts of two waltzes by Aleksander Świeszewski.

Świeszewskis in Warsaw. While Chopin's use of the plural indicates that there
were at least two Świeszewskis, perhaps brothers, only one of them published
waltz music in Warsaw–Aleksander Świeszewski. Chopin's comparison of
the Świeszewskis to Lanner and Strauss Sr. is entirely appropriate, for out
of all the Warsaw dance composers whose music I examined, Aleksander
Świeszewski comes closest to Viennese practice. The majority of his publications are piano transcriptions of waltzes and mazurkas originally performed
by a dance orchestra (presumably his own) at balls given in Warsaw's Resursa
dance halls during the carnival seasons of 1829 and 1830. Diagram 6.4 provides form charts of two of Świeszewski's waltzes. Both contain seven themes
organized in a medley format that favors open-ended thematic variety. In
neither are the individual themes notationally paired into a succession of
separate waltzes. As I have argued, though, the grouping of Viennese waltz
themes into a series of five or six individual waltzes is done more as a notational convenience rather than as reflecting a listener's perception. The first

of Świeszewski's two waltzes runs through all seven themes without any thematic reprise (abcdefg). The second waltz contains one internal repetition scheme (dded), which could be interpreted as a self-standing waltz; and at the end of the medley Świeszewski indicates *dal segno*, but he (or the publisher) does not provide a *fine*. Although not shown, Świeszewski's melodies also stylistically reflect Viennese practice, and their violinistic nature suggests that Aleksander Świeszewski was himself a violinist, which perhaps may have also prompted Chopin's comparison.

TONAL STRUCTURE AND THEMATIC REPETITION

John Rink observes a marked change in Chopin's compositional practice toward the end of the 1820s that is especially evident in the works he composed while he was living in Vienna. "Perhaps the most significant development brought about by Chopin's eight months in Vienna," Rink says, "was a new sensitivity to the 'structural momentum' of his music, which he learnt to maximize by using 'dynamic' harmonic progressions as remote tonal structures" (1992, 88). In addition to all-encompassing harmonic progressions that unite sections within a single trajectory, Rink also notes that forward impulse is achieved by a "new approach to recapitulation and closure," whereby "Chopin emphasizes completion of the tonal structure spanning the main body of the piece (to which the coda functions literally as a 'tail'), differentiating the last statement of the recurrent A section from earlier ones and, more importantly, generating momentum towards closure" (1992, 89).

As I previously noted, in his Warsaw waltzes Chopin does not vary the return of the opening A section, nor does he provide codas. By using the same cadential material for both the opening and closing A sections, Chopin makes no attempt to draw attention to the process of global closure. However, in both KK 1213–14 and op. 18 Chopin varies the return of the opening material. Through the compositional techniques of reharmonization, intensification, and phrase expansion, Chopin problematizes the final return of the opening theme. The resolution of the musical crisis at the ensuing perfect authentic cadence, as in KK 1213–14, or at the entrance of the coda, as in op. 18, draws attention to the process of closure and in so doing dramatizes it. Such disruptions at or near the beginning of the coda are a signature technique of Lanner and Strauss Sr.

The "structural momentum" brought about by all-encompassing progressions that Rink observes in Chopin's post-Warsaw works is especially evident in op. 18 (refer to Diagram 6.3). An all-encompassing tonal progression unites the succession of seven sharply contrasting waltz themes within a single tonal trajectory. Not unusual for Viennese waltzes, the second theme (theme b) of the first waltz is set within a different key—here A♭ major, the key of the subdominant. This opening gambit initiates a large-scale descending fifths progression (E♭–A♭–D♭–G♭) that ultimately leads to a structural cadence at the return of waltz 1. The arrival of G♭ major in bar 165 is a special moment in the piece. Tonally, it is the point of farthest remove, and, marked with the expression *dolce* and infused with the rhythmic motive of the female dancer, it is the most intimate theme in the piece. At a middleground level, G♭ major functions as the flatted mediant within the overarching tonic arpeggiation I–♭III–V–I. Thus, the surface design and deep tonal structure mutually reinforce each other.

In chapter 3 I observed that during the early 1830s Lanner and Strauss Sr. also began experimenting with more sophisticated large-scale tonal progressions. However, it seems unlikely that this particular shift in Chopin's compositional practice was motivated in any way by his exposure to the music of Lanner and Strauss Sr. Certainly, Chopin was already well aware of sophisticated strategies for large-scale tonal organization from the music of J. S. Bach, Mozart, and other composers he studied and performed while living in Warsaw.[19] It is possible, however, that Chopin recognized these tonal techniques in the music of Lanner and Strauss Sr. and, as he did with other features of Viennese waltzes, intentionally employed them in an attempt to model op. 18 as closely as possible on the waltzes he heard while he was in Vienna. As we shall see, except for op. 64, no. 3, Chopin takes a much more conservative approach to tonal organization in his published waltzes after op. 18.

Chopin does not embrace all aspects of Lanner's and Strauss Sr.'s compositional practice, however: he rejects the technique of open-ended thematic variety. Perhaps the principle of thematic return was too strongly engrained in his compositional mindset to override; and/or perhaps he felt a bit uncomfortable with the hedonistic aesthetics of unending variety and its undertones of unmitigated sensual pleasure. Whatever the reason, the profusion of themes in op. 18 is regulated within ternary patterns of contrast and return. Although Chopin does employ a medley layout, waltz 1 returns near the end right before the coda. Moreover, each of the individual waltzes (except for waltz 4) exhibits some pattern of contrast and return, most typically an ABA design.

Table 6.2 summarizes the similarities and dissimilarities between Chopin's Warsaw waltzes, the waltzes of Lanner and Strauss Sr. that were composed around 1830, and Chopin's two Viennese waltzes KK 1213–14 and op. 18. In comparison to the Warsaw waltzes, KK 1213–14 and op. 18 represent an altogether different category in Chopin's conception of the waltz. The striking similarities between these two waltzes and the Viennese waltzes of Lanner and Strauss Sr., especially in cases where the similarities involve characteristics that are out of character for Chopin (absence of phrase overlap, absence of half cadences, Viennese melodic style), suggest that Chopin not only heard the music of Lanner and Strauss Sr. but also listened and took note. Given the strong Viennese dialect of op. 18, it is curious that, in a letter written to his family just four days before he left Vienna for Paris, Chopin writes: "I have picked up nothing that is essentially Viennese. For example, I can't dance a waltz properly–that speaks for itself! My piano has heard nothing but mazurkas" (1963, 88).

While it is true that much of Chopin's creative focus during his time in Vienna centered on the composition of his first nine published mazurkas (op. 6 and op. 7), his claim still seems a bit exaggerated, especially considering the evidence of KK 1213–14 and op. 18. His outright denial of any foreign influence perhaps may be explained by the historical circumstances surrounding his visit to Vienna. Shortly after Chopin arrived in Vienna, he learned of the Polish revolt that had started in Warsaw–commonly referred to as the November Uprising, beginning the night of 29 November–against the repressive Russian occupation of Czar Alexander. Many of Chopin's closest friends were directly involved in the fighting, and his family was living in Warsaw at that time. Deeply concerned about the safety and welfare of his family and friends and about Poland's political plight, pricked by anti-Polish sentiments he experienced firsthand in Vienna, and bitter about his failure to recapture the musical glory he had achieved during his first trip to Vienna, Chopin perhaps wanted to assure his family and himself that in the midst of it all his Polish heart was pure. As Jim Samson notes: "Chopin was no revolutionary. But his sympathies were undoubtedly with the Polish cause, and the effect of the uprising was immeasurably to strengthen those sympathies." Evidence of a nationalistic attitude can be heard in a "new note of seriousness with which he approached Polish national dances" (Samson 1996, 73–74). Nonetheless, while Chopin may have wished not to admit it, he did learn to speak the language of the Viennese waltz, and while perhaps not entirely Viennese, it comes very close.

TABLE 6.2. SUMMARY OF STYLISTIC DISTINCTIONS BETWEEN CHOPIN'S WARSAW WALTZES, THE VIENNESE WALTZES OF LANNER AND STRAUSS SR., AND CHOPIN'S TWO VIENNESE WALTZES, KK 1213–14 AND OP. 18

	CHOPIN'S WARSAW WALTZES: OP. 69, NO. 2, OP. 70, NO. 3, AND KK 1207–1208 (1829–30)	VIENNESE WALTZES OF LANNER AND STRAUSS SR. COMPOSED BETWEEN 1829 AND 1832	KK 1213–14 (1830)	OP. 18 (1833)
half cadences	50 percent of all phrases	2 percent of all phrases	not used	not used
phrase overlap	common	not used	not used	not used
overall form	three-part *da capo* (ABA)	medley (ABCD . . .)	three-part (ABA)	medley
number of themes	3–4	c. 16	4	7
form of each waltz	rounded binary	simple binary	rounded binary	rounded binary
introduction and coda	not used	standard practice	yes	yes
crisis point at or near the beginning of the coda	not used	standard practice	yes	yes
melodic style	pianistic and vocal	violinistic and vocal	pianistic and vocal	violinistic and vocal
melodic hemiola	not used	common	not used	common
nontonic phrase openings	29 percent of all phrases	58 percent	100 percent of all phrases	89 percent of all phrases

CHOPIN'S APPROACH TO FORM IN HIS
WALTZES PUBLISHED AFTER OP. 18

The seven waltzes Chopin composed and published after op. 18 (op. 34, nos. 1–3, op. 42, and op. 64, nos. 1–3) are a diverse group of works exhibiting a wide range of approaches to thematic design and tonal structure–from the most complicated tonal structure of all his waltzes (op. 64, no. 3) to the simplest tonal structure (op. 64, no. 1), from the expression of deep melancholy (op. 34, no. 2) to exuberant virtuosity (op. 34, no. 3), and from simple ABA ternary designs (op. 64, no. 1) to more complex rondo designs (op. 42). It is as if once he mastered the essential elements of the Viennese waltz in op. 18, he felt free to experiment with those elements and combine them with other elements not characteristically Viennese–in effect, individualizing the *grande valse* genre to suit his own aesthetic taste and compositional sensibilities. Partly as a result of this process of hybridization, Chopin's published waltzes after op. 18 are more stylized than op. 18 and his unpublished waltzes; that is, to varying degrees they contain musical elements not typically found in waltzes composed for the ballroom as well as musical elements that are not suitable for dance accompaniment, the most obvious of which are faster tempi and intricate ornamental filigree that would be lost in the acoustics of a crowded and bustling dancing space.

In the face of such diversity, however, several general trends are evident throughout this group of waltzes from the first to the last. As shown in Table 6.3, there is a gradual move away from thematic extravagance to thematic economy. Additionally, in the waltzes after op. 18, Chopin gradually returns to the practice of cadential variety and phrase overlaps. Ultimately, by his last published waltz, op. 64, no. 3, which has only two distinct themes, Chopin rejects all aesthetic premises of the Viennese waltz except repetitive continuity.

Although after op. 18 Chopin gradually turns away from the aesthetic principles of the Viennese waltz, there is one domain in which the influence of Lanner and Strauss Sr. runs deep: rhythm. Op. 18 may be read as Chopin's attempt to capture the rhythmic techniques of Lanner and Strauss Sr. as best he understood them. Specifically, Chopin exploits techniques of melodic hemiola and the progression from metrical dissonance to metrical consonance within a phrase. In his subsequent waltzes, he experiments with these techniques and introduces new types of metrical dissonances. In the section that follows, I discuss the formal organization of the remaining published waltzes. During the course of this discussion, I shall also track Chopin's development of these Viennese rhythmic techniques.

TABLE 6.3. NUMBER OF THEMES IN CHOPIN'S PUBLISHED WALTZES

op. 18	7 themes
op. 34, no. 1	6 themes
op. 34, no. 2	5 themes
op. 34, no. 3	4 themes
op. 42	5 themes
op. 64, no. 1	3 themes
op. 64, no. 2	3 themes
op. 64, no. 3	2 themes

Op. 34, Nos. 1–3

As discussed, op. 18 is closely aligned with the Viennese ballroom, and although I have found no direct evidence that it was ever used as dancing music, aside from the coda, it is entirely danceable.[20] Two of the three waltzes of op. 34—no. 1 and, to a lesser degree, no. 3—also follow the Viennese ballroom waltz model. Indeed, the strong parallels between these two waltzes and the ballroom waltzes of Lanner and Strauss Sr. may have prompted Schumann's observation that "they seem to have been actually improvised in the ballroom" (1952, 139). The Viennese elements are the use of an introduction and coda; the high number of themes; the high percentage of authentic cadences, resulting in tonally closed themes with clear-cut phrase boundaries; the use of Viennese melodic types, many of which, especially in the case of op. 34, no. 1, are violinistic in nature; and the presence of crisis points within the coda (op. 34, no. 1, bars 273–77; op. 34, no. 3, bars 155–60). As can be seen in Diagram 6.5, they also both employ dynamic middleground progressions that provide tonal momentum into the final returns of their opening themes.

Alongside these Viennese characteristics, we also see Chopin interjecting a greater degree of virtuosic passagework that showcases the physical gestures and technical capabilities of the pianist (Chopin) over the musical representation of the waltzers. In op. 18 Chopin relegates the virtuosic element to the coda. In op. 34, nos. 1 and 3 it is extended into the waltz themes themselves; and this may be interpreted as one of Chopin's solutions to the problematic associations of the ballroom waltz music with femininity, pleasure, and entertainment music. The problem, of course, is that these associations run counter to the aesthetics and functions of "serious" art music (music for a cultivated audience, earned pleasure, music for music's sake, innovation,

Waltz in A♭ Major, op. 34, no. 1 (1835)   abcdef
Grande valse brillante
thematic design: ternary (ABA)
305 bars

        waltz 1   waltz 2   waltz 1

   17   16 16   16 16   16 19 (61)
  intro ‖: a a   b b :‖ c c   d d d d e e d d   c c   a a   b b   c c   coda (f)
         TD TD XT XT   XT XT   XT XT XT XT XD XD XT XT XT XT   TD TD XT XT XT XD

          I   IV   V–I   I

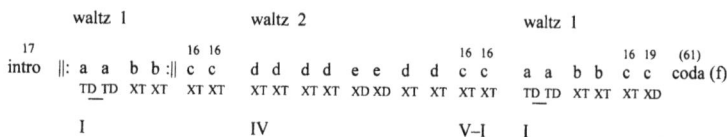

Waltz in F Major, op. 34, no. 3 (1838)   abcd
Grande valse brillante
thematic design: ABCA
173 bars

   16   (29)
  intro a a a a   b b b b   c c c c c c   a a   coda (dc)
         TT TT TT TT   XT XT XT XT   XT XD XT XD XT XD   TT TT

          I   IV   IV   ♭VI–V   I

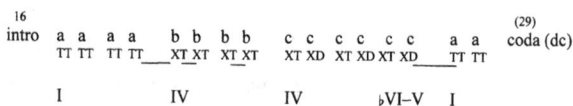

DIAGRAM 6.5. Form charts of Chopin's waltzes op. 34, nos. 1 and 3.

and the avoidance or concealment of conventions). The virtuosic element has two consequences in this regard: the associations of unmitigated pleasure are counterbalanced with the physical sense of effort and technical skill needed to perform the bravura passages; and the waltz's strong associations with feminine beauty are mitigated with the male authorial presence of Chopin. A common strategy in this regard is that when Chopin does use lyrical (feminine) themes, he most often surrounds them with themes exhibiting a strong virtuosic element. In reformulating the waltz genre to suit his own aesthetic aims, Chopin carves out an artistic niche for himself in the very crowded market of popular dance music and in the process legitimize the *grande valse* genre as a viable avenue of publication for a "serious" composer of art music. This was particularly important for Chopin, since he apparently had no interest in writing for other instrumental or vocal genres that did not include the piano. As a composer, he staked his entire reputation on his piano music.

Op. 34, no. 1, the opening of which is provided in Example 6.6, begins with a seventeen-bar introduction organized as a large sentence (4 + 4 + 9). The basic idea of the opening four bars is a combination of three motives: *x*, the post horn rhythm; *y*, a descending cascade; and *z*, a progression of four

EXAMPLE 6.6. Chopin's Waltz in A♭ Major, op. 34, no. 1, bars 1–17.

chromatically ascending block chords that throughout the opening eight bars prolong the dominant of A♭ major. A large arch is created in the nine-bar continuation through the registrally ascending and descending repetitions of motive *y*. In bar 13 Chopin rhythmically contracts the length of the motive by changing the duration of the last note from a quarter note to an eighth note. This results in a group of five eighth notes that is repeated five times. The shortening of the motive also completes a phrase acceleration in which the durations of the musical groups get progressively smaller during the course of the introduction, from two-bar groups (bars 1–10), to one-bar groups (bars 11–12), to contracted one-bar groups (bars 13–16).

Notice that the final pitch of the last five-note group overlaps with the entrance of the first theme. Importantly, this overlap preserves the succession of strong hyperbeats every four bars. Thus, the rhythmic and metrical irregularities of this passage are confined only to the foreground and not to larger levels of meter and grouping organization. It is also important to note that Chopin does not include a ritardando leading into bar 17, which would help prepare the listener for the entrance of the first theme. Instead, if one maintains the tempo, the effect should be a kind of shock, in that the tumultuous and virtuosic introduction is suddenly replaced by the metrical clarity and gentle lyricism of the first theme.[21] Interestingly, older recordings tend to adhere to the vivace tempo throughout the introduction, while more recent recordings favor the use of a ritardando.[22]

While the opening theme of waltz 1 is a model of Viennese lyricism replete with a tight-knit cantabile melody in parallel sixths, the second theme of waltz 1 returns to virtuosic passagework motivically related to the melodic material of the introduction. Thus, the lyrical opening theme of op. 34, no. 1 is flanked by Chopin's individual brand of virtuosic pianism. The third theme of waltz 1 (theme c) maintains the virtuosic element, and motivically it is also related to the introduction: it is a large sentence (4 + 4 + 8) in which the opening four-bar motive begins with a tonal inversion of the opening two-bar motive of the introduction. With its strongly emphasized cadential progressions, it serves as a closing theme not only for the first waltz but also for the second. In its third and final appearance, Chopin extends its length, creating a structural tension that highlights the process of global closure. The structural tension is not only maintained but also heightened in the coda through extended virtuosic passagework, harmonic disruptions, and the avoidance of structural closure until the final two bars.

Chopin's virtuosic pianism also dominates the *Grande valse brillante* in F Major, op. 34, no. 3. This waltz is a single waltz organized as a succession of four themes (abca) framed by the return of theme a and by an introduction and coda. The virtuosic element is found in the perpetually whirling passagework of the introduction, which Chopin extends into theme a. Thus, the lyrical theme b and the Viennese "laughing" c theme are subordinated within Chopin's performative presence. Although the whirling passagework is pure Chopin, the Viennese influence may be seen in Chopin's continuing experimentation in the realm of metrical dissonance.

As in op. 34, no. 1, Chopin employs the technique of using successively smaller groups as a phrase progresses toward its goal, an accelerando of sorts that increases momentum and rhythmic excitement as the end approaches. The internal repetitions of these groups and the shift to smaller-sized units imagined result in metrical shifts and, when sounded against a $\frac{3}{4}$ accompaniment, metrical dissonances as well. The opening four bars of the introduction, as shown in Example 6.7, may be grouped into two two-bar units that prolong $\hat{5}$. Beginning in bar 5, the motive from bar 3 is repeated four times, thus effecting a shift from two-bar units to one-bar units. A swirling three-note figure commences in bar 9 that through its repetition emphasizes the level of the dotted quarter note.[23] The dotted-quarter-note grouping is maintained until the second half of bar 16, at which point the final part of the ascent to the high A accelerates to single eighth notes. Thus, as the grouping durations given above the staff illustrate, during the course of this introduction the durations progressively get smaller: from two bars, to one bar, to a dotted quarter note, to single eighth notes.

EXAMPLE 6.7. Chopin's Waltz in F Major, op. 34, no. 3, bars 1–26.

Admittedly, once we reach the eighth notes in bar 9, the vivace tempo and predominantly half-step motion make it difficult to track a dotted-quarter-note pulse. Chopin, however, initiates another acceleration, beginning in bar 9 in the ascent from C^5 to A^5, that can be more readily heard. As shown by the reduction given in Example 6.8, the durational design of this passage, until the last measure, replicates the acceleration of bars 1–9. The first two notes of the ascent, C and C♯, are each prolonged for two bars; the next three pitches, D, E♭, and E, are prolonged for one bar each; and the final four pitches complete the acceleration from a dotted quarter note to eighth notes. The climactic arrival on A in bar 17 overlaps with the entrance of a stable accompaniment pattern and a slower durational pattern in the melody of the first theme, both of which help release the tension engendered by the introduction's rhythmically exciting and multileveled accelerandos.

Theme a's melodic grouping structure, which is comprised of repeated groupings of four eighth notes, results in a steady succession of half-note

EXAMPLE 6.8. Durational reduction of Chopin's Waltz
in F Major, op. 34, no. 3, bars 1–17.

pulses that conflicts with the one-bar pulses of the accompaniment. Example 6.9 provides a metrical analysis of this passage. While it is possible to hear the half-note pulses falling into the standard Viennese hemiolic pattern of $\frac{3}{2}$ against the accompaniment's $\frac{6}{4}$ meter, there is another possible reading. The near literal threefold repetition of the eight-note groups in bars 17–20, together with the vivace tempo, permit the possibility of hearing a duration pattern of three whole notes forming a large $\frac{3}{1}$ measure. In this way, Chopin shifts the Viennese hemiola to a metrically higher level in which four bars of the notated meter are metrically organized as a single bar in triple meter. A metrical acceleration occurs in bars 21–22 whereby the melody shifts back to the more typical $\frac{3}{2}$ hemiola; and in the final two bars the resolution of the metrical dissonance is coordinated with the tonal resolution of the perfect authentic cadence. Thus, the melody can be heard as a succession of three different meters– $\frac{3}{1}$, $\frac{3}{2}$, and $\frac{6}{4}$–that progress from metrical dissonance to metrical consonance. As noted earlier, Lanner and Strauss Sr. similarly use the technique of organizing a phrase by the progression of metrical dissonance to metrical consonance. Lanner's and Strauss Sr.'s metrical dissonances are entirely danceable because both the downbeats of the melody and accompaniment are coordinated every two bars. Thus, there is no conflict between the music and the dancers' two-bar twirl. In op. 34, no. 3, Chopin, free from the constraints of composing for the pleasure of ballroom dancers, is able to expand and develop this technique on a higher level. In the process, though, he leaves the dancers behind.

The intense rhythmic energy of the first theme is released into the beautifully lyric and spacious theme b, set within the key of the subdominant, B♭ major. Example 6.10 provides the music. In this theme, we see the return of a signature feature of Chopin's approach to phrase rhythm, a feature he studiously avoided in op. 18: the artful play of phrase boundaries. Theme b opens with an auxiliary progression IV⁶–V⁶₅–I that establishes the new key of B♭

EXAMPLE 6.9. Chopin's Waltz in F Major, op. 34, no. 3, bars 15–32.

major. The IV⁶, however, in the larger tonal context, functions as a passing chord connecting the F triad in bars 47–48, which is the cadential tonic of theme a, to the V⁶₅ in bar 50. The bass's B♭ in bar 51 completes the ascent. While this fourth ascent (F–G–A–B♭) does not result in a phrase overlap, it does create a noticeable tonal continuity across the phrase boundary.

Theme b appears to be a sixteen-bar period segmented into two parallel eight-bar phrases, each, in standard Viennese fashion, articulated with an authentic cadence. The melody, however, does not abide by such a clean-cut organization. A remarkable feature of this theme is that all of its individual melodic segments are anacrustic, that is, they all begin with a pickup on a metrically weak beat. The melodic segment in bar 54, above what appears to be a cadential dominant, begins with a two-beat anacrusis that one expects

EXAMPLE 6.10. Chopin's Waltz in F Major, op. 34, no. 3, bars 46–59.

will lead in some way to the end of the first eight-bar phrase. The eighth-note motion, however, pushes through to the downbeat of bar 57, which begins a varied repetition of the first phrase. Thus, we are never given a satisfying melodic ending to the antecedent–the anacrusis beginning in bar 54 leads to the beginning of the consequent, not to the end of the antecedent. In the reharmonized consequent phrase, Chopin intensifies the tonal tension by avoiding a tonic until the very last bar of the period (not shown). We have seen this type of blurring of phrase boundaries previously as a characteristic feature of Chopin's unpublished waltzes. It will continue to be, as we shall see, an important feature of most of the remaining published waltzes.

While op. 34, nos. 1 and 3 are clothed with Chopin's virtuosic pianism and the accoutrements of the Viennese ballroom waltz, op. 34, no. 2 in A minor inhabits a wholly different sonic world. The title *Grande valse brillante* seems inappropriate, for it contains no whirling virtuosic passagework, it is set in the minor mode and in a slow tempo (lento), and it is consumed with a lyricism tragic in tone. Wilhelm von Lenz (1809–83), a former student of Chopin, refers to it as a *valse mélancolique* (1872, 37). Chopin's friend Stephen Heller (1811–85) reports that this was Chopin's personal favorite.[24] Given Chopin's commitment to express his Polish identity through his music, it would make sense that he felt deeply about this waltz, for in its tone, expression, and melodic style it is modeled on the unpublished Warsaw waltzes, and thus its Polishness is a foregrounded feature. Samson (1985, 125) even goes so far as to suggest that it is related to the slow *kujawiak*-style mazurkas, and Jean-Jacques Eigeldinger notes that this waltz "is one of the richest in Polish

Waltz in A Minor, op. 34, no. 2 (1838)   abcde
Grande valse brillante
thematic design: ABBA
204 bars

```
              waltz 1                        waltz 1 repeated (no changes)
              12    9                        12    9                        20!
     a a   b b  c c  d d  d d      b b  c c  d d  d d      a a   e    a a
     TD TT TD TT XT XT TD TT TD TT TD TT XT XT TD TT TD TT TD TT XD TD TT

     i      i    i    I    i        i    i    I    i        i    i–V  i
```

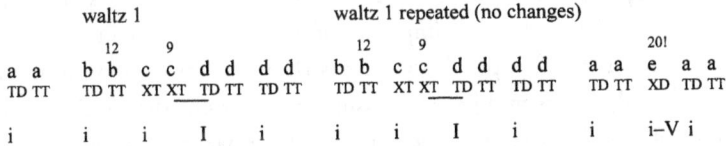

DIAGRAM 6.6. Form chart of Chopin's Waltz in A Minor, op. 34, no. 2.

folkloric elements" (1986, 158). It would seem that Chopin has taken his private Polish style of waltz composition into the very cosmopolitan and public arena of the *grande valse* genre.

As shown in Diagram 6.6, this piece is comprised of a single waltz (bbccdddd) repeated without notated variation. Chopin dispenses with the Viennese "call to the floor" introduction and crisis-laden coda. In place of these, the piece opens and closes with a lugubrious theme set in a deep, dark register. The opening theme features the circling waltz motive that also opens op. 34, no. 3 and op. 64, no. 1. The tempo is so slow that the motive loses much of its physical association with the dance, but it gains an emotional intensity, especially given that the $\hat{5}$-$\hat{6}$-$\hat{5}$ neighboring motion in the minor mode is often associated with death and grief.[25]

We see in this waltz a return to cadential variety characteristic of Chopin's Warsaw waltzes. Nearly half the phrases are articulated by half cadences. And in the instances where two tonic cadences follow each other, there is a contrast of mode (A major/A minor). Also noteworthy is the simple tonal design. Although Chopin does not use a large-scale tonal progression to provide the piece structural momentum from beginning to end, as he does for op. 18 and op. 34, nos. 1 and 3, the changes in mode provide deeply expressive shifts in the music and provide the music a narrative structure and momentum. The recasting of the prayerful theme d from the major mode to the minor mode, especially, along with the sudden drop in dynamics and the Phrygian reharmonizations, suggest for this piece a tragic expressive genre. Chopin could easily have ended the waltz after the return of the desolate theme a in bar 168. However, an improvisatory bass melody enters and steers the music briefly to C major and then to a bright, redemptive E major, whose upward arpeggiation imbues the music with a sense of newfound hope, all of which makes the final return of theme a sound all the more inevitably tragic.

In the next two waltzes, op. 42 and op. 64, no. 1, Chopin further limits himself by eliminating not only modulations but also changes in mode. This is a rather remarkable, self-imposed limitation, especially in light of Rink's observation that Chopin, beginning with his works composed in Vienna, increasingly favors middleground tonal progressions that "unite all the sections of a work into a single gesture directed towards long-range resolution of V to I" (1992, 88). Indeed, the absence of structural modulations is a noticeable trait in Chopin's formulation of the *grande valse* genre—four out of eight of Chopin's published waltzes never move beyond their tonic keys (op. 34, no. 2, op. 42, and op. 64, nos. 1 and 2), and out of those four, two maintain the same mode throughout (op. 42 and op. 64, no. 1). One way to interpret this unusual feature is as a relocated emphasis on "tonicness." A defining characteristic of Viennese themes is their tendency to end with a tonic. Chopin adopts this practice for op. 18 and op. 34, no. 1. In subsequent waltzes, however, Chopin sheds himself of this trait and returns to his natural inclination toward cadential variety. Perhaps as a means to retain tonic stability but at a higher level, Chopin compensates by remaining in the tonic key. Whatever the reason, the result is a greater focus on the melodic and rhythmic intricacies of the musical surface and, in the case of op. 42 and op. 64, no. 2, a greater reliance on patterns of thematic repetition to generate a sense of cyclic motion.

Op. 42

The *Grande valse* in A♭ Major, op. 42, is organized as a twelve-part rondo with an introduction and a coda (Diagram 6.7). While this waltz does not possess the strong sense of tonal momentum a middleground progression would provide (it remains in or close to the tonic major key from beginning to end), a cyclic motion is instead achieved by a predictable pattern of thematic contrast and return. The refrain, which is the second (b) theme (bar 41), consists of virtuosic passagework that traces a succession of four four-bar arches. Tonally, the refrain is open-ended; the last four-bar arch concludes with a dominant seventh chord. This open-endedness provides Chopin the opportunity to play with the way in which the refrain tonally connects into the following theme.

Waltz in A♭ Major, op. 42 (1840) abcde
Grande valse
289 bars
thematic design: rondo ABCBDBEBABDB

```
                  9      7                          16 28                          16  16 17        13
intro  a a a a   b b   c c   b b   d d   b b   e e   b b   a a a a   b   d d   b b   coda (a)
       TT TT TT TT  XT XT  TT TT  XT XD  XD XD  XT XD  XT XD  XT XD  TT TT TT TD  XD  XX XD  XT XD

       I           I     I     I     I     I     I     I     I       I   I     I
```

DIAGRAM 6.7. Form chart of Chopin's Waltz in A♭ Major, op. 42.

To illustrate Chopin's subtle play of phrase boundaries, Example 6.11 presents three of these connections. The V⁷ at the end of the refrain in bars 53–56 resolves into a tonic that appears to begin theme c, thereby producing a phrase overlap. Supporting this reading is the entrance of a stable (and new) accompaniment pattern in bar 57. However, the motivic design and harmonic rhythm of this passage suggest hearing bar 57 as the final bar of the refrain and the pickup to bar 58 as marking the opening of theme c. The first four bars of theme c are organized as a sentence (1 + 1 + 2) supported by a two-bar harmonic rhythm. This reading reveals two unusual features, at least within Chopin's waltzes: a nonoverlapping nine-bar phrase and the succession of two hyperdownbeats.[26] Thus, what at first appeared to be an overlap turns out to be a nonoverlapping phrase boundary.

On the next occurrence the end of the refrain *does* overlap with the entrance of the next theme. Here the concluding dominant in bars 85–88 resolves to a tonic that begins theme d. The accompaniment, however, immediately transforms the tonic into a secondary dominant of IV, which resolves to a locally stable IV in the next bar. The tonal momentum of the refrain thus extends into the second bar of the ensuing theme.

At the conclusion of the next statement of the refrain, Chopin plays with the listener's expectations. On the downbeat of bar 121, Chopin lands on the same chord as in bars 89 and 57 (the tonic, A♭). And on beats 2 and 3 the chord contains the same pitches as in bar 89, slightly revoiced. Chopin, though, renotates the G♭ as an F♯, thus transforming it into a German augmented sixth chord, and resolves it as such in a brief tonicization of the mediant. The tonal processes of the third statement of the refrain thus spill over into the third bar of theme e. The larger point to this discussion is that Chopin, in the waltzes he composed and published after op. 18, gradually returns to the practice of creating rhythmic and tonal continuities across phrase boundaries, a compositional technique of which he was a master.

a. Bars 53–61

b. Bars 85–92

c. Bars 117–124

EXAMPLE 6.11. Comparison of three passages in Chopin's Waltz in
A♭ Major, op. 42 (bars 53–61, 85–92, 117–24).

While Chopin turns away from the Viennese aesthetic of self-containment, he continues to experiment with metrical dissonance. In op. 34, no.
3, Chopin transplants the quintessential Viennese metrical dissonance ($\frac{3}{2}$
against $\frac{6}{4}$) to a metrically higher level ($\frac{3}{1}$ against $\frac{6}{2}$); in op. 42, Chopin explores
lower levels of metrical dissonance by juxtaposing a melody in $\frac{12}{8}$ against the $\frac{6}{4}$
of the oom-pah-pah accompaniment (Example 6.12). Chopin previously used
the dotted quarter note as a melodic grouping duration and as a metrical
pulse in the introduction to op. 34, no. 3, bars 9–16. In that case, the swirling
melody was not sounded against the accompaniment; thus, there was no direct metrical dissonance (although one could argue that metrical dissonance
is created by the fact that one hears the $\frac{12}{8}$ meter against the generic expecta-
tion of a $\frac{6}{4}$ meter). In the opening theme of op. 42, however, both are present.

EXAMPLE 6.12. Chopin's Waltz in A♭ Major, op. 42, bars 9–24.

As illustrated in Example 6.13, in the two types of metrical dissonance that Chopin employs in op. 18 and op. 34, metrical conflict resides at the levels of the half note and dotted half note and, in the case of op. 34, no. 3, at the next higher level (the circled notes in the example are the pulses that conflict with the opposing meter). In the case of op. 42, the metrical conflict resides at a lower level between the dotted quarter notes of the melody and the quarter notes of the accompaniment. The higher levels are congruent. Thus, since both $\frac{6}{4}$ and $\frac{12}{4}$ are congruent at the level of the dotted whole note (two notated bars), there is no (inferred) conflict with the two-bar rotations of the dancers.

Op. 64, Nos. 1–3

Diagram 6.8 provides form charts of Chopin's three op. 64 waltzes. Composed in 1847, these late waltzes are marked by thematic economy, continuing experiments in metrical dissonance, and the use of rhythmic and tonal continuities across phrase boundaries. The vast majority of the phrases are open-ended either at the beginning or the end (rarely both) by means of auxiliary progressions or half cadences. The first waltz is the simplest of all of Chopin's published waltzes, and the third is the most complex.

Op. 64, no. 1 in D♭ major is comprised of two waltzes organized in a modified *da capo* ternary form (ABA). The repetition of the first waltz is

1. Op. 18, Op. 64, nos. 1 and 3 (Viennese type)

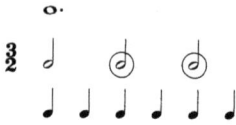

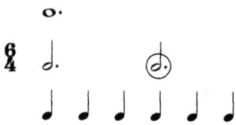

2. Op. 34, no. 3

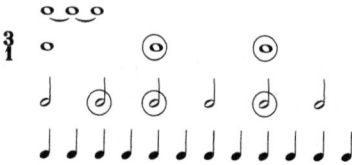

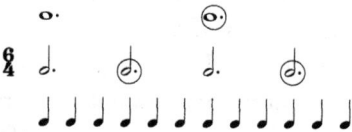

3. Op. 42

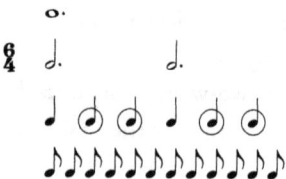

EXAMPLE 6.13. Types of metrical dissonance in Chopin's published waltzes.

a.   Waltz in D♭ Major, op. 64, no. 1 (1847)   abc

    Valse
    124 bars
    thematic design: ternary (ABA)

```
                waltz 1                 waltz 2              waltz 1
      4
    intro   a a ‖: b b :‖      c  c   c  c    "intro"  a a   b b   b b
            TD TD   XT XT      XT XT  XT XT             TD TD  XT XT  XT XT
            I                  I                        I
```

b.   Waltz in C♯ Minor, op. 64, no. 2 (1847)   abc

    Valse
    192 bars
    thematic design: rondo (ABCBAB)

```
    16 16                 16 16                16 16
    a a   b b  b b   c c   b b  b b      a a   b b  b b
    TD TT  XT XT XT XT  TT TX   XT XT XT XT  TD TT  XT XT XT XT
    i     i          I     i              i     i
```

c.   Waltz in A♭ Major, op. 64, no. 3 (1847)   ab

    Valse
    171 bars
    thematic design: ternary (ABA)

```
              9    15          12  9  16                    17   (23)
    a a  a a  a a  trans    b  b  b  b    a a  a a         coda
    TX XD TX XD TD TX  T  D   TD TD_TT XD____TX XD TX TT
    I             ii ( ——→ )  III        vi –V–I          ♭VI–V–I
```

DIAGRAM 6.8. Form charts of Chopin's op. 64 waltzes.

near literal except for the final two bars, in which Chopin provides a bravura flourish over the final cadence. This variation gesturally calls attention to global closure, which for this piece is especially important, since there is no coda. The second waltz does not modulate, nor does it offer a change of mode from major to minor. Rather, contrast is achieved by a shift in melodic style in which the soft, lyrical, sostenuto theme of the second waltz is flanked by the swirling virtuosic passagework of the first waltz, which suggests the authorial presence of Chopin.

The famous opening bars, the music of which is provided in Example 6.14, is largely constructed out of a repeating four-note neighboring figure that, beginning in bar 3, establishes a series of two-beat groups. In bars 1 and 2, however, Chopin elongates the motive by one beat. In bar 1 he introduces the motive with a quarter-note A♭, and in bar 2 he interpolates two notes in the middle of the motive, thereby expanding it to a length of six eighth notes. The

a. Chopin, Op. 64, no. 1, bars 1–12

b. Chopin, Op. 18, bars 1–8

EXAMPLE 6.14. Chopin's Waltz in D♭ Major, op. 64, no. 1, bars 1–12, and op. 18, bars 1–8.

end result is that the opening two bars may be heard as two beats of a $\frac{6}{4}$ meter leading into three beats of a $\frac{3}{2}$ meter. This same metrical acceleration is used in the introduction to op. 18, as shown at the bottom of the example. Unlike op. 18, however, in op. 64, no. 1 Chopin maintains the melodic hemiola into the entrance of the accompaniment, at which point it becomes a metrical dissonance. With the arrival of the climactic B♭ in bar 9, the melody resolves to a metrically consonance $\frac{6}{4}$. The overall effect is that the entire opening eight bars may be heard as an extended anacrusis leading to the B♭ in bar 9, which, as discussed in chapter 5, creates a middleground motivic repetition of the neighboring motion of the musical surface. While Chopin uses the same rhythmic techniques as found in Viennese waltzes, in op. 64, no. 1 he clothes them with a virtuosic pianism all his own.

EXAMPLE 6.15. Chopin's Waltz in C♯ Minor, op. 64, no. 2, bars 65–81.

The rondo design of the Waltz in C♯ Minor, op. 64, no. 2 is similar to that of op. 42: the second theme of each serves as a *moto perpetuo* refrain, and neither strays far from the tonic key. There are some notable differences, though. In op. 64, no. 2, Chopin employs a modal shift for the luxurious seventeen-bar theme c (notated in D♭ major). Also, there are fewer themes (three as opposed to five in op. 42), and in op. 64, no. 2, Chopin dispenses with the introduction and coda. In fact, the end of op. 64, no. 2 comes as a bit of a surprise, since there is nothing in the music to indicate that global closure is imminent. And that may very well be the point for this waltz. The second of each paired statement of the refrain is marked *pp* and ends with a two-octave ascent that, with the help of a four-bar decrescendo, seemingly evaporates into thin air.

Chopin does not employ metrical dissonances in this waltz. Instead, he continues to explore tonal continuities across phrase boundaries. The expansive third theme of this waltz (theme c), provided in Example 6.15, is a particularly beautiful example of Chopin's artful play of phrase boundaries. Rhythmically, both the accompaniment and melody lean toward two-beat groups but never seriously call into question the controlling $\frac{6}{4}$ meter. Tonally, the first half of the melody is supported by an ascending 5–6 sequence. Coordinated with the four-bar harmonic rhythm, the melody also ascends in parallel tenths with the bass. Against this structural ascent, however, the melody continuously falls mostly by step, adjusted occasionally by register transfers so as to keep the melody in the soprano register. The final goal of the descent, the A♭ in bar 81, overlaps with a varied restatement of the theme, which itself overlaps with the return of the refrain. The theme, sentential in design, is based on a 5 + 5 + 9 model.[27] Chopin, however, rhythmically displaces the melodic entrances of the second and third segments as well as the melodic entrance of the varied restatement (the diagonal lines in between the staves indicate these displacements). This results in a series of anacrustic segments that never quite seem to arrive at a stable resting point, and ultimately the melody is thrown back into the swirling refrain. Thus, the simplicity of this work's tonal design and episodic thematic layout is offset by a refinement of detail and sophisticated treatment of phrase rhythm.

The third waltz of op. 64 is the furthest removed in style and compositional practice from op. 18 and the Viennese waltzes of Lanner and Strauss Sr. It is marked by extreme motivic economy (it has only two thematic sections) and an almost obsessive adherence to tonally open-ended phrases. As Diagram 6.8 illustrates, Chopin appears to be intentionally going against the grain of the Viennese practice. Whereas all of the phrases of op. 18 (and most of the phrases of the waltzes of Lanner and Strauss Sr.) are tonally closed with authentic cadences, the overwhelming majority of phrases in op. 64, no. 3 avoid tonic closure, more so than any other waltz he wrote.

The opening theme (not shown), eight bars long, is presented in paired statements. The first statement (bars 1–8) ends with a V/vi; the second statement (bars 9–16) opens with vi and continues the descending fifths motion to the concluding half cadence. Chopin builds rhythmic momentum through the second statement and into the second paired statement by means of a phrase accelerando. In bars 9–12 both the accompaniment and the melody support a $\frac{6}{4}$ meter. In bars 13–14 the melody slips into a $\frac{3}{2}$ hemiola and again shifts meter in bars 15–16 into a $\frac{12}{8}$ pattern. Thus, the basic pulse accelerates from a dotted half note, to a half note, to a dotted quarter note, the latter two of which are metrically dissonant with the accompaniment.

Typically, Chopin will present only two paired statements of a theme; here he offers a third pair. This final paired statement initiates a series of modulations that eventually lead, via a short transition, to the major mediant (C major), the key of the second theme.

EXAMPLE 6.16. Chopin's Waltz in A♭ Major, op. 64, no. 3, bars 71–86.

There is very little of the waltz to be found in the second theme. Chopin's op. 34, no. 2, op. 34, no. 3, op. 42, and op. 64, no. 2 all contain lyrical themes that are relatively loose knit and improvisatory in nature, and as such they run counter to the well-formed, tight-knit lyrical themes of Lanner and Strauss Sr. The second theme of op. 64, no. 3 extends these tendencies to a far greater degree. It is the only theme out of all of Chopin's published waltzes that dispenses with the oom-pah-pah accompaniment. As in theme e of op. 34, no. 2, beginning in bar 73 the melody resides in the bass voice. In op. 34, no. 2 the "pah-pahs" of the waltz accompaniment were maintained in the right hand. In the second theme of op. 64, no. 3, part of which is given in Example 6.16, the right hand begins with a steady stream of twelve C-major quarter-note chords. The twelve quarter notes could be organized as two bars of $^6_4$ (or four bars of $^3_4$), three bars of $^4_4$, or two bars of $^3_2$. With nothing in the score (beyond the bar lines) to indicate possible beat groupings, it is left to the *sotto voce* bass melody to determine the meter. The low melody begins with a repetition of a motive previously heard in bars 67–68 and 71–72, and its duple groupings suggest, at least initially, a $^3_2$ interpretation (although it is certainly possible to maintain a $^6_4$ reading). The durational patterns of the two bars that follow, bars 75–76, however, are ambiguous at best, not clearly supporting $^6_4$ or $^3_2$. This passage would certainly have disoriented a listener participating mimetically in this music as a waltz. Only by bar 78 does a $^6_4$ meter begin to emerge, but it is constantly questioned by syncopations in the melody and accompaniment. Metrical clarity in this passage is not a foregrounded element, and without it the music loses its ability to serve effectively as a sonic analogue of the dance.

With the reprise of the opening theme in bar 109 we return to the domain of the ballroom. The second paired statement of the theme touches the flatted submediant before resolving in an expanded passage to the tonic. Here, global closure is signaled by the coordination of the cadential tonic with a hyperdownbeat (bar 149) and an ensuing virtuosic coda that continuously accelerates to the end (*poco a poco accelerando al fine*).

CONCLUSION

In this final chapter I have attempted to show the similarities between Chopin's conception of op. 18 and the Viennese waltzes of Lanner and Strauss Sr. The striking similarities in formal design, melodic design, tonal design, and cadential design suggest that Chopin used the waltzes he heard while he resided in Vienna as compositional models. While in the waltzes composed and published after op. 18 Chopin gradually turns away from the Viennese aesthetics of self-containment and open-ended variety, he adapts and transforms two rhythmic techniques of Lanner and Strauss Sr., absorbing them into his own aesthetic. The first is metrical dissonance between the melody and accompaniment. In op. 18, Chopin explores the traditional Viennese type ($\frac{3}{2}$ against $\frac{6}{4}$); in subsequent waltzes, he introduces two new types ($\frac{3}{1}$ against $\frac{6}{4}$ and $\frac{12}{8}$ against $\frac{6}{4}$). The second is the technique whereby a phrase progresses from a state of metrical dissonance to a state of metrical consonance. A third rhythmic technique, one not rooted in the Viennese waltz, is the use of rhythmic and metrical accelerations, which are especially prominent in the introductions of Chopin's published waltzes.

It is difficult to generalize the characteristics of Chopin's published waltzes since, as I have shown, his conception of the *grande valse* genre was not fixed but evolved from op. 18 to op. 64. While not applicable to all of his published waltzes, certain key characteristic elements recur significantly often, especially when compared to their relative absence in his unpublished waltzes. His published waltzes are conceived on a larger scale, they often use introductions and codas, their lyricism is often surrounded by virtuosic themes, and they often employ metrical dissonances. Once he had formulated it in Warsaw, Chopin's conception of his private, unpublished waltzes did not substantially change throughout his life: they are shorter in length and do not use introductions and codas, they are often set in the minor mode and strongly lean toward the expression of melancholy, they are more lyrical and avoid virtuosic passagework, and they are infused with the rhythmic motive of the female waltzer.

The nineteenth century witnessed a virtual explosion of popular dance music that was fueled by an insatiable appetite for light entertainment music on the part of upper- and middle-class consumers. One outcome of this robust market was that gifted and savvy composers could support themselves solely on the composition, performance, and publication of popular music. As popular music making became more isolated from high art music, it increasingly developed its own musical language and supported its own community of composers. As Jim Samson (1985, 127) observes, one of Chopin's great achievements was his unmatched ability to move fluently between these two levels of music making. Much attention has been given to Chopin's achievements as a composer of art music—so much, in fact, that his dance music tends to be viewed solely through the lens of the autonomous artwork, completely separated from any association with ballroom dance music. Although such approaches are valuable inasmuch as they reveal inner artistic beauty and compositional craft, they may neglect an entire domain of musical associations and influences based on social dance practices of Chopin's time. In the last three chapters of this book, I have integrated analytical, stylistic, and dance-based cultural approaches to the waltz. My goal has been to place Chopin and his waltz music back within the hustle and bustle of this once vital and ubiquitous domain, a domain that has gradually receded from our collective consciousness as the dance practices upon which his waltzes were based fell from common use.

NOTES

INTRODUCTION

1. For discussions of the types and locations of dancing events and the social functions of western European ballroom dancing in the eighteenth century, see Reichart (1984), Harris-Warrick (1986), Leppert (1988), Fink (1996), Cohen (2000), and Semmens (2004). For similar discussions of social dancing during the first half of the nineteenth century, see Historisches Museum der Stadt Wien (1979), Hanson (1985), Fink (1996), and Clark (2002).

2. Concerning the politics of the dancing body and its iconic representation in the eighteenth century, see Leppert (1988, 99–103).

3. For a discussion of the use of dance in eighteenth-century composition pedagogy, see Ratner (1956) and Sisman (1982). As a paradigm of musical simplicity, the minuet was considered so simple to compose that even dilettantes who knew little about music could compose them through dice games or other systems of *ars combinatoria*. The title page of one publication published in London around 1770 reads: "A Tabular System Whereby the Art of Composing Minuets Is made so Easy that any Person, without the least knowledge of Musick, may compose ten thousand" (cited by Ratner 1970, 344). In the nineteenth century, the waltz replaced the minuet as the gateway to musical composition. In 1829 Warsaw composer Józef Damse published a small booklet in which he claimed: "A million waltzes or a way to compose a million waltzes even for those who know nothing about music" (see W. Tomaszewski 1992a, 110).

4. Riepel (1754), quoted and translated in Sisman (1982, 448).

5. See Geiringer (1966, 270). Kirnberger cites this pedagogical practice in the preface to his *Recueil d'airs de danse caractéristique*: "The number of partitas and suites that we have inherited from our forebears and which are no more than collections of dances demonstrates that this was the chief study of the young musicians of their time, as much for those that dedicated themselves to composing as well as those that applied themselves only to performing" (quoted and translated in Powell 1967, 68).

6. The *Neue Mozart-Ausgabe* has devoted two volumes to compositional exercises that survive from Mozart's youth (IX/27/1) and exercises from Mozart's students (X/30/1–2). Concerning Mozart's education, see Halliwell (2006).

7. Ratner cites this letter in a discussion of the influence of dance music in eighteenth-century music (1956, 444).

8. Translated by Krzysztof Komarnicki. See also Walery Gostomski's book *Polonez i menuet: Szkic estetyczno-obyczajowy* (1891).

9. See Scott (2008) for a discussion of these terms.

10. In his text *Nineteenth-Century Music*, Carl Dahlhaus, for example, is particularly severe. He relegates all music that falls outside the category of "art music" as "trivial" and includes within this category music of the ballroom, promenade concerts, salons, and *variétés* (1989, 311). The "monotony of musical banality" found in this rather broad category of works, says Dahlhaus, not only "leaves us awestruck" but renders musical analysis pointless (1989, 311). See Bohlman (1993) and Gramit (2000) for discussions of these attitudes in academic literature.

11. Concerning the emergence of a popular style of composition, see Scott (2008, 119–31).

12. As one would expect, there is a substantial body of research by German and Austrian scholars. The two main thrusts of this literature are social history of the waltz and biographical research on Lanner and the Strauss family. See Schönherr and Rienhöhl (1954), Linke (1987, 1992, 1996), Salmen (1988, 1989), and Fink (1996).

1. INFLUENCES OF THE EARLY EIGHTEENTH-CENTURY BALLROOM MINUET ON THE MINUETS FROM J. S. BACH'S FRENCH SUITES, BWV 812–817

1. "The absorption of operatic style into pure instrumental genres lies at the heart of the development of music in the eighteenth century" (Rosen 1980, 43). For most if not all of the eighteenth century, vocal music held a privileged status over instrumental music. Because of its specificity in depicting meaning and emotion, vocal music was considered aesthetically superior to instrumental music. Accordingly, composition pedagogues commonly instructed their students to imitate the voice, from which their art is derived. To take but one of many examples, Bernard Germain Lacépède, in his treatise *La poétique de la musique*, instructs a composition student to compose a symphony as though "he were writing a grand aria in which one or more voices were trying to express emotions that were more or less vivid; he will substitute for these voices the first violin, or other instruments that are easily distinguished; from time to time he will seek to imitate the inflections of the human voice by means of instruments capable of sweet or pathetic inflections" (1785, 2:331, quoted and translated in Bonds 1991, 63).

2. For example, roughly one-third of Lully's minuets exhibit irregular phrase structures (Little 1967, 75–77). Russell reports that "in a survey of almost 100 eighteenth-century *recueils*, only about one in four contains only minuets in which the number of measures in every reprise is divisible by four; in the slightly more than 100 manuscripts surveyed, the ratio is even smaller" (1999, 399).

3. The contredanse is the other important dance of the eighteenth century. While the minuet held a privileged place in the ballroom as "the queen of dances" (Feldtenstein 1767, 37), during the course of a ball the contredanse was typically danced more often, by more people, and by a wider range of social classes.

4. After the French Revolution, the popularity of the minuet sharply declined, especially in France and England. It did, however, continue to be practiced as a social dance well into the first quarter of the eighteenth century in Germany and Austria. Concerning the longevity of the minuet as a social dance, see Aldrich, Hammond, and Russell (2000, 13–18).

5. A convenient way to view a historically informed performance of the *pas de menuet* is to visit the Library of Congress's digitized dance collection at http://memory.loc.gov/ammem/dihtml/dihome.html (accessed 20 July 2011).

6. The English dancing master Kellom Tomlinson is widely regarded as one of the most important dance pedagogues of the eighteenth century. His work, which is representative of French court dancing in the first half of the eighteenth century in England and on the Continent, is particularly valuable for my study because it contains a detailed discussion of the relationship between the minuet as danced and minuet music. The most important German source for court dancing from the first half of the eighteenth century is Gottfried Taubert's monumental *Rechtschaffener Tanzmeister* (1717). Like Tomlinson, Taubert's treatise represents a transmission of the French style and not of an independent German style.

In a study of Taubert's work, Angelika Gerbes believes that it is unlikely that a distinct German style existed (1972, 251). For a discussion of the significance of Taubert's work, see Russell (2006).

7. The type of dance notation used here by Tomlinson was most likely an invention of the principal choreographer of the Paris Opéra, Pierre Beauchamp (Witherell 1983, 5). It was first used in publication by the French dancing master Raoul-Auger Feuillet (1700) and quickly thereafter became the accepted form of dance notation throughout the eighteenth century.

8. Out of the roughly forty surviving minuet choreographies contained in dance manuals, only one is not tailored to fit the phrase organization of the music (Russell 1999, 386).

9. Besides their pedagogical function, Tomlinson informs the owner of his treatise that "these Prints are also designed as proper Furniture for a Room . . . and when hung up in their regular Order in Frames with Glasses, they will be a beautiful and instructive Representation of the whole Dance at one View" ([1735] 1970, book 2, introduction to plate I).

10. Tomlinson's detailed visual display of fourteen plates presents all the music, including the internal repetitions (AABB AABB AABB), and in doing so provides interesting insight into the contemporary performance practice of dance music. Not only is each large-scale repetition of the A$\|$B tune varied, but the repetitions of each strain within the A$\|$B tune are varied as well ($A^1A^2B^1B^2$ $A^3A^4B^3B^4$ $A^5A^6B^5B^6$).

11. The term "hypermeter" refers to levels of meter operating above the no-

tated meter. My concept of hypermeter is based on the work of Rothstein (1989) and Lerdahl and Jackendoff (1983).

12. Concerning the improvisatory nature of the minuet, see Thorp (2003) and Russell (2006).

13. Riepel (1754, 30), quoted and translated in Russell (1992, 119).

14. The standardization of phrase lengths found in minuets written for Vienna's Imperial Ballrooms (*Redoutenmenuetten*) is, perhaps, tied to the minuet's decline in popularity in the second half of the eighteenth century, alongside a general decline in the technical proficiency of the dancers. If the minuet was no longer a frequent and creative part of a dancer's repertoire, then it would stand to reason that the dancers' footwork would become more prosaic, less embellished, and thus more predictable. The most likely model for their performance would be the pedagogical minuet, which, as we have seen, is characterized by quadratic syntax and close congruence between the dance and music. The previously cited quote by Leopold Mozart in which he observes that dancers could only dance to the tunes that were used when they learned to dance would seem to support this explanation. Another possible avenue of influence for *Redoutenmenuetten*, especially in regard to the predominance of rounded binary form and a ternary *da capo* layout, is the art minuet (Russell 1992, 134–38).

15. It should be noted that there are occasional examples of hypermetrical irregularities in the repertoire of dance minuets (Russell 1992, 1999). On the whole, though, they are rare. Experienced dancers would have perhaps

enjoyed the challenge of dancing against the metrical grain and devising an artful way of realigning their step-units to the music (or not).

16. See Tomlinson ([1735] 1970, 148–49), Malpied (1770, 90–91, 100–104), and Magri ([1779] 1988, 189).

17. For examples of minuets notated in $\frac{6}{4}$ rather than $\frac{3}{4}$, see the minuets contained in E. Pemberton's treatise *An Essay for the Further Improvement of Dancing* ([1711] 1970). Loulié observes that "the only reason for using $\frac{6}{4}$ instead of twice $\frac{3}{4}$ [in the minuet] is because in $\frac{3}{4}$ the good beat is not distinguished from the false beat; and it is for this reason that dancers beat the Minuet in $\frac{6}{4}$ although it is notated in $\frac{3}{4}$" ([1696] 1965, 61–62).

18. See Saint Lambert ([1702] 1984, 38), Taubert ([1717] 1976, 523–29, 879–89), and Tomlinson ([1735] 1970, 149).

19. In his dictionary Sébastien de Brossard defines a passepied as "in all respects very like a minuet, except that 'tis more brisk and lively" ([1740] 1966, 175).

20. Again, Tomlinson makes the connection between the minuet step and a two-bar hypermeter very clear: "The *Time* of these Movements, in *Dancing*, ought never to be beat after every Bar but every other Measure, by Reason, as has been said, one *Menuet Step* takes two Measures of these Movements; and it is to be noted that . . . the *Time* is to be mark'd the first Measure down, and the second up, instead of twice down" ([1735] 1970, 149).

21. The treatise, "A New Treatise on the Art of Dancing," first published in the *Lady's Magazine* in six installments in 1785, has been republished in *Dance Research: The Journal of the Society for Dance Research* 11, no. 2 (1993): 43–59.

22. Geiringer (1966, 11), quoted in Little and Jenne (1991, 3–4). For more recent scholarship concerning Bach's exposure to French culture while attending the Ritterakademie, see Wolff (2001, 65–66).

23. See Lester (1986, 13–44) for a comprehensive discussion of accents in tonal music.

24. Minuets typically begin directly on the downbeat without any upbeat preparation.

25. Most often, Bach organizes his simple binary forms as a succession of parallel phrases in which each recurrence of the opening phrase exhibits a heightened level of musical activity. Concerning Bach's employment of this compositional technique, see Lester (2001).

26. The term "sentence" in connection with a particular type of phrase structure was first coined by Arnold Schoenberg (1967, 20–24, 58–81) and his student Erwin Ratz (1973, 23–24). In his groundbreaking study of Classical form, William Caplin (1998) examines the use of this phrase type in the instrumental music of Haydn, Mozart, and Beethoven. My concept of the sentence is based on Caplin's work.

27. For example, see Telemann's two sets of fifty minuets published in 1728 and 1730.

28. The concept of structural uniformity in Bach's music has been most recently addressed by Lester (1999, 2001) and Beach (2005). According to Lester, one of the basic premises of Bach's compositional style is that "the opening of a piece states a core of material that is then worked with throughout the composition" (2001, 52).

29. Bach employs a similar strategy in the second half of the first minuet of the French Suite in D Minor, BWV 812.

30. See Laskowski (1990), Smith (1995), and Beach (2005) for other interpretations of this work's tonal structure.

31. *Stufe(n)* is a term used in Schenkerian theory to refer to diatonic triads that through the process of composing-out (*Auskomponierung*) provide unity and content to music.

32. In *Fundamentals of Music Composition,* Arnold Schoenberg refers to sentence form as a "higher form of construction than the period" (1967, 58). With one exception, his examples are drawn from Classical and Romantic repertoires. While one may take issue with Schoenberg's evolutionary model of music history, sentences appear with far more frequency in the Classical and Romantic repertoires than in Baroque music.

33. This relative lack of specific musical characteristics in comparison to other court dances may in part help explain why the minuet was able to adopt so many different affects and topics without losing its sense of "minuet." Allanbrook states that the "minuet can admit of almost any figuration which does not disguise its essential movement" and that it "can also tolerate the overlay of another style or topical reference" (1983, 35). Other dances, such as the sarabande, were not as flexible. As hypermeter became more of a standard feature in the second half of the eighteenth century, the minuet lost a unique defining feature.

2. MOZART IN THE BALLROOM

1. For an extended discussion of minuet form in the eighteenth century, see Russell (1999).

2. Tilden Russell observes that "the minuet-trio relationship is a huge topic that has barely been touched" and that "the trio is probably the most ignored element in dance-movement studies" (1983, 3, 220). Furthermore, studies of Mozart's Redoutensäle minuets, written during the last four years of his life, are scarce, despite passing observations by Erik Smith (1982, 64; 1990, 217), H. C. Robbins Landon (1988, 41–43), and David Wyn Jones (1990, 276–77) that the trios of these late minuets contain some of Mozart's boldest experiments in orchestration and rhythm. Russell (1983) provides the most detailed and illuminating discussion to date concerning the issue of contrast between minuets and trios. In answer to the question as to why minuet-trio contrast became standard practice, Russell cites contemporary Classical compositional aesthetics in which contrast, as achieved through variety, new forms, and surprise, emerged as a highly valued compositional trait (1983, 225–26).

Since Tilden's 1983 dissertation, two important studies have been published that address the issue of minuet-trio contrast: Gretchen A. Wheelock's book *Haydn's Ingenious Jesting with Art: Contexts of Musical Wit and Humor* (1992) and Melanie Lowe's article "Falling from Grace: Irony and Expressive Enrichment in Haydn's Symphonic Minuets" (2002). Both studies focus principally on minuets not intended as ballroom dance music. The types of expressive and stylistic oppositions the authors find in this repertoire are peculiar to Haydn and are not commonly found in Mozart's dance or art minuets.

3. On the longevity of the minuet, see Aldrich, Hammond, and Russell (2000, 13–17).

4. See Nissen ([1828] 1964, 692). At a very early age Mozart's father arranged instruction for him in dance from the French dancing master Gaetano Appolino Baldassare Vestris. His letters contain numerous accounts of his activities during carnival as a dancer, observer, and critic of the dance and also as a dance choreographer and composer. For a detailed discussion of Mozart's activities as a dancer, see Busch-Salmen (1990, 65–81).

5. In 1787, partly in order to keep Mozart in Vienna, Joseph II appointed Mozart as Imperial Chamber composer. It was a nominal position that paid 800 guilder a year, "too little for what I could do and too much for what I do" (Solomon 1995, 423–24). His only responsibility was to provide dance music for the court balls in the Redoutensäle.

6. Simple binary form is typically defined as a two-part form that exhibits the thematic design A:‖:B or A:‖:A². It is often defined in opposition to rounded binary form, which is characterized by a thematic return midway through the second part (A:‖:BA²). That the term "simple binary" can be applied to both Bach's minuets and Mozart's minuets reveals the crudeness and inadequacy of formal terminology, especially when applied across stylistic periods. Bach, whose music is characterized by thematic unity, typically organizes his binary dance movements as a succession of two to three parallel phrases (A:‖:A² or A:‖:A²A³). As Joel Lester notes, if contrasting material is introduced, it typically is combined with material previously heard (2001, 52–53). Furthermore, Bach often will heighten some aspect of musical activity within each phrase as well as between phrases (Lester 2001, 53). The first phrase will thereby be the most stable; the last phrase will be the most

unstable (i.e., up until the final cadence). Mozart's minuets, on the other hand, are characterized by thematic contrast and strongly articulated phrase organizations. Typically, Mozart introduces new material at the beginning of the second section. The second section will either continue with new material or conclude with a restatement of material from the first section. While Mozart's Salzburg minuets show a wide range of proportional layouts, including minuets with six-bar phrases, his Viennese minuets, except for two, fall into a symmetrical 8 + 8 layout.

7. Feldtenstein (1767), quoted and translated in Allanbrook (1983, 33).

8. Sulzer ([1792–97] 1994, 3:339), quoted and translated in Lowe (2002, 174).

9. Melanie Lowe discusses the associations of the minuet with noble simplicity in her book *Pleasure and Meaning in the Classical Symphony* (2007, 107–108). Johann Winckelmann, in his 1755 treatise *Gedancken über die Nachahmung der griechischen Wercke in der Mahlerey und Bildhauer-Kunst* (Reflections on the imitation of Greek works in painting and sculpture), was the first to cite the aesthetic categories of noble simplicity and quiet grandeur as essential attributes of classical beauty. It was largely his work, along with archaeological excavations in Herculaneum and Pompeii, that initiated the "Greek revival" and deeply influenced the rise of the neoclassical movement during the late eighteenth century.

10. For a discussion of the concept of complaisance in dance, see Wynne (1970).

11. Weaver (1712, 65), quoted in Wynne (1970, 31).

12. While little is known concerning the origin of the minuet, dance scholars are agreed that the *branle de Poitou* was not its predecessor. See Sutton (1985, 133–36) and Little (2001, 16:740).

13. The works of Jean-Baptiste-Joseph Pater (1695–1736) and Nicolas Lancret (1690–1743), both followers of Watteau, contain many scenes of pastoral minuets (see Ingersoll-Smouse 1928; Holmes 1991). For other pastoral minuet depictions, see Franz Christoph Janneck's *Der Tanz* (c. 1750), Norbert Grund's *Le Menuett-Tänzerin* (1760), the title page from Johann Kirnberger's *Recueil d'airs de danse caractéristiques* (1777), Philibert-Louis Debucourt's *Le menuet de la mariée* (1786), and Adam Buck's *Un minuet à l'angloise* (1800). Although it makes no reference to the pastoral, Johann Zoffany's *A Family Party, the Minuet* (n.d.) beautifully captures the artful simplicity and gracefulness of the minuet as danced by a young girl. Such paintings, in which minuet dancers are framed within a pastoral setting, provide a visual corollary to the expression marking *minuetto grazioso*.

14. The dual visual representation of the minuet as the embodiment of both aristocratic power and natural beauty is repeated in artwork throughout the century. For further examples, see note 13.

15. Hogarth's eloquent description of minuet dancing found its way into at least one dancing treatise whose author passed it off as his own. See Cassidy (1810, 66–67).

16. For an extended discussion of eighteenth-century theories of beauty, see Dieckmann (1973–74).

17. Although not identified in this same sense, Edward Lowinsky dis-

cusses the quality of "rhythmic ease" in his seminal 1956 article, "On Mozart's Rhythm."

18. In a recent article, Scott Burnham (2005) identifies murmuring accompaniments as a key feature of Mozart's beautiful music, along with simple harmonies, simple melodies, slow harmonic rhythms, and transparent and straightforward textures. In his biography of Mozart, Maynard Solomon devotes two chapters to the beautiful in Mozart's music. Although he does not explicitly cite murmuring accompaniments as a characteristic of Mozart's musical beauty, almost every musical example he discusses includes this kind of texture (1995, chaps. 12 and 24).

19. For an example of this type, see the trio from the eighth minuet of K. 585.

20. See also Rameau ([1725] 1967, 92–98) and Russell (2006, 146–53).

21. The melodic doubling of the flute (or piccolo) with the violin is a distinguishing feature of Mozart's Salzburg trios.

22. My concept of "auxiliary progression" is based on Schenker ([1935] 1979, 87–90). See Burstein (2005) for a recent discussion of this compositional technique.

23. For an in-depth discussion of the articulative impact of auxiliary progressions, see McKee (1996).

24. Mozart and Johann Baptist Vanhal were the first composers in Vienna to publish *Deutsche* in 1787. Mozart's only published set of *Ländler* dates from the last year of his life, after he had composed his last set of minuets.

25. The minuet is included in a manuscript bearing the title "Kleine Clavier-Stücke von J. S. Bach. C. P. E. Bach.

J. C. Bach. J. C. F. Bach. Altnickol" (Staatsbibliothek Preussischer Kulturbesitz, West Berlin). Reproduced in Warburton (1989, 17).

26. For example, see Blom (1941, 162–80), Nettl (1963, 90–91), and Russell (1983, 230).

27. Women wore long, full, hooped dresses. The only way a woman could expose her feet was to extend her leg outward or lift the fabric of her dress. Tightly tied whale-bone corsets restricted breathing and movement of the upper body. As a result of the clothing, women would appear to glide across the ballroom floor with a minimum of physical activity. Commenting on the visual effect of hooped petticoats and stiff corsets, one observer noted that "ladies now walk as if they were in a go-cart" (quoted in Ewing 1986, 42). The men's footwork, on the other hand, was completely exposed by short trousers and skin-tight silk stockings. Men's calves were considered sexually attractive and were appropriately displayed by the outward turn of the legs and, at times, by artificial enlargement (stuffed stockings).

28. Concerning the use of dialogue textures in minuet trios in the second half of the eighteenth century, see Kirkendale (1979, 148–49), Finscher (1974, 144–45), and Russell (1983, 225, 240–41).

29. See Mozart's "Là ci darem la mano" from *Don Giovanni* for an operatic example of a seduction aria that employs a similar compositional strategy.

30. See, for example, the tenth minuet of K. 568 and the first, seventh, eighth, ninth, tenth, and twelfth minuets of K. 585.

31. It is important to note that, while the minuet music signifies historical

authority and class membership, it still maintains essential musical qualities of a minuet dance: $\frac{3}{4}$ meter, melodic groups initiated on odd-numbered bars, and, most important, a clearly maintained two-bar hypermeter. In other words, underneath the minuet's fancy aristocratic attire, it is still music that is eminently danceable.

32. For an insightful survey on the Habsburg monarchy during the eighteenth century, see Ingrao (2000).

33. While its elevated position was a result of practical concerns such as acoustics and visibility, the prominence of the orchestral space set the stage for the emergence of the "dance composer/conductor as hero" in the early nineteenth century. In the 1790s the iconography of ballroom orchestras begins to change. Prior to 1790, dance ensembles were most often depicted without a leader; beginning in the 1790s, images of orchestra leaders begin to appear. See, for example, Seyner Königl's 1795 ballroom print reproduced in Busch-Salmen and Salmen (1990, 55).

34. For a history of the European ballroom in the eighteenth century, see Fink (1996).

35. "One hundred musical instruments" is hyperbole. Payment records for the Redoutensäle dance orchestras indicate that the standard sizes were forty-three players in the large hall and twenty-seven players in the small hall (Edge 1992, 82–83). Pezzl (1786–90), quoted and translated in Landon (1991, 149–50).

36. Mozart also uses this loud-soft technique in his other Redoutensäle dance music (*Deutsche, Tänze,* and *Kontretänze*). However, in those cases the loud-soft alteration does not participate in the opposition of aristocratic power and natural grace but rather is used simply as a practical means of making sure that the music is heard.

37. Only within the last three decades has the frame as an object of historical and aesthetic inquiry received sustained critical attention from art historians. The frame's neglect can be most readily seen in art histories, of which, as Paul Mitchell and Lynn Roberts sadly observe, 99 percent exclude the frame from their illustrations (1999, II:378).

38. Gallini advises minuet dancers to assume an expression of "sprightly vacancy, an openness of the face, without the least tincture of any indecent air of levity" ([1762] 1967, 165).

3. THE MUSICAL VISIONS OF JOSEPH LANNER AND JOHANN STRAUSS SR.

1. Feldtenstein (1767, 36–37), quoted and translated in Allanbrook (1983, 33).

2. The contredanse is a French version of the English country dance, which was imported into France at the end of the seventeenth century. The French contredanse initially used the English "longways" formation, in which couples were arranged in two opposing rows, with men on one side and women on the other side. During the dance, each couple worked their way to the head of the line. Once at the head, they danced a duet by themselves, after which they returned to the back of the line, giving way to the next couple. By midcentury the longways formation had been abandoned in favor of four couples arranged in a square. For discussions

comparing the choreography and social roles of the contredanse to the minuet, see Allanbrook (1983, 60–63) and Leppert (1988, 94–99).

3. The word "waltz" is derived from the German verb *walzen*, which means simply "to turn" or "to revolve." Concerning the early history of the waltz and other turning dances, see Aldrich (1990, 1997) and Aldrich, Hammond, and Russell (2000).

4. Although relatively simple and unsophisticated, especially in comparison to the minuet, the early waltz was more varied and technically more difficult than styles of waltzing after 1820.

5. Using the term "ilinx" (the Greek word for "whirlpool"), the social theorist Roger Caillois classifies the waltz as a type of "game" based on the "pursuit of vertigo and which consists of an attempt to momentarily destroy the stability of perception and inflict a kind of voluptuous panic upon an otherwise lucid mind" (1961, 23).

6. What makes this scene truly amazing, beyond Mozart's brilliant use of these dances for character development and plot advancement, is that while the three dances enter successively, once one begins it continues while the next begins, until all three are being played simultaneously by three different onstage orchestras. This results in polymeter (the simultaneous projection of different meters): the minuet is in $\frac{3}{4}$, the contredanse is in $\frac{2}{4}$, and the *Deutscher* is in $\frac{3}{8}$. Allanbrook (1983, 277–87) and Heartz (1990, 179–93) both provide in-depth discussions of this scene. Heartz provides evidence showing that it was not uncommon in large dance halls to have two dance orchestras situated at either end of

the room playing different dances. This would stand to reason in that it would be difficult for a single dance ensemble to be heard across a large dance hall filled with noisy carnival revelers. Not cited by Heartz is a print reproduced in Becker (1991, 196–97) illustrating a ball held in the National Theater in Prague in 1790 in commemoration of the coronation of Leopold II. A large hall is depicted from one end looking lengthwise down toward the other end of the hall. Two dance orchestras in opposing balconies are shown at the end closest to the viewer; two larger orchestras are shown in the middle of the hall in opposing balconies; and, although they are not visible, because of the symmetry of the hall it is reasonable to assume that two additional orchestras are performing at the far end. Thus, it is possible that on this occasion six different orchestras were performing simultaneously for six different groups of dancers! In moving through and in between the different dancing spaces, one would experience a fantastic mixture of different musics in different tempi. Mozart's idea of simultaneous dances in *Don Giovanni* is not just a clever artistic device born out of his imagination but rather was most likely based on his actual experiences as an observer and participant in ballroom dancing. See also Semmens (2004, 181–84) for a discussion of multiple dance orchestras in public balls at the Paris Opéra in the eighteenth century.

7. Most ballroom dances of the eighteenth and nineteenth centuries have step patterns no longer than one bar.

8. Early critics believed not only that a woman's honor and reputation

would be sullied by dancing a waltz but also that the waltz would bring about a downfall in morality of all mankind. One of the earliest tracts decrying the moral dangers of the waltz was published in 1797 with the title *Discussions of the Most Important Causes of the Weakness of Our Generation in Regard to The Waltz*. After quickly selling out, it was republished two years later with the new title *Proof that the Waltz is the Main Source of the Weakness of Body and Mind of Our Generations, Most Urgently Recommended to the Sons and Daughters of Germany*. These publications are cited in Sachs (1952, 431–32).

9. See Yaraman (2002, 8) for a discussion of the voyeuristic nature of published waltz criticism.

10. Dance orchestras in eighteenth-century depictions of balls are rarely given such visual prominence, if they are shown at all. In the Rameau print presented in Figure 1.3, for example, only the backs of the musicians are shown. As will be discussed later in the chapter, the visual prominence of the dance orchestra leader in nineteenth-century iconography of the dance reflects the emergence of the waltz composer/conductor as a popular figure in society and as the most important person in the hall.

11. The sketches are reproduced in Grandville (1986).

12. Nicolai (1781), quoted in Jacob (1948, 21).

13. The Vienna Congress was famous for its endless succession of balls, which prompted Prince de Ligne's well-known quip "le congrès ne marche pas, mais il danse" (the Congress doesn't work; it dances). Quoted in La Garde-Chambonas (1902, 380).

14. Concerning exhibitionism and fetishism in women's fashions in the nineteenth century, see Steele (1985, 24–30).

15. Laura Mulvey (1975), who coined the term "the male gaze," was the first to theorize in psychoanalytical terms the ways in which women are looked at in cinema.

16. Surprisingly, some of the most sexually charged literary descriptions of waltzing women were penned by religious authorities. The stated purpose of their publications was to warn their readers about the dangers of what could, should, and would happen to unmarried women who dared to waltz. The authority of the church made dance criticism a literary forum where it was socially permissible to describe and read about "improper" sexual conduct. And the majority of these publications contain extended lyrical descriptions of sexual behavior, often voyeuristic in nature. Their widespread popularity suggests that they were not so much read for their moral message as for their sexual content; in other words, they represent a form of literary erotica.

An interesting sidebar on this topic is a small publication by the American author Ambrose Bierce. Playing off the public's seemingly insatiable appetite for sexually explicit dance criticism, Bierce pulled off one of the great literary hoaxes of the nineteenth century. Passing himself off as a man of the world turned reformed moralist and using the pseudonym William Herman, Bierce wrote and published a small book in 1877 titled *The Dance of Death* in which he strongly condemns the waltz. Framing his story as a voyeuristic adventure, Bierce invites the reader to attend a ball with him at the home of a church deacon in San Francisco. Instead of going directly to the ballroom, Bierce first takes the reader into the game room to play cards. It is not until 2:00 AM, at the height of the ball, that the reader is led out to the ballroom to view the dancers. Bierce then describes, in explicit and extended detail, the waltzing couples as if they were engaged in sexual intercourse. After the dance, the sexual desires of some of the dancers are consummated during the carriage ride home.

Within one year this little book went through three printings and sold over eighteen thousand copies. It was endorsed by the Methodist Church Conference and favorably reviewed by most national publications, including the *Evening Post* and many religious journals. In the second printing, Bierce added an appendix of glowing reviews and letters, many from prominent church officials. To top it off, Bierce, under his own name, published a scathing review of the book in which he reveals its true nature.

I have not that bold bad volume before me (the editor of this paper virtuously burned the office copy after gloating over it during the whole of one day . . .). . . . From cover to cover it is one sustained orgasm of a fevered imagination – a long revel of intoxicated propensities. . . . To his perverted discernment this rather silly but harmless enough amusement is a seductive, naughty rite performed behind too thin a veil. . . . [The critics'] asinine praises may perhaps have this good effect: "William Herman" may be tempted forth, to disclose his disputed iden-

tity and gather his glory. Then he can be shot. (Quoted in Bierce 1998, 136–37)

17. Cellarius cautions dancing masters against enforcing in their students too strict a uniformity of style: "This waltzer shines by his impetuosity, his animation – his attitude, without being precisely disordered, has not, perhaps, a strict regularity. . . . Another waltzes placidly, and without the least agitation. . . . [H]e impresses upon [his partner] a calm and gentle motion, and moves with soft undulation. . . . The master should be upon his guard against endeavouring to reform these peculiarities . . . which are often the result of constitution and nature. . . . These diversities . . . constitute one of the attractions of the [waltz]" (1840, 47–48).

18. Quoted in Messer-Krol (1995, 9).

19. Concerning the perceptual interaction of dance and music, see Mitchell and Gallaher (2001) and Krumhansl and Schenck (1997). Krumhansl and Schenck suggest that "there appear to be a large number of dimensions available [in dance and music] to establish structural mappings between the two domains" (1997, 78). The dimensions they cite are emotion, tempo, dynamics, texture, contour, and large-scale grouping organization. Mitchell and Gallaher review various types of cognitive matches that may exist between music and different types of visual events, including dance.

20. Cook's "enabling similarities" correspond to Lakoff and Johnson's "invariant principle." See Zbikowski (2002–2003) for a critique and extension of Cook's work as it relates to the field of metaphor theory.

21. For a detailed discussion of the construction of feminine beauty in the nineteenth century, see Steele (1985).

22. For an example, see Texier (1853, 1:57).

23. Sevin Yaraman (2002, 37–41) cites repetition as a defining feature of the *valse à trois temps* and of the music composed to accompany it.

24. At a higher metrical level, the $\frac{6}{4}$ hypermeasures can be heard as hyperbeats within duple or quadruple patterns.

25. Max Schönherr (1976, 70) also cites the use of grand pauses at the opening of codas as a characteristic feature of Lanner and Strauss Sr. waltzes.

26. Hanslick (1870, 37), quoted and translated in Gartenberg (1968, 138).

27. Berlioz ([1837] 2001, 334–35), quoted and translated in Barzun (1969, 1:339).

28. Concerning the concept of "metrical dissonance," see Krebs, who classifies this type of hemiola as a "G$\frac{3}{2}$ dissonance" (1999, 31–34, 71).

29. Quoted and translated in Barzun (1969, 1:474).

30. And this is perhaps the principal reason why the Viennese waltz has met resistance as a legitimate art form. In the music academic community, there is a deep mistrust and anxiety over musical pleasure, especially if unearned, because it engages the supposedly irrational body rather than the rational mind. Concerning the anxieties of listening pleasure, see Cumming (2000, 274–77). See also Lowe (2007, 99–132) for a discussion of listening pleasure in the late eighteenth century.

31. Laube ([1834–37] 1973, 4:34–39), quoted and translated in Schnitzler (1954, III–12).

32. Quoted and translated in Fantel (1971, 48).

33. Langenschwarz (1836, 22–23), quoted and translated in Hanson (1985, 163).

34. Metternich (1970), quoted and translated in Wechsberg (1973, 44).

35. Prior to 1830 the number of waltzes ranged from six to twelve. By 1830 the standard number was six, and by 1835 it had settled into a succession of five waltzes. The reduction of waltzes was motivated in part by an expansion of the standard length of the theme from eight to sixteen (and sometimes thirty-two) bars. Also, the high demand for new waltzes, especially during carnival season, perhaps strained the creative imagination.

36. See also Strauss's two "Waltz Garlands," opp. 67 and 77, and Lanner's "Waltz Quodlibet," op. 97.

37. By the end of the 1830s, sixteen-bar phrases would become the standard.

38. Zbikowski (2008, 291) discusses the variability of correspondences that are available between music and dance. He conceives of dances as situated on a continuum between two extremes: on the one end, no correlation between the dance and music, and, on the other end, complete correlation. He views the waltz as having an unusually tight correlation between the dance and the music. The correlation for most other ballroom dances, he believes, are characterized by a looser relationship.

4. DANCE AND THE MUSIC OF CHOPIN

1. A notable exception is Sevin Yaraman's book *Revolving Embrace: The Waltz as Sex, Steps, and Sound* (2002), a

chapter of which explores Chopin's waltz music in relation to the choreography of the waltz.

2. Concerning Chopin's purported connection to Polish folk traditions, see Milewski (1999).

3. I am indebted to Krzysztof Komarnicki for the Polish translations contained in this chapter.

4. Attendance reports in Warsaw's newspapers indicate that during carnival the National Theater routinely accommodated fifteen hundred to two thousand dancers. Reported in Museum Historyczne Warszawy (1992, 1324).

5. Concerning Chopin's musical education, see Goldberg (2008, 107–46).

6. In 1827 approximately 72 percent of Warsaw's population was Roman Catholic. Reported in *Przewodnik warszawski 1827*, 46.

7. See Ciepliński (1983, 33). Warsaw's connection to French culture was particularly strong during the Napoleonic campaigns.

8. The ballet *Wesele krakowskie* (Crakow wedding), which premiered in Warsaw in 1823, was the first Polish ballet based on traditional national dances (Pudełek 1998, 216). For a discussion of the introduction of folk dance in Polish opera, see Milewski (1999, 113–35).

9. In his treatise *Fashionable Dancing* (1840, 8–11), Henri Cellarius was one of the first dancing masters to articulate the division between theatrical and ballroom dancing techniques and the need for specialized instruction in one or the other.

10. Those dancing masters and the dates of their notices are Ludwik Thiery [sic] (5 September), Jacób Zielińsky [sic] (15 September), F. Kunicki (5 October),

Piort. Tomasini (12 October), Franciszek Domagalski (15 October), Jan Zurkowski [sic] (17 October), and Karol Göbel (26 October).

11. For a discussion of dance instruction in Warsaw's school curricula, see Magier (1963, 58–60). For information on dance instruction in Warsaw's military academies, see Gołębiowski ([1831] 1983, 327, 333), Bukar (1913, 65–66), Miterzanka (1931, 33), Niemcewicz (1957, 1:57), and Ćwięka-Skrzyniarz (1983, 65–66).

12. Niemcewicz (1957, 57), quoted and translated in Ćwięka-Skrzyniarz (1983, 66).

13. Ogiński (1956), quoted and translated in Ćwięka-Skrzyniarz (1984, 30).

14. See Goldberg (2008, 54–106) and W. Tomaszewski (1992b, 167–70).

15. Gołębiowski ([1831] 1983, 264), quoted and translated in Goldberg (2008, 61).

16. Travel writers of the opening part of the nineteenth century constantly compared the Poles to the French in their dress, manners, and fondness for amusements. See, for example, Stephens (1838, 213) and Granville (1828, 542, 569–70). For an extended discussion of French influence in Warsaw's society, see Jedlicki (1999, 3–50).

17. The first newspaper advertisement for Kurpiński's "Polonez" appears on 19 February 1829 in the *Kurier warszawski*.

18. These figures are reported in *Przewodnik warszawski 1827*, 46.

19. Kattfuss (1800), quoted and translated in Lamb (2001, 27:73).

20. Such compositional manuals for the dilettante in which pieces were composed using simple formulas or by games of chance using dice, spinning tops, and random number selection were not un-

common and belong to the eighteenth-century tradition of *ars combinatoria*. See Ratner (1970).

21. I examined 116 waltzes by 36 composers published in Warsaw between 1816 and 1830. These waltzes are housed in the Jagiellonian Library, Cracow, Poland. Wojciech Tomaszewski's (1992a) bibliography of music published in Warsaw lists 525 waltzes published during this time period. In the discussion that follows, I identify Warsaw waltz publications by Tomaszewski's index numbers.

22. Very shortly after the beginning of the November Uprising of 1830, Kasper Napoleon Wysocki composed and published a musical depiction of the uprising titled "The Revolutionary Waltz" (1830, Tom. 1433). The waltz is divided into eight sections (abcdefa coda), each representing a different event in the uprising: (1) "The revolt of minds and their courageous actions"; (2) "Oppressed and imprisoned Brothers call for help"; (3) "An assault near Belweder and the Arsenal and the taking of the latter"; (4) "Brothers liberated from prisons"; (5) "Astonishment and emotion of the unexpectedly liberated"; (6) ". . . their acting together with us"; (7) "General commotion among the citizenry . . ."; (8) ". . . slowly to reestablish order and peace." Despite their initial success, which Wysocki's waltz portrays, the Poles were eventually crushed by the Russian army the following September.

Johann Nepomuk Hummel was one of the earliest composers of programmatic "battle" waltzes. See his Twelve German Dances with Battle Coda, op. 25 (1807) and New Waltzes with Trios and a Grand Battle Coda, op. 91 (1820).

23. The first Warsaw publication of a Strauss Sr. waltz appears in 1830 (Tom. 1410); the first Warsaw publication of a Lanner waltz appears in 1834 (Tom. 1789).

24. Other Warsaw waltz composers of notable talent were Maria Szymanowska-Wołowska, Ludwik Nidecki, and Józef Nowakowski.

25. Concerning Elsner's approach to the pedagogy of composition and its influence on Chopin, see Goldberg (2006). Elsner was strongly influenced by the eighteenth-century German theorists Johann Philipp Kirnberger and Heinrich Koch. In this German tradition the succession of cadence types was tightly prescribed, and in most cases Koch advises the student to avoid using the same cadence successively.

26. See Goldberg (2008, 147–76) for a discussion of Chopin's connection to these and other Warsaw salons.

27. Chopin relates the account in a letter to his family written on 26 August 1825; for an English translation of this letter, see Zamoyski (1980, 26–27).

28. Reported by Kazimierz Wójcicki (1855, 1:18).

29. See Kobylańska (1955, 231).

30. Chopin describes Rembieliński's technique in a letter dated 30 October 1825 (1954–60, 1:142). Previously that year, Rembieliński had returned from an extended stay in Paris, where he studied piano and composition (Sowiński [1857] 1971, 476).

31. Chopin uses the same "metrical dissonance" in the opening section (bars 9–40) of his Waltz in A♭ Major, op. 42. Concerning the concept of metrical dissonance, see Krebs (1999).

32. Note that the second waltz is by itself in a *da capo* layout.

33. For other supporting sources, see Azoury (1999, 10).

34. Quoted in Szulc (1998, 262).

35. Indeed, almost all of Chopin's earliest critics and biographers use the ballroom as an imaginary reference point in their interpretations of Chopin's waltzes. In his 1879 biography of Chopin, Arnold Niggli remarks that Chopin's waltzes are "full of perfect grace and elegance, their sparkling, animated rhythm magically conjuring up the image of a glittering ballroom, packed with dancers in full flight" (quoted in Ballstaedt 1994, 32). See also Niecks (1902, 2:248–51), Finck (1889, 44), Hallé ([1896] 1972, 74), Huneker (1900, 136), and Hadden (1903, 223).

36. More memorial than biography, Liszt's book was the result of a collaboration between Liszt and Princess Caroline Sayn-Wittgenstein, his Polish-born lover.

5. THE MUSICAL VISIONS OF CHOPIN

1. The dates of composition provided in Table 5.1 are based on those given by Chomiński and Turło (1990) and Samson (1996).

2. The German word "waltz" is derived from the verb *walzen*, which means "to turn," "to revolve," or "to wander." *Waltzen* is related to the Latin verb *volvere*, meaning "to turn" or "to rotate."

3. The appropriation of astronomic metaphors (e.g., orbits, spheres, planets) in describing the motion of waltzers is common in the literature of the waltz. Johann Wolfgang von Goethe was one of the earliest writers to use such terms in print. In a scene from *Die Leiden des jungen Werthers*, quoted earlier in chapter 3, the characters Werther and Lotte "whirled round each other like planets in the sky" (Goethe 1988, 17).

4. Although many dancing masters were able violinists or keyboard players, very few had the musical training to be able to describe in any meaningful way what makes a good dance tune. Nor was it their primary concern. As Sevin Yaraman (2002, 31–32) points out, the most detailed account on how to compose danceable waltz music comes from the German composer, theorist, and critic Adolph Bernhard Marx. In the section that follows, I use Marx as a guide in locating points of correspondence between the music and the dance.

5. Concerning structural highpoints in music, see Agawu (1982) and Eitan (1997).

6. In this brief prelude, Chopin employs the waltz as the controlling musical topic.

7. At the largest level the entire waltz is organized in a circular form, ABA, and the A and B sections themselves are in rounded binary form.

8. Yaraman also identifies neighboring motion as an important feature of nineteenth-century waltz music (2002, 33–36).

9. See Niecks (1902, 2:249).

10. According to Chopin's student Wilhelm von Lenz (1872, 37), Chopin referred to this waltz as a *valse mélancolique*.

11. Quoted in Aldrich (1991, 154–55).

12. And drop they did, although not always just from dizziness. At the beginning of the 1830 carnival season, the *Kurier warszawski* (3 January 1830) published a story about a mother whose beautiful and talented daughters, age

fifteen, seventeen, and eighteen, all died within one month of each other. Cause of death: "too much dancing." More likely they died from respiratory illness, which was a leading cause of death in urban centers. Respiratory illnesses were aggravated by the conditions in dance halls, which were typically dusty, smoky, overheated, crowded, and poorly ventilated.

13. In some instances, the first segment overlaps with the beginning of the second, resulting in the proportion 2 + 3. In such cases, I still use the label 1 + 3.

14. In this phrase, Chopin cleverly introduces an enharmonic pun. The phrase begins with B♭ as ♭$\hat{6}$ of D major but ends with A♯ as $\hat{7}$ of B minor. The shift to the diatonic collection of B minor is prepared in bar 37, where Chopin uses B♮ rather than B♭. Also notice how Chopin tonally dovetails the phrase ending in bar 32 with the phrase beginning with the pickup into bar 33. The V/III, which begins the new phrase, functions as a passing chord, connecting the tonic B-minor chord of bar 32 to the D-major chord in bar 34. In bar 37 the V/III functions as a neighboring chord to the mediant. The grouping boundaries between the phrase structure and the tonal structure are thus in conflict with each other.

15. For example, melodic arches are also a characteristic feature of Chopin's mazurkas, as are oom-pah-pah accompaniments. In fact, at times it is difficult to distinguish between the two genres. This potential ambiguity is reflected in the title and music of a dance published in Warsaw in the 1820s, "Mazurka – though not really a mazurka – but a waltz" (cited in Stadnicki 1962, 70, 124–26). See also Goldberg (2008, 66–69) concerning the sometimes hazy generic boundaries between mazurkas and waltzes. Goldberg argues that their generic identities, which are at times obscured by notational similarities, are clarified by the unique performance style of each genre.

16. Across Europe popular tunes from the stage were routinely arranged and published as ballroom dance music, including waltzes. In Warsaw, for example, arias from Rossini's opera *Barber of Seville* were extremely popular as waltz music (Stadnicki 1962, 154).

17. Quoted in Chopin (1954–60, 2:151).

18. In his essay "Harmony at the Tea Table: Gender and Ideology in the Piano Nocturne," Jeffery Kallberg (1996, 30–61) discusses the female-gendered associations of musical finery in the genre of the nocturne.

19. Notice that against the small ornamental neighbor motions of the melody, the repeating bass line composes out a large double-neighbor motion around $\hat{5}$ in its first seven bars.

20. Rink (1997, 58–59), for example, reads the opening section of the third movement as a "mazurka-like variation."

21. See Chopin's concert piece *Rondo à la mazur*, op. 5, for a clear opening presentation of the genre of the mazurka.

22. The dates of the letters are 27 March 1830, 10 April 1830, and 17 April 1830. It should be noted that it was not uncommon for composers of this time, including Orłowski, to take a melody from one genre and recast it in another genre, and Chopin's silence could be read as indifference to this practice. Thus, my case rests more on the musical evidence rather than on Orłowski's arrangements.

23. This movement is an example of what Robert Hatten would call "troping," which he defines as the mixture of "two style types in a single location to produce a unique expressive meaning from their collision or fusion" (2004, 68).

6. CHOPIN'S APPROACH TO WALTZ FORM

1. For a summary of different interpretations, see Kobylańska (1979, 224).

2. Chopin apparently never used the term "melancholy" in describing these waltzes. He does, however, use the term *dolente* in the surviving autograph manuscript of op. 69, no. 2. Moreover, when op. 69, no. 2 was first published in 1852, it was paired with the Waltz in F Minor, op. 70, no. 2. On the title page the publisher, J. Wildt of Kraków, added the description "Deux valses mélancholiques."

3. It is possible that this is the same waltz that Nidecki refers to as "Walc melancholiczny" in an advertisement published in the *Kurier warszawski* (9 November 1830, 1574).

4. While Lanner and Strauss Sr. appear not to have composed melancholy waltzes, there are examples by other Austro-German composers. In the first edition (1821) of Franz Schubert's *36 Originaltänze für Klavier*, op. 9 (D. 365), the second waltz appears under the name *Trauerwalzer*. Both Carl Czerny and Robert Schumann composed sets of variations on this waltz, which was later given the name *Sehnsuchtswalzer*. In 1834 Schumann wrote a short article, "Der Psychometer," in which he classifies waltzes into three types: head waltzes, foot waltzes, and heart waltzes. The third type, says Schumann, has its origins in "the *Sehnsuchtswalzer*, evening flowers, twilight shapes, and memories of long-gone youth and a thousand loves" (quoted in Daverio 1997, 107). For a discussion on the origins and veracity of the cliché "Gay Vienna," see Schnitzler (1954).

5. For interpretation #2, listen to Vladimir Ashkenazy's recording (London 414600-2); for interpretation #3, compare Dinu Lipatti's recording (EMI 5669652).

6. For this approach, listen to Alfred Cortot (EMI 7673592) and Dinu Lipatti (EMI 5669652).

7. Just three summers later, Wagner reports that "the hot summer air of Vienna was . . . impregnated for me almost solely by *Zampa* and Strauss" (1983, 63).

8. In 1829 Lanner was appointed music director of the Redoutensäle in Vienna, a position Mozart once held at the end of his life. Lanner also regularly played at many restaurants and dance halls in the city and suburbs as well as at private parties. Strauss's principal job during the early 1830s was as music director of the Sperl. First opened in 1806 by Johann Georg Scherzer, the Sperl, along with the Apollo, were the most popular dancing establishments in Vienna. Concerning the quantity and variety of dancing activities and establishments in Vienna during the opening decades of the nineteenth century, see Hanson (1985, 150–68) and Fink (1996, 95–211).

9. Quoted in Hanson (1985, 150).

10. For a summary of different interpretations, see Kobylańska (1979, 38–39). Chomiński and Turło (1990, 210) give 1833 as the year of its composition.

11. An "incomplete" authentic cadence occurs when a composer, through various means, leads the listener to expect a V–I authentic cadence. This is often achieved by the repetition of an eight-bar phrase that had previously concluded with an authentic cadence. At the point the tonic should have arrived, however, the music breaks off into silence. As a result, the length of the phrase is typically one bar shorter than expected. The most well known example is found in the opening instrumental introduction of the drinking song "Libiamo ne' lieti calici" from Verdi's *La Traviata*. See also the repetition of the second theme (bars 52–61) from the first movement of Schubert's Symphony No. 8 in B Minor.

12. The arabic numbers between the staves indicate the hypermeter.

13. For crisis points in Chopin's published waltzes, see op. 18, bar 233, op. 34, no. 3, bars 159–60, and op. 42, bars 210–12.

14. For octave designations, I use the system developed by the Acoustical Society of America: middle C equals C^4, the next highest C equals C^5, and so on.

15. For examples of melodies specifically scored for post horn or trumpet and that contain the rhythm quarter note/two eighth notes/quarter note, see Strauss Sr. op. 13, waltz no. 1, op. 19, waltz no. 3, and op. 60, waltz no. 5. See Schönherr (1976, 89–90) for further discussion of post horn melodies in the waltzes of Lanner and Strauss Sr.

16. For additional examples of spiccato melodies, see also Strauss Sr. op. 5, waltz no. 6, op. 13, coda, and op. 45, waltz 1 as well as Lanner op. 26, waltz 4.

17. For detailed studies of cadential hemiolas in Baroque music, see Willner (1991, 1996a, 1996b, 2007).

18. It is important to note that the earlier Viennese waltzes of Pamer, Hummel, and Beethoven do not employ hemiolas. While Schubert occasionally employs melodic hemiolas (see especially waltz no. 13 from D. 779), they are not a characteristic feature of his waltzes.

19. As Goldberg observes, aside from exposure to a wealth of music from his formal training at the Warsaw Conservatory, Chopin frequented Warsaw's music bookstores on a daily basis, "where he spent long hours browsing and playing through works of old masters, recently published scores, and newly arrived works from abroad" (2008, 54).

20. It is interesting to note that one of the surviving autograph manuscripts, dated 10 July 1833, does not include the coda, which with its virtuosic accelerando is the only section of the waltz that would be unsuitable for dancing. Instead, it concludes with a *da capo* repetition on the opening waltz. A reproduction of this manuscript is provided in Drath (1979, 3–6).

The distinction between functional and stylized dance music is often ambiguous and false. Chopin, for example, states quite clearly in a letter from Vienna written during the winter of 1830 that a set of mazurkas he had just composed "are not meant for dancing" (1963, 72). He is here most likely speaking of his op. 6 and op. 7 mazurkas, which were composed during his stay in Vienna. We may interpret Chopin's comment as an attempt to establish for himself a reputation as a serious composer of concert music apart from the dance hall and in so doing distance himself from the flood of published dance music, most of it second-rate. But also it is precisely because much of his dance music is so danceable – perhaps originally conceived as dance improvisations – that he felt the need to clarify the music's artistic function as he wanted it to be defined. Despite his intentions, we know that some of his mazurkas did make their way back to the dance floor. His Mazurka in B♭ Major, op. 7, no. 1 was published in Warsaw twice, first in 1835 and then again in 1842. The title page of the 1835 publication announces: "Newest Mazurka composed for fortepiano by Fr. Chopin as danced at the National Theater and at dancing evenings at the Old Ressursa" (Tom. 1874). Even Chopin's sister Ludwika expressed a certain degree of anxiety over the danceability of Chopin's music. In a letter written to Fryderyk from Warsaw in February 1835, she confesses:

> Your mazurka, the one that goes Bam Bum Bum in the third part [possibly op. 17, no. 1] . . . was performed by the full orchestra at the Variety Theater [and] played all night at the ball at the Zamoyskis, [who] were extremely pleased with it for dancing. What do you say about being profaned like that? . . . The Mazurka is more properly for listening. . . . What will you say about my being at the Lebruns one evening and having had to profane you? They had asked me if I could play your magnificent Mazurka, and . . . I played for dancing with the approval of the dancers. My dear, tell me whether you wrote it in the spirit of a dance;

perhaps we have understood you incorrectly. (Quoted in Szulc 1998, 115–16)

21. Chopin's pedaling indication also heightens the contrast between the end of the introduction and the beginning of the first theme. Chopin indicates the pedal to be held throughout bars 9–16, resulting in a hazy swirl of notes. Sonic clarity is restored in bar 17. Chopin's pedaling also supports hearing and performing the opening four bars as two two-bar groups. In this reading the opening gesture concludes with E♭^{3} on the third beat of bar 2 rather than continuing to the E♭^{2} on the downbeat of bar 3.

22. The recordings of Arthur Rubinstein (EMI 64933) and Ignaz Paderewski (Nimbus 8816) maintain the beginning tempo throughout the introduction. The more recent recordings of Evgeny Kissin (BMG-RCA 88697 625302) and Zoltán Kocsis (Decca 475 8046) prepare the entrance of the first theme with a ritardando.

23. Another interpretation of bars 9–16, suggested by Robert Hatten in a personal communication, is to hear the eighth notes grouped into twos, resulting in a quarter-note pulse. In this reading the durational pattern that results highlights an ascending chromatic line in paired pitches (C–D♭, C♯–D, etc.) that further intensifies the move to the climactic initiation of the theme at bar 17.

24. Quoted in Niecks (1902, 2:249).

25. Walter Everett (1990) explores the use of the 5̂–6̂–5̂, motive (in the minor mode) as a sonic symbol of grief in Schubert's *Winterreise*.

26. For this interpretation, listen to Rachmaninoff's recording (2005, Fono Enterprise Srl). See Rothstein (1995a, 233–37) for an insightful interpretation of this work's hypermeter. My reading of theme c corresponds to his alternative durational reduction, which he presents as a secondary meter in opposition to the primary meter.

27. Paul Hamburger (1966, 91–92) makes a similar observation as to the grouping organization of this theme.

BIBLIOGRAPHY

Agawu, Kofi. 1982. "The Structural Highpoint as Determinant of Form in Nineteenth-Century Music." Ph.D. diss., Stanford University.

———. 1991. *Playing with Signs: A Semiotic Interpretation of Classic Music*. Princeton, N.J.: Princeton University Press.

Aldrich, Elizabeth. 1990. "A New Look at an Old Dance: The Waltz." In the proceedings of the Hong Kong International Dance Conference, 29–46. Hong Kong.

———. 1991. *From the Ballroom to Hell*. Evanston, Ill.: Northwestern University Press.

———. 1997. "Social Dancing in Schubert's World." In *Schubert's Vienna*, ed. Raymond Erickson, 119–40. New Haven, Conn.: Yale University Press.

Aldrich, Elizabeth, Sandra Noll Hammond, and Armand Russell. 2000. *The Extraordinary Dance Book T.B. 1826: An Anonymous Manuscript in Facsimile*. Stuyvesant, N.Y.: Pendragon Press.

Allanbrook, Wye Jamison. 1983. *Rhythmic Gesture in Mozart*. Chicago: University of Chicago Press.

Allanbrook, Wye Jamison, and Wendy Hilton. 1992. "Dance Rhythms in Mozart's Arias." *Early Music* 20, no. 1:142–49.

Azoury, Pierre. 1999. *Chopin through His Contemporaries*. Westport, Conn.: Greenwood Press.

Ballstaedt, Andreas. 1994. "Chopin as 'Salon Composer' in Nineteenth-Century German Criticism." In *Chopin Studies 2*, ed. John Rink and Jim Samson, 18–34. Cambridge: Cambridge University Press.

Balzac, Honoré de. 1899. *A Daughter of Eve*. Trans. Katherine Prescott Wormeley. Boston: Little, Brown.

Barzun, Jacques. 1969. *Berlioz and the Romantic Century*. 2 vols. New York: Columbia University Press.

Batteux, Charles. [1746] 1981. *Les beaux-arts réduits à un même principe*. In *Music and Aesthetics in the Eighteenth and Early-Nineteenth Centuries*, ed. Peter le Huray and James Day, 40–56. Cambridge: Cambridge University Press.

Beach, David W. 2005. *Aspects of Unity in J. S. Bach's Partitas and Suites: An Analytical Study*. Rochester, N.Y.: University of Rochester Press.

Becker, Howard. 1982. *Art Worlds.* Berkeley: University of California Press.

Becker, Max. 1991. *Mozart: Sein Leben und seine Zeit in Texten und Bildern.* Frankfurt: Insel.

Berlioz, Hector. 1969. *The Memoirs of Hector Berlioz.* Trans. and ed. David Cairns. New York: Knopf.

———. [1837] 2001. *Strauss: Son orchestre, ses valses – de l'avenir du rythme.* In *Hector Berlioz: Critique musicale, 1823–1863,* ed. Yves Gerard, 3:329–35. Paris: Buchet/Chastel.

Bierce, Ambrose. 1877. *The Dance of Death.* 2nd ed. San Francisco: Henry Keller.

———. 1998. *A Sole Survivor: Bits of Autobiography.* Ed. S. T. Joshi and David E. Schultz. Knoxville: University of Tennessee Press.

Blom, Eric. 1941. "The Minuet-Trio." *Music and Letters* 22, no. 2:162–80.

Bohlman, Philip V. 1993. "Musicology as a Political Act." *Journal of Musicology* 11, no. 4:411–36.

Bonds, Mark Evans. 1991. *Wordless Rhetoric: Musical Form and the Metaphor of the Oration.* Cambridge, Mass.: Harvard University Press.

Brainard, Ingrid. 1986. "New Dances for the Ball: The Annual Collections of France and England in the 18th Century." *Early Music* 14, no. 2:164–73.

Brodziński, Kazimiérz. 1829. "Wyjątek z pisma o tańcach." In *Melitele,* ed. Antoni Edward Odyńiec, 85–101. Warsaw: A. E. Odyńiec.

Brossard, Sébastien de. [1740] 1966. *Dictionary of Music.* Trans. James Grassineau. Reprint. New York: Broude Brothers.

Budday, Wolfgang. 1983. *Grundlagen musikalischer Formen der Wiener Klassik: An Hand der zeitgenössischen Theorie von Joseph Riepel und Heinrich Christoph Koch dargestellt an Menuetten und Sonatensätzen (1750–1790).* Kassel: Bärenreiter.

Bukar, Seweryn. 1913. *Pamiętniki.* Warsaw: Biblioteka Dzieł Wyborowych.

Burke, Edmund. [1757] 1958. *A Philosophical Enquiry into the Origins of Our Ideas of the Sublime and Beautiful.* Ed. J. T. Boulton. New York: Columbia University Press.

Burnham, Scott. 2005. "On the Beautiful in Mozart." In *Music and the Aesthetics of Modernity: Essays,* ed. Karol Berger and Anthony Newcomb, 39–52. Cambridge, Mass.: Harvard University Press.

Burstein, L. Poundie. 2005. "Unraveling Schenker's Concept of the Auxiliary Cadence." *Music Theory Spectrum* 27, no. 2:159–85.

Busch-Salmen, Gabriele, and Walter Salmen. 1990. *Mozart in der Tanzkultur seiner Zeit.* Innsbruck: Edition Helbling.

Byron, George Gordon, Baron. [1813] 1907. "The Waltz: An Apostrophic Hymn." In *The Complete Poetical Works of Lord Byron,* ed. Sir Leslie Stephens, 156–64. New York: Macmillan.

Caillois, Roger. 1961. *Man, Play, and Games.* Trans. Meyer Barash. New York: Free Press of Glencoe.

Caplin, William E. 1998. *Classical Form: A Theory of Formal Functions for the Instrumental Music of Haydn, Mozart, and Beethoven.* New York: Oxford University Press.

Carner, Mosco. 1948. *The Waltz*. London: Max Parrish.

Cassidy, James P. 1810. *A Treatise on the Theory and Practice of Dancing*. Dublin: W. Folds.

Castiglione, Baldassare. [1528] 1976. *The Courtier*. Trans. George Bull. Rev. ed. London: Penguin Books.

Cellarius, Henri. 1840. *Fashionable Dancing*. Illustrated by Paul Gavarni. London.

Chomiński, Józef M., and Teresa D. Turło. 1990. *Katolog dzieł Fryderyka Chopina*. Cracow: Polskie Wydawnictwo Muzyczne.

Chopin, Fryderyk. 1954–60. *Correspondance de Frédéric Chopin, l'Aube 1816–1831*. Ed. Bronisław Edward Sydow, Suzanne and Denise Chainaye, and Iréne Sydow. 3 vols. Paris: Richard-Masse.

———. 1963. *Selected Correspondence of Chopin*. Collected and annotated by Bronisław Edward Sydow. Ed. and trans. Arthur Hedley. New York: McGraw-Hill.

Ciepliński, Jan. 1983. *A History of Polish Ballet*. Trans. Anna Ema Lesiecka. London: Veritas Foundation Publication Center.

Clark, Maribeth. 2002. "The Quadrille as Embodied Musical Experience in 19th-Century Paris." *Journal of Musicology* 19, no. 3:503–26.

Cohen, Sarah R. 2000. *Art, Dance, and the Body in French Culture of the Ancien Régime*. Cambridge: Cambridge University Press.

Compan, Charles. [1787] 1974. *Dictionnaire de danse*. Reprint. New York: Broude Brothers.

Cone, Edward T. 1968. *Musical Form*. New York: W. W. Norton.

Cook, Nicholas. 1998. *Analysing Musical Multimedia*. Oxford: Clarendon Press.

Cumming, Naomi. 2000. *The Sonic Self: Musical Subjectivity and Signification*. Bloomington: Indiana University Press.

Ćwięka-Skrzyniarz, R. 1983. *The Great Polish Walking Dance*. Irvington, N.J.: R. Ćwięka.

———. 1984. *The Elegant Polish Running-Sliding Dance*. Irvington, N.J.: R. Ćwięka.

Dahlhaus, Carl. 1989. *Nineteenth-Century Music*. Trans. J. Bradford Robinson. Berkeley: University of California Press.

Damse, Józef. 1829. *Milion walców czyli Sposób układania miliony walcow dla tych nawet, którzy muzyki nie znaja*. Warsaw: A. Brezina.

Daverio, John. 1997. *Robert Schumann: Herald of a "New Poetic Age."* New York: Oxford University Press.

Davies, Peter J. 1989. *Mozart in Person: His Character and Health*. London: Greenwood.

Dieckmann, Herbert. 1973–74. "Theories of Beauty to the Mid-Nineteenth Century." In *Dictionary of the History of Ideas*, ed. Philip P. Wiener, 1:195–206. New York: Charles Scribner's Sons.

Drath, Jan Bogdan. 1979. *Waltzes of Fryderyk Chopin: Sources*. 2 vols. Kingsville: Texas A&I University Publications.

Duindam, Jeroen. 2003. *Vienna and Versailles: The Courts of Europe's Dynastic Rivals, 1550–1780*. Cambridge: Cambridge University Press.

Edge, Dexter. 1992. "Mozart's Viennese Orchestras." *Early Music* 20, no. 1:64–88.

Eigeldinger, Jean-Jacques. 1986. *Chopin: Pianist and Teacher as Seen by His Pupils.* Trans. Naomi Shohet. Cambridge: Cambridge University Press.

Eitan, Zohar. 1997. *Highpoints: A Study of Melodic Peaks.* Philadelphia: University of Pennsylvania Press.

Everett, Walter. 1990. "Grief in 'Winterreise': A Schenkerian Perspective." *Music Analysis* 9, no. 2:157–75.

Ewing, Elizabeth. 1986. *Dress and Undress: A History of Women's Underwear.* London: Bibliophile.

Fantel, Hans. 1971. *Johann Strauss, Father and Son, and Their Era.* Newton Abbot, England: David & Charles.

Feldtenstein, C. J. von. 1767. *Die Kunst nach der Choreographie zu tanzen und Tänze zu schreiben.* Brunswick: Schröderschen Buchhandlung.

Feuillet, Raoul-Auger. 1700. *La pavane des saisons.* Paris: l'auteur.

———. [1700] 1968. *Chorégraphie.* Reprint. New York: Broude Brothers.

Finck, Henry Theophilus. 1889. *Chopin and Other Musical Essays.* New York: Scribner's.

Fink, Monika. 1996. *Der Ball: Eine Kulturgeschichte des Gesellschaftstanzes im 18. und 19. Jahrhundert.* Innsbruck: Studien Verlag.

Finscher, Ludwig. 1974. *Die Entstehung des klassischen Streichquartetts: Von den Vorformen zur Grundlegung durch Joseph Haydn.* Kassel: Bärenreiter.

Flaubert, Gustave. [1869] 1989. *Sentimental Education.* Trans. Douglas Parmée. Oxford: Oxford University Press.

Gallini, Giovanni Andrea Battista. [1762] 1967. *A Treatise on the Art of Dancing.* Reprint. New York: Broude Brothers.

Gartenberg, Egon. 1968. *Vienna: Its Musical Heritage.* University Park: Pennsylvania State University Press.

———. 1974. *Johann Strauss: The End of an Era.* University Park: Pennsylvania State University Press.

Geiringer, Karl. 1966. *Johann Sebastian Bach: The Culmination of an Era.* New York: Oxford University Press.

Gerbes, Angelika Renate. 1972. "Gottfried Taubert on Social and Theatrical Dance of the Early Eighteenth-Century." Ph.D. diss., Ohio State University.

Gmeiner, Josef. 1979. *Menuett und Scherzo: Ein Beitrag zur Entwicklungsgeschichte und Soziologie des Tanzsatzes in der Wiener Klassik.* Tutzing: H. Schneider.

Goethe, Johann Wolfgang von. 1988. *The Sorrows of Young Werther.* In *Goethe: The Collected Works,* ed. David E. Wellbery, trans. Victor Lange and Judith Ryan, 11:1–88. Princeton, N.J.: Princeton University Press.

———. 1994. *Italian Journey.* In *Goethe: The Collected Works,* ed. Thomas P. Saine and Jeffrey L. Sammons, trans. Robert R. Heitner, 6:11–466. Princeton, N.J.: Princeton University Press.

Goldberg, Halina. 1997. "Musical Life in Warsaw during Chopin's Youth, 1810–1830." Ph.D. diss., City University of New York.

———. 2006. "Phrase Structure of Chopin's Early Works in Light of Elsner's Instruction." Manuscript.

———. 2008. *Music in Chopin's Warsaw.* Oxford: Oxford University Press.

Goldmann, Helmut. 1956. "Das Menuett in der deutschen Musikgeschichte des 17. und 18. Jahrhunderts." Ph.D. diss., University of Erlangen.

Gołębiowski, Łukasz. [1827] 1979. *Opisanie historyczno-statystyczzne miasta Warszawy.* Warsaw: Wyd. Artstyczne i Filmowe.

———. [1831] 1983. *Gry i zabawy różnych stanów.* Warsaw: Wyd. Artstyczne i Filmowe.

Gostomski, Walery. 1891. *Polonez i menuet: Szkic estetyczno-obyczajowy.* Warsaw.

Graf, Max. 1945. *Legend of a Musical City.* New York: Philosophical Library.

Gramit, David. 2000. "Between Täuschung and Seligkeit: Situating Schubert's Dances." *Musical Quarterly* 84, no. 2:221–37.

Grandville, J. J. 1986. *Grandville dessins originaux.* Ed. S. Guillaume. Nancy: Le Musée.

Granville, A. B. 1828. *St. Petersburgh: A Journal of Travels to and from That Capital; Through Flanders, the Rhenich Provinces, Prussia, Russia, Poland, etc.* London: H. Colburn.

Hadden, J. Cuthbert. 1903. *Chopin.* London: J. M. Dent.

Hallé, Charles, Sir. [1896] 1972. *The Autobiography of Charles Hallé, with Correspondence and Diaries.* Ed. C. E. Hallé and Marie Hallé. London: Elek.

Halliwell, Ruth. 2006. "Education." In *The Cambridge Mozart Encyclopedia,* ed. Cliff Eisen and Simon P. Keefe, 322–24. Cambridge: Cambridge University Press.

Hamburger, Paul. 1966. "Mazurkas, Waltzes, and Polonaises." In *Frédéric Chopin: Profiles of the Man and the Musician,* ed. Alan Walker, 73–113. London: Barrie and Rockliff.

Hanslick, Eduard. 1870. *Geschichte des Concertwesens in Wien.* Vienna: Wilhelm Braumüller.

———. 1950. *Music Criticisms: 1849–99.* Trans. and ed. Henry Pleasants. Baltimore, Md.: Penguin Books.

Hanson, Alice. 1985. *Musical Life in Biedermeier Vienna.* London: Cambridge University Press.

Harris-Warrick, Rebecca. 1986. "Ballroom Dancing at the Court of Louis XIV." *Early Music* 14, no. 1:41–49.

Hatten, Robert. 1994. *Musical Meaning in Beethoven: Markedness, Correlation, and Interpretation.* Bloomington: Indiana University Press.

———. 2004. *Interpreting Musical Gestures, Topics, and Tropes: Mozart, Beethoven, Schubert.* Bloomington: Indiana University Press.

Heartz, Daniel. 1990. *Mozart's Operas.* Berkeley: University of California Press.

———. 1995. *Haydn, Mozart and the Viennese School.* New York: W. W. Norton.

Herder, Johann Gottfried. [1800] 1981. *Kalligone.* In *Music and Aesthetics in the Eighteenth and Early-Nineteenth Centuries,* ed. Peter le Huray and James Day, 253–57. Cambridge: Cambridge University Press.

Hilton, Wendy. 1981. *Dance of Court and Theater: The French Noble Style 1690–1725.* London: Dance Books.

———. 1997. *Dance and Music of the Court and Theater.* Stuyvesant, N.Y.: Pendragon Press.

———. 1998. "Minuet." In *International Encyclopedia of Dance,* ed. Selma Jeanne Cohen, 4:431–33. New York: Oxford University Press.

Historisches Museum der Stadt Wien. 1979. *Fasching in Wien: Der Wiener Walzer 1750–1850.* Vienna: Historisches Museum der Stadt Wien.

Hogarth, William. [1753] 1997. *The Analysis of Beauty*. Ed. Ronald Paulson. New Haven, Conn.: Yale University Press.

Holmes, Mary Tavener. 1991. *Nicolas Lancret 1690–1743*. New York: Harry N. Abrams.

Houle, George. 1987. *Meter in Music, 1600–1800*. Bloomington: Indiana University Press.

Huneker, James. 1900. *Chopin: The Man and His Music*. New York: C. Scribner's Sons.

Ingersoll-Smouse, Florence. 1928. *Pater*. Paris: Les Beaux-Arts, édition d'études et de documents.

Ingrao, Charles W. 2000. *The Habsburg Monarchy, 1618–1815*. 2nd ed. Cambridge: Cambridge University Press.

Jacob, H. E. 1948. *Johann Strauss, Father and Son*. Trans. Marguerite Wolff. New York: Crown.

Jahn, Otto. 1882. *Life of Mozart*. Trans. Pauline D. Townsend. London: Novello, Ewer.

Jedlicki, Jerzy. 1999. *A Suburb of Europe: Nineteenth-Century Polish Approaches to Western Civilization*. English ed. New York: Central European University Press.

Jones, David Wyn. 1990. "Dance and Ballet." In *The Mozart Compendium: A Guide to Mozart's Life and Music*, ed. H. C. Robbins Landon, 276–83. New York: Schirmer Books.

Kallberg, Jeffery. 1996. *Chopin at the Boundaries: Sex, History and Musical Genre*. Cambridge, Mass.: Harvard University Press.

Kamien, Roger. 2005. "Quasi-auxiliary Cadences Beginning on a Root-Position Tonic Chord: Some Preliminary Observations." In *Essays from the Third International Schenker Symposium*, ed. Allen Cadwalleder, 37–50. Hildesheim: Georg Olms.

Karasowski, Moritz. 1970. *Frederic Chopin: His Life and Letters*. Trans. Emily Hill. Westport, Conn.: Greenwood Press.

Kelly, Michael. [1826] 1968. *Reminiscences of Michael Kelly*. New York: Da Capo Press.

Kirkendale, Warren. 1979. *Fugue and Fugato in Rococo and Classical Chamber Music*. Trans. Margaret Bent and Warren Kirkendale. Durham, N.C.: Duke University Press.

Kirnberger, Johann Philipp. [1771–79] 1982. *The Art of Strict Musical Composition*. Trans. David Beach and Jurgen Thym. New Haven, Conn.: Yale University Press.

———. [c. 1777] 1995. *Recueil d'airs de danse caractéristiques, pour servir de modele aux jeunes compositeurs et d'exercice à ceux qui touchent du clavecin*. Wiesbaden: Breitkopf & Härtel.

Kivy, Peter. 1984. *Sound and Semblance: Reflections on Musical Representation*. Princeton, N.J.: Princeton University Press.

Kobylańska, Krystyna. 1955. *Chopin in His Own Land*. Trans. Claire Grece-Dabrowska and Mary Filippi. Cracow: Polish Music Publications.

———. 1979. *Frédéric Chopin: Thematisch-bibliographisches Werkverzeichnis*. Munich: G. Henle.

Koch, Heinrich. [1787] 1983. *Introductory Essay on Composition*. New Haven, Conn.: Yale University Press.

Koźmian, Andrzej Edward. 1867. *Wspomnienia*. 2 vols. Poznań: Nakł. Mieczysława Leitgabra.

Krebs, Harald. 1999. *Metrical Dissonance in the Music of Robert Schumann*. New York: Oxford University Press.

Krumhansl, Carol L., and D. L. Schenck. 1997. "Can Dance Reflect the Structural and Expressive Qualities of Music? A Perceptual Experiment on Balanchine's Choreography of Mozart's Divertimento N. 15." *Musicae Scientiae* 1:63–85.

Kurier warszawski. 1821–30. Warsaw.

Lacépède, Bernard Germain. 1785. *La poétique de la musique.* 2 vols. Paris.

La Garde-Chambonas, Auguste-Louis-Charles, comte de. 1902. *Anecdotal Recollections of the Congress of Vienna.* Introduction and notes by Comte Fleury, trans. Albert Dresden Vandam. London: Chapman & Hall.

Lakoff, George, and Mark Johnson. 1980. *Metaphors We Live By.* Chicago: University of Chicago Press.

Lamb, Andrew. 2001. "Waltz." In *The New Grove Dictionary of Music and Musicians,* ed. Stanley Sadie. 2nd ed. London: Macmillan.

Landon, H. C. Robbins. 1988. *Mozart's Last Year: 1791.* New York: Schirmer Books.

———. 1991. *Mozart and Vienna.* New York: Schirmer Books.

Langenschwarz, Maximilian. 1836. *Europäische Geheimnisse eines Mediatisierten.* Hamburg: Georg Boormann.

Laskowski, Larry. 1990. "J. S. Bach's 'Binary' Dance Movements: Form and Voice Leading." In *Schenker Studies,* ed. Hedi Siegel, 84–93. New York: Cambridge University Press.

Laube, Heinrich. [1834–37] 1973. *Reisenovellen.* 5 vols. Reprint. Frankfurt: Athenäum.

Lenz, Wilhelm von. 1872. *Die grossen Pianoforte-Virtuosen unserer Zeit aus persönlicher Bekanntschaft.* Berlin: B. Behr.

Leppert, Richard. 1988. *Music and Image.* Cambridge: Cambridge University Press.

Lerdahl, Fred, and Ray Jackendoff. 1983. *A Generative Theory of Tonal Music.* Cambridge, Mass.: MIT Press.

Lester, Joel. 1986. *The Rhythms of Tonal Music.* Carbondale: Southern Illinois University Press.

———. 1999. *Bach's Works for Solo Violin: Style, Structure, Performance.* New York: Oxford University Press.

———. 2001. "Heightening Levels of Activity and J. S. Bach's Parallel-Section Constructions." *Journal of the American Musicological Society* 54, no. 1:49–96.

Linke, Norbert. 1987. *Musik erobert die Welt: Wie die Wiener Familie Strauss die "Unterhaltungsmusik" revolutionierte.* Vienna: Herold.

———. 1992. *"Es mußte einem was einfallen": Untersuchungen zur kompositorischen Arbeitsweise der "Naturalisten."* Tutzing: Hans Schneider.

———. 1996. *Johann Strauss.* Reinbek bei Hamburg: Rowohlt.

Liszt, Franz. [1851] 1963. *Frederic Chopin.* Trans. Edward N. Waters. London: Free Press of Glencoe.

Little, Meredith. 1967. "The Dances of J.-B. Lully (1632–1687)." Ph.D. diss., Stanford University.

———. 1980. "Minuet." In *The New Grove Dictionary of Music and Musicians,* ed. Stanley Sadie, 12:353–58. London: Macmillan.

———. 2001. "Minuet." In *The New Grove Dictionary of Music and Musicians,* ed. Stanley Sadie, 2nd ed., 16:740–46. New York: Grove's Dictionaries.

Little, Meredith, and Natalie Jenne. 1991. *Dance and the Music of J. S. Bach.* Bloomington: Indiana University Press.

Loulié, Étienne. [1696] 1965. *Elements or Principles of Music.* Reprint. Trans. Albert Cohen. New York: Institute of Mediaeval Music.

Lowe, Melanie. 1998. "Expressive Paradigms in the Symphonies of Joseph Haydn." Ph.D. diss., Princeton University.

———. 2002. "Falling from Grace: Irony and Expressive Enrichment in Haydn's Symphonic Minuets." *Journal of Musicology* 19, no. 1:171–221.

———. 2007. *Pleasure and Meaning in the Classical Symphony.* Bloomington: Indiana University Press.

Lowinsky, Edward E. 1956. "On Mozart's Rhythm." *Music Quarterly* 42, no. 2:162–86.

Magier, Antoni. 1963. *Estetyka miasta stołecznego Warszawy.* Wrocłow: Wydawnicto Ossolińskich.

Magri, Gennaro. [1779] 1988. *Theoretical and Practical Treatise on Dancing.* Reprint. London: Dance Books.

Malpied, M. 1770. *Traité sur l'art de la danse.* Paris: Boüin.

Marks, Lawrence. 1978. *The Unity of the Senses: Interrelations among the Modalities.* New York: Academic Press.

Marx, Adolph Bernhard. 1837–38. *Die Lehre von der musikalischen Komposition.* 2 vols. Leipzig: Breitkopf und Härtel.

———. [1856] 1997. "Form in Music." In *Musical Form in the Age of Beethoven: Selected Writings on Theory and Method,* trans. and ed. Scott Burnham, 55–90. Cambridge: Cambridge University Press.

McKee, Eric. 1996. "Auxiliary Progressions as a Source of Conflict between Tonal Structure and Phrase Structure." *Music Theory Spectrum* 18, no. 1:51–76.

———. 1999. "The Influence of the Functional Minuet in the French Suites of J. S. Bach." *Music Analysis* 18, no. 2:235–60.

———. 2004. "Dance and the Music of Chopin: The Waltz." In *The Age of Chopin: Interdisciplinary Inquiries,* ed. Halina Goldberg, 106–61. Bloomington: Indiana University Press.

———. 2005. "Mozart in the Ballroom: Minuet-Trio Contrast and the Aristocracy in Self-Portrait." *Music Analysis* 24, no. 3:383–434.

Mendelssohn-Bartholdy, Felix. 1972. *Briefe aus Leipziger Archiven.* Ed. Hans-Joachim Rothe and Reinhard Szeskus. Leipzig: Deutscher Verlag für Musik.

Messer-Krol, Ulrike, ed. 1995. *The Viennese Opera Ball: On the Myth of the Waltz.* Trans. Renée V. Paschen-Landschauer. Vienna: C. Brandstätter.

Metternich, Clemens Wenzel Lothar, Fürst von. 1970. *Memoirs of Prince Metternich.* Trans. Alexander Napier. New York: H. Fertig.

Milewski, Barbara. 1999. "Chopin's Mazurkas and the Myth of the Folk." *19th-Century Music* 23, no. 2:113–35.

Mitchell, Paul, and Lynn Roberts. 1999. "Frame." In *The Dictionary of Art,* ed. Jane Turner, 11:372–96. New York: Macmillan.

Mitchell, Robert W., and Matthew C. Gallaher. 2001. "Embodying Music: Matching Music and Dance in Memory." *Music Perception* 19, no. 1:65–85.

Miterzanka, Mieczysława. 1931. *Działalność pedagogiczna Adam Ks.*

Czartoryskiego. Warsaw: Naukowe Towarzystwo Pedagogiczne.

Molière. 1989. *The Would-Be Gentleman.* In *Don Juan and Other Plays,* ed. Ian Maclean, trans. George Graveley and Ian Maclean, 259–336. Oxford: Oxford University Press.

Monelle, Raymond. 2000. *The Sense of Music.* Princeton, N.J.: Princeton University Press.

Morrow, Mary Sue. 1989. *Concert Life in Haydn's Vienna: Aspects of a Developing Musical and Social Institution.* Stuyvesant, N.Y.: Pendragon Press.

Mozart, Wolfgang Amadeus. 1966. *The Letters of Mozart and His Family.* Trans. and ed. Emily Anderson. New York: St. Martin's Press.

———. 2000. *Mozart's Letters, Mozart's Life: Selected Letters.* Ed. and trans. Robert Spaethling. New York: W. W. Norton.

Muffat, Georg. [1695] 2001. *Florilegium Secondum.* In *Georg Muffat on Performance Practice,* trans. and ed. David K. Wilson, 23–66. Bloomington: Indiana University Press.

Mulvey, Laura. 1975. "Visual Pleasure and Narrative Cinema." *Screen* 16, no. 3:6–18.

Museum Historyczne Warszawy. 1992. *Bibliografia Warszawy: Wydawnictwa ciągłe. 1795–1863.* Wrocław: Zakład Nardowy Imienia Ossolińskich – Wydawnictwo.

Nettl, Paul. 1963. *The Dance in Classical Music.* New York: Philosophical Library.

Neumeyer, David. 2006. "The Contredanse, Classical Finales, and Caplin's Formal Functions." *Music Theory Online* 12, no. 4.

Nicolai, Friedrich. 1783–96. *Beschreibung einer Reise durch Deutschland und die Schweiz im Jahre 1781.* Berlin: Stettin.

Niecks, Frederick. 1902. *Frederick Chopin as a Man and Musician.* 2 vols. 3rd ed. London: Novello.

———. 1917. "Historical and Aesthetical Sketch of the Waltz." *Monthly Musical Record* 47:560–61.

Niemcewicz, Julian Ursyn. 1957. *Pamiętniki czasów moich.* 2 vols. Warsaw: Państwowy Instytut Wydawniczy.

Nissen, Georg Nikolaus von. [1828] 1964. *Biographie W. A. Mozarts.* Reprint. Hildesheim: Georg Olms.

Ogiński, Michał Kleofas. 1956. *Lisy o muzyce.* Cracow: Polskie Wydawnictwo Muzyczne.

Ohnet, Georges. 1882. *Serge Panine.* Paris: Paul Ollendorff.

Pemberton, E. [1711] 1970. *An Essay for the Further Improvement of Dancing.* Reprint. Westmead: Gregg International.

Pezzl, Johann. 1786–90. *Skizze von Wien.* 2 vols. Vienna: Krauß.

Powell, Newman W. 1967. "Kirnberger on Dance Rhythms, Fugues, and Characterization." In *Festschrift Theodore Hoelty-Nickel,* ed. Newman W. Powell, 65–76. Valparaiso, Ind.: Valparaiso University.

Praetorius, Michael. [1612] 1971. *Terpsichore.* Reprint. Wolfenbüttel: Möseler Verlag.

Przewodnik warszawski 1827. Warsaw: Glücksberg.

Przewodnik warszawski 1829. Warsaw: Glücksberg.

Pudełek, Janina. 1998. "Poland: Theatrical Dance." In *International Ency-*

clopedia of Dance, ed. Selma Jeanne
Cohen, 5:215–21. New York: Oxford
University Press.

Radziwiłł, Louise, Princess. 1912.
Forty-Five Years of My Life (1770–1815).
Trans. A. R. Allinson. New York:
McBride, Nast.

Rameau, Pierre. [1725] 1967. *Le maître à
danser*. Reprint. New York: Broude
Brothers.

Ratner, Leonard. 1956. "Eighteenth-
Century Theories of Musical Period
Structure." *Musical Quarterly* 42, no.
4:439–54.

———. 1970. "*Ars Combinatoria*: Choice
and Chance in Eighteenth-Century
Music." In *Studies in Eighteenth-Century Music*, ed. H. C. Robbins Landon,
343–63. New York: Oxford University
Press.

———. 1980. *Classic Music: Expression,
Form, and Style*. New York: Schirmer
Books.

Ratz, Erwin. 1973. *Einführung in die
musikalische Formenlehre*. 3rd ed. Vienna: Universal Edition.

Reeser, Eduard. 1949. *The History of the
Waltz*. Stockholm: Continental.

Reichart, Sarah. 1984. "The Influence
of Eighteenth-Century Social Dance
on the Viennese Classical Style."
Ph.D. diss., City University of New
York.

Riepel, Joseph. 1754. *Anfangsgründe zur
musikalischen Setzkunst*. Vol. 1: *De
Rhythmopoeïa oder von der Tactord-
nung*. 2nd ed. Regensburg: Johann
Leopold Montag.

Rink, John. 1992. "Tonal Architecture in
the Early Music." In *The Cambridge
Companion to Chopin*, ed. Jim Samson.
Cambridge: Cambridge University
Press.

———. 1997. *Chopin: The Piano Concer-
tos*. Cambridge: Cambridge University
Press.

Roschitz, Karlheinz. 1995. "On the Myth
of the Waltz." In *The Viennese Opera
Ball: On the Myth of the Waltz*, ed.
Ulrike Messer-Krol, trans. Renée V.
Paschen-Landschauer, 7–48. Vienna:
C. Brandstätter.

Rosen, Charles. 1980. *Sonata Forms*.
New York: W. W. Norton.

Rothstein, William. 1989. *Phrase Rhythm
in Tonal Music*. New York: Schirmer
Books.

———. 1995a. "Analysis and the Act of
Performance." In *The Practice of Performance: Studies in Musical Interpretation*, ed. John Rink, 217–40. Cambridge: Cambridge University Press.

———. 1995b. "Beethoven with and
without *Kunstgepräng*: Metrical Ambiguity Reconsidered." In *Beethoven
Forum* 4:165–94.

Rousseau, Jean-Jacques. 1751–72. "Menuet." In *Encyclopédie*, ed. Denis Diderot
and Jean d'Alembert, 10:346. Paris:
Briasson.

Russell, Tilden A. 1983. "Minuet, Scher-
zando, and Scherzo: The Dance
Movement in Transition, 1781–1825."
Ph.D. diss., University of North
Carolina.

———. 1992. "The Unconventional
Dance Minuet: Choreographies of the
Menuet d'Exaudet." *Acta Musicologica*
64:118–38.

———. 1999. "Minuet Form and Phrase-
ology in *Recueils* and Manuscript
Tunebooks." *Journal of Musicology* 17,
no. 3:386–419.

———. 2006. "The Minuet According
to Taubert." *Dance Research* 24, no.
2:138–62.

Sachs, Curt. 1952. *World History of the Dance*. Trans. Bessie Schönberg. New York: Seven Arts.

Saint-Lambert, Monsieur de. [1702] 1984. *Principles of the Harpsichord*. Trans. and ed. Rebecca Harris-Warrick. Cambridge: Cambridge University Press.

Salmen, Walter. 1988. "Tanz im 17. und 18. Jahrhundert." In *Musikgeschichte in Bildern*, Bd. 4, Lfg. 4. Leipzig: Deutscher Verlag für Musik.

———. 1989. "Tanz im 19. Jahrhundert." In *Musikgeschichte in Bildern*, Bd. 4, Lfg. 5. Leipzig: Deutscher Verlag für Musik.

———, ed. 1990. *Mozart in der Tanzkultur seiner Zeit*. Innsbruck: Edition Helbling.

Samson, Jim. 1985. *The Music of Chopin*. Oxford: Oxford University Press.

———. 1996. *Chopin*. New York: Schirmer Books.

Sand, George. 1994. *The Master Pipers*. Trans. Rosemary Lloyd. Oxford: Oxford University Press.

Schachter, Carl. 1989. "Review of *The Music of Chopin* by Jim Samson." *Music Analysis* 8, nos. 1–2:187–97.

Schenker, Heinrich. [1935] 1979. *Free Composition*. Trans. and ed. Ernst Oster. New York: Longman.

Schnitzler, Henry. 1954. "'Gay Vienna' – Myth and Reality." *Journal of the History of Ideas* 15, no. 1:94–118.

Schoenberg, Arnold. 1967. *Fundamentals of Musical Composition*. Ed. Gerald Strang and Leonard Stein. New York: St. Martin's Press.

Schönherr, Max. 1976. "Ästhetik des Walzers: Erfahrungen aus Geschichte und Musizierpraxis, vorgelegt in Form eines alphabetischen Katalogs." *Österreichische Musikzeitschrift* 31, no. 2:57–127.

Schönherr, Max, and Karl Rienhöhl. 1954. *Johann Strauss Vater: Ein Werkverzeichnis*. Vienna: Universal.

Schulenberg, David. 2006. *The Keyboard Music of J. S. Bach*. 2nd ed. New York: Schirmer Books.

Schumann, Robert. 1952. *On Music and Musicians*. Ed. Konrad Wolff, trans. Paul Rosenfeld. New York: Pantheon.

Scott, Derek B. 2008. *Sounds of the Metropolis: The Nineteenth-Century Popular Music Revolution in London, New York, Paris, and Vienna*. New York: Oxford University Press.

Semmens, Richard. 2004. *The Bals publics at the Paris Opera House in the Eighteenth Century*. Hillsdale, N.Y.: Pendragon Press.

Sisman, Elaine. 1982. "Small and Expanded Forms: Koch's Model and Haydn's Music." *Musical Quarterly* 68, no. 4:444–75.

Smith, Erik. 1982. *Mozart Serenades, Divertimenti and Dances*. London: British Broadcasting Corp.

———. 1990. "Dances." In *The Compleat Mozart: A Guide to the Musical Works of Wolfgang Amadeus Mozart*, ed. Neal Zaslaw, 216–25. New York: W. W. Norton.

Smith, Peter H. 1995. "Structural Tonic or Apparent Tonic?: Parametric Conflict, Temporal Perspective, and a Continuum of Articulative Possibilities." *Journal of Music Theory* 39, no. 2:245–84.

Smith, Richard. 1827. *Notes Made during a Tour in Denmark, Holstein, Mecklenburg-Schwerin*. London: C. & J. Rivington.

Solomon, Maynard. 1995. *Mozart: A Life.* New York: Harper Collins.

Sowiński, Albert. [1857] 1971. *Les musiciens polonais et slaves: Dictionnaire biographique.* Reprint. New York: Da Capo.

Spohr, Louis. 1961. *The Musical Journeys.* Trans. and ed. Henry Pleasants. Norman: University of Oklahoma Press.

Stadnicki, Edwin Kornel. 1962. *Walc fortepianowy w Polsce w latasch 1800–1830.* Cracow: Polskie Wydawnictwo Muzyczne.

Stanhope, Philip Dormer. *The Letters of Philip Dormer Stanhope, Earl of Chesterfield.* Ed. Lord Mahon. 4 vols. London: S. & J. Bentley, Wilson and Fley.

Steele, Valerie. 1985. *Fashion and Eroticism: Ideals of Feminine Beauty from the Victorian Age to the Jazz Age.* Oxford: Oxford University Press.

Stephens, John Lloyd. 1838. *Incidents of Travel in Greece, Turkey, Russia, and Poland.* New York: Harper & Bros.

Strobel, Desmond F. 2004. "Waltz." In *International Encyclopedia of Dance,* ed. Selma Jeanne Cohen, 6:359–62. New York: Oxford University Press.

Sulzer, Johann Georg. [1792–97] 1994. *Allgemeine Theorie der schönen Künste.* Rev. ed. 4 vols. Hildesheim: Georg Olms.

Sutton, Julia. 1985. "The Minuet: An Elegant Phoenix." *Dance Chronicle* 8, no. 4:119–52.

Szulc, Tad. 1998. *Chopin in Paris.* New York: Scribner.

Taubaut, Karl Heinz. 1968. *Höfische Tänze: Ihre Geschichte und Choreographie.* Mainz: B. Schotts Söhne.

Taubert, Gottfried. [1717] 1976. *Rechtschaffener Tanzmeister, oder gründliche Erklärung der frantzösischen Tantz-Kunst.* Reprint. Documenta Choreologica 22. Leipzig: Zentralantiquariat der DDR.

Texier, Edmond. 1852. *Tableau de Paris.* 2 vols. Paris: Paulin et le Chevalier.

Thorp, Jennifer. 2003. "In Defence of Danced Minuets." *Early Music* 31, no. 1:100–108.

Tomaszewski, Mieczysław. 1990. *Fryderyk Chopin: A Diary in Images.* Warsaw: Arkady.

Tomaszewski, Wojciech. 1992a. *Bibliografia warszawskich druków muzycznych 1801–1850.* Warsaw: Biblioteka Narodowa.

———. 1992b. *Warszawskie edytorstwo muzyczne w latach 1772–1865.* Warsaw: Biblioteka Narodowa.

Tomlinson, Kellom. [1735] 1970. *The Art of Dancing Explained by Reading and Figures.* Reprint. Westmead, England: Gregg International Publishers.

Trollope, Frances. 1838. *Vienna and the Austrians; With Some Account of a Journey through Swabia, Bavaria, the Tyrol, and Salzburg.* 2 vols. London: Richard Bentley.

Wagner, Richard. 1983. *My Life.* Trans. Andrew Gray. Cambridge: Cambridge University Press.

Warburton, Ernest, ed. 1989. *The Collected Works of Johann Christian Bach.* Vol. 42. New York: Garland.

Weaver, John. 1712. *An Essay Towards an History of Dancing.* London: J. Tonson.

Wechsberg, Joseph. 1973. *The Waltz Emperors.* New York: G. P. Putnam's Sons.

Wheelock, Gretchen A. 1992. *Haydn's Ingenious Jesting with Art: Contexts of Musical Wit and Humor.* New York: Schirmer Books.

Willner, Channan. 1991. "The Two-Length Bar Revisited: Handel and the Hemiola." In *Göttinger Händel-Beiträge* 4:208–31.

———. 1996a. "Handel, the Sarabande, and Levels of Genre: A Reply to David Schulenberg." *Music Theory Online* 2, no. 7.

———. 1996b. "More on Handel and the Hemiola: Overlapping Hemiolas." *Music Theory Online* 2, no. 3.

———. 2007. "Metrical Displacement and Metrically Dissonant Hemiolas." Manuscript.

Winckelmann, Johann. 1755. *Gedancken über die Nachahmung der griechischen Wercke in der Mahlerey und Bildhauer-Kunst*. Friedrichstadt: Christian Heinrich Hagenmüller.

Witherell, Anne L. 1983. *Louis Pécour's 1700 Recueil de dances*. Ann Arbor: UMI Research Press.

Wójcicki, Kazimierz Władysław. 1855. *Cmentarz powązkowski w Warszawie*. 3 vols. Warsaw: Gebethner i Wolff.

———. 1877. *Społeczność Warszawy w początkach naszego stulecia*. Warsaw: Gebethner i Wolff.

———. 1974. *Pamiętniki dziecka Warszawy i inne wspomnienia warszawskie*. 2 vols. Warsaw: Panstwowy Instytut Wydawniczy.

Wolff, Christoph. 2001. *Johann Sebastian Bach: The Learned Musician*. New York: W. W. Norton.

Wynne, Shirley. 1970. "Complaisance: An Eighteenth-Century Cool." *Dance Scope* 5, no. 1:22–35.

Yaraman, Sevin. 2002. *Revolving Embrace: The Waltz as Sex, Steps, and Sound*. Hillsdale, N.Y.: Pendragon Press.

Zamoyski, Adam. 1980. *Chopin: A New Biography*. New York: Doubleday.

Zbikowski, Lawrence. 2002–2003. "Music Theory, Multimedia, and the Construction of Meaning." *Intégral* 16–17:251–68.

———. 2008. "Dance Topoi, Sonic Analogues and Musical Grammar: Communicating with Mßusic in the Eighteenth Century." In *Communication in Eighteenth-Century Music*, ed. Danuta Mirka and Kofi Agawu, 283–309. Cambridge: Cambridge University Press.

INDEX

Aldrich, Elizabeth, 95, 96, 127–128
Allanbrook, Wye Jamison, 8, 148, 225n33, 230n6
Attwood, Thomas, 5
auxiliary progression, 69–70, 228n22. *See also* waltz (Chopin, Lanner, and Strauss, Sr.)

Bach, Johann Christian, 71–72, 72
Bach, Johann Sebastian: as a composition teacher, 42–43; connection to the French court, 28; French Suites, 27–30; minuet from the French Suite in D Minor, BWV 812, 30–33, 31; minuet from the French Suite in B Minor, BWV 814, 34–37, 35, 36; minuet from the French Suite in E♭ Major, BWV 815, 33–34, 34; minuet from the French Suite in E Major, BWV 817, 37–41, 38, 40, 41
Bach, Wilhelm Friedmann, 43
Balzac, Honoré de, 101–102, 103, 106
Batteux, Charles, 21, 25, 29, 62, 113
Berlioz, Hector, 114, 116, 190
Bierce, Ambrose, 231n16
Blom, Eric, 89
Brodziński, Kazimiérz, 6
Brossard, Sébastien de, 56, 224n19
Budday, Wolfgang, 4
Burke, Edmund, 61

Burnham, Scott, 228n18
Byron, George Gordon, Baron, 149

Caplin, William, 9, 115, 225n26
Carner, Mosco, 187
Castiglione, Baldassare, 53–54
Cellarius, Henri, 94, 108–109, 113, 161, 232n17, 234n9
Chopin, Fryderyk, 129, 131–132, 139, 140, 146, 148;
approach to waltz form, 192–197;
cadences and phrase connections, 175–180, 185–186, 198, 205–206, 209, 215–216, 217–218;
dance-music relations in his waltzes, 148–171, 239n20;
as a dancer, 141–145;
distinctions between published and unpublished waltzes, 146–148;
Mazurka in B♭ Major, op. 7, no. 1, 239n20;
melodic hemiola and metrical dissonance, 198, 203–204, 210–211, 212, 213–214, 216, 218;
Piano Concerto in F Minor, op. 21, 139, 166–167, 168–171, 169;
Prelude in A Major, op. 28, no. 7, 152, 152;
published waltzes (*brillante* waltzes), 187, 198–219;

trip to Vienna, 180–182;
unpublished waltzes, 163–171, 218–219;
valse mélancolique, 155, 174–175, 180,
　206–207;
Viennese influence, 178–197, 198, 199;
virtuosic passagework, 200, 201–202,
　214;
waltzes (by opus number): Waltz in
　E♭ Major, op. 18, 152, 165, 172, 182–184,
　183, 185, 186, *187–192, 188,* 195, 197, 198,
　199, 214, 239n20; Waltz in A♭ Major,
　op. 34, no. 1, 199, 200–203, *201;* Waltz
　in A Minor, op. 34, no. 2, 154, *155–157,*
　155, 156, 198, 206–208; Waltz in F Ma-
　jor, op. 34, no. 3, 152, 157, *157,* 192, 198,
　199, 202–206, *203, 204, 205, 206;* Waltz
　in A♭ Major, op. 42, 152, 198, 208–211,
　210, 211, 215; Waltz in D♭ Major, op.
　64, no. 1, 152, 157–159, *158,* 198, 211,
　213–214, *214;* Waltz in C♯ Minor, op.
　64, no. 2, 215–216, *215;* Waltz in A♭
　Major, op. 64, no. 3, 152, 195, 216–218;
　Waltz in A♭ Major, op. 69, no. 1,
　165–166, *166,* 167; Waltz in B Minor,
　op. 69, no. 2, 162, *162,* 172–174, 175,
　176–178, *177, 178,* 185, 197; Waltz in
　G♭ Major, op. 70, no. 1, 162–163, *163;*
　Waltz in D♭ Major op. 70, no. 3, 152,
　153, 166–170, *168, 169,* 172–174, 175, 185,
　197; Waltz in E Major, KK 1207–
　1208, 160–161, *160,* 170, 172–174, 175,
　185, 197; Waltz in A♭ Major, KK 1209–
　1211, 165, 172–174, 176; Waltz in E
　Minor, KK 1213–14, 149–153, *150,*
　151, 159, 170, 172, 182–186, *183, 184,* 197;
　Waltz in A Minor, KK 1238–1239, 165;
　Waltz in D Minor, KK 1252, 174;
　Warsaw waltzes, 172–180, 194, 196, 197;
　waltzes and "circles," 148–159;
　waltzes and gender, 161–171
Chopin, Ludwika, 240n20
Clark, Maribeth, 11
Compan, Charles, 56

Cone, Edward T., 42, 65, 175–176
contredanse, 1, 9, 12, 24, 47, 49–50, 91,
　92, 223n3, 229n2
Cook, Nicholas, 107, 232n20
Cortot, Alfred, 177, 238n6
Cruickshank, Robert, *104,* 105
Czartoryska, Princess Izabela, 141

Dahlhaus, Carl, 222n10
Damse, Józef, 139, 140, 221n3
dance: and expression, 7; as a model for
　aristocratic behavior, 2–3, 141; social
　functions of, 2; as used in teaching
　composition, 3–6, 42–43. *See also* con-
　tredanse; *Deutsche; Ländler;* minuet;
　polonaise; waltz (Chopin, Lanner, and
　Strauss, Sr.)
Deutsche, 49, 50, 76, 89, 91, 92, 228n24,
　229n36, 230n6; "artless simplicity," 55,
　73–75, 180; oom-pah-pah accompani-
　ment, 71–72
Doux, François Gabriel Le, 133
Duindam, Jeroen, 83

Elsner, Józef, 131–132, 141, 175, 181, 235n25
enabling similarity (Cook), 107, 108, 120,
　128, 232n20

Feldtenstein, C. J. von, 51, 82, 223n3
Flaubert, Gustave, 103–104, 118, 119
Freystädtler, Franz Jacob, 5

Gallini, Andrea Battista, 51–52, 56,
　229n38
Geiringer, Karl, 28, 42–43
Gerbes, Angelika, 223n6
Gładkowska, Konstancja, 166–167, 168
Glasbrenner, Georg Adolph, 119
Gmeiner, Josef, 89
Goethe, Johann Wolfgang von, 95, 96,
　100, 236n3
Goldberg, Halina, 131, 170–171, 180,
　234n5, 235n25, 237n15, 239n19

Gołębiowski, Łukasz, 130–131, 134–135, 137

Grabowski, Stanisław, 174–175

Graf, Max, 106

Grandville, J. J., 98–99, *98*, *99*

Hanslick, Eduard, 10, 114, 119

Harris-Warrick, Rebecca, 86

Hatten, Robert, 238n23

Heartz, Daniel, 84, 85, 92, 230n6

Herder, Johann Gottfried, 7

Hiller, Stephen, 155

Hilton, Wendy, 17, 27, 47, 66, 76

Hogarth, William, 59–61, 62, 74, 227n15

Hohenzollern, Princess Louise, 138

Hummel, Johann Nepomuk, 6–7, 235n22, 239n18

hypermeter (defined), 223n11. *See also* minuet; waltz (Chopin, Lanner, and Strauss, Sr.)

incomplete authentic cadence, 182, 239n11

Jenne, Natalie, 8–9, 17, 28

Kallberg, Jeffery, 237n18

Kelly, Michael, 46, 100

Kirnberger, Johann Philipp, 3–4, 7, 8, 221n5, 227n13, 235n25

Kivy, Peter, 107

Koch, Heinrich, 4, 175

Krebs, Harald, 233n28, 235n31

Kurpiński, Karol, *136*, 137, 234n17

La Garde-Chambonas, Auguste Louis Charles, comte de, 100–101, 118

Lacépède, Bernard Germain, 222n1

Ländler, 49, 50, 76, 89, 91, 228n24; "artless simplicity," 55; oom-pah-pah accompaniment, 71–72

Langenschwarz, Maximilian Leopold, 119

Lanner, Joseph, 13, 90, 97, 106, 109, 139, 140, 141, 175, 178–181, 182, 188, 192, 195, 198, 204, 238n8; "Abschied von Pest," op. 95, *117*; "Ankunfts-Walzer," op. 34, *189*; "Annen-Einladungs-Walzer," op. 48, *188*; and the development of a vernacular musical language 10–11, 180; "Flora-Walzer," op. 33, *189*; "Fortsetzung der Katharinen-Tänze," op. 41, 112, *112*; "Die Humoristiker Walzer," op. 92, *117*; "Paradies Soirée Walzer," op. 52, *117*, 120–124, *121*; as a popular musician, 113–114; "Redout-Carneval-Tänze," op. 30, *188*; "Redout-Carneval-Tänze," op. 42, 120–124, *121*, *188*; rhythm, 190–191; showmanship, 182–183; treatment of the violin, 187, 190; "Die Werber," op. 103, 109–110, *110*, 124–127, *124*, *125*. *See also* waltz (Chopin, Lanner, and Strauss, Sr.)

Laube, Heinrich, 118

Leppert, Richard, 47

Lester, Joel, 225n28, 226n6

Liszt, Franz, 145, 180, 236n36

Little, Meredith, 8–9, 17, 28, 29

Louis XIV, 2, 10, 11, 16, 47, 56, 86

Louis XV, 26, 27, 86, 102

Lowe, Melanie, 9, 226n2, 227n9, 233n30

Lowinsky, Edward, 227n17

Magri, Gennaro, 15, 25, 42, 52, 56, 76, 95

Marks, Lawrence, 107

Marx, Adolph Bernard, 122, 148, 149, 159, 174, 236n4

mazurka, 128, 129, 130, 132, 135, 140, 141, 142, 170–171, 172, 180, 193, 196, 206–207, 237n15, 240n20

Mendelssohn, Felix, 124, 190

metaphor, 107

Metternich, Prince Clemens von, 119

minuet: aesthetics of, 51–62; *ars combinatoria*, 221n3; in artwork, 56–58; and beauty (Hogarth and Burke), 58–62; choreography of (*menuet ordinaire*), 16–17, 48; as compared to the waltz, 11–12; complaisance, 52–54; as a cultural and historical icon, 82–83; dance-music relations, 17–23, 24–27, 41, 48, 54–55, 62, 223n8; difficulty of, 11, 47, 95; duets, 76–79; eroticism, 76, 77–79; formal design, 46, 51, 226n6; improvisatory nature, 22, 66–67, 224n12; influence on Classical style, 4, 15–16, 42; minuet-trio contrast, 46–47, 54–55, 57–58, 65, 82–83, 87–89; mixed styles (grace and power), 79–82; as a model for aristocratic behavior, 3; and nature, 55–58; oom-pah-pah accompaniment, 67–72; performance practice, 223n10; popularity of, 47, 90–91, 223n4, 224n14; reverences in, 17, 19, 23, 27, 48, 83, 89, 95; "rhythmic ease" in Mozart's trios, 63–67; sentence form, 32–33, 34–37, 41–43, 51; as a spectacle, 27, 76, 95; "time," 22, 23, 24–27; two-bar hyper-meter as a defining feature, 21, 25–27, 30–34, 41–43, 48, 55, 58, 65, 75, 87; as used in pedagogy, 4–5, 42–43

Molière, 1, 2
Monelle, Raymond, 115
Morrow, Mary Sue, 84
Mozart, Leopold, 5, 21, 49, 224n14
Mozart, Wolfgang Amadeus: as a composer of dance music, 6, 49–50, 62, 72, 83, 88, 92; as a composition teacher, 5; as a dancer, 46, 49, 62, 226n4; *Don Giovanni*, 92, 228n29, 230n6; fourth minuet of K. 461, 67, 68; second minuet and trio of K. 461, 64, 65–66; third minuet and trio of K. 601, 80, 81–82; third minuet of K. 599, 51, 52, 54, 54, 63; trio from the eighth minuet of K. 176, 67–69, 69, 70; trio from the first *Deutsche* of K. 571,

74–75, 75; trio from the first minuet of K. 176, 77, 78; trio from the fourth minuet of K. 599, 70–71, 71; trio from the ninth minuet of K. 568, 77–79, 79; trio from the second minuet of K. 176, 76–77, 77; trio from the seventh *Deutsche* of K. 567, 73, 73–74; trio from the sixth minuet of K. 104, 69–70, 70. *See also* minuet

Muffat, Georg, 3
multimedia, 1
Mulvey, Laura, 231n15

Neumeyer, David, 9, 24
Nicolai, Christoph Friedrich, 100
Nidecki, Ludwik, 175, 235n24, 238n3
November Uprising, 181, 196, 235n22

Ogiński, Michał Kleofas, 134
Ohnet, Georges, 104
Orłowski, Antoni, 139, 170, 237n22

Pezzl, Johann, 85–86
Ployer, Barbara, 5
polonaise, 83, 128, 130, 135, 137, 138, 140, 180; as compared to the minuet, 5–6
Potocka, Countess Aleksandra, 141
Powell, Newman, 7, 8
Praetorius, Michael, 55–56

Rachmaninoff, Sergei, 177, 241n26
Rameau, Pierre, 26, 27, 86, 231n10
Ratner, Leonard, 8, 16, 81, 221n3, 222n7
Ratz, Erwin, 42, 115, 225n26
Redoutensäle, 51, 84–87, 84, 85
Reeser, Eduard, 71
Reicha, Anton, 175
Reichart, Sarah, 8, 17, 27
Rembieliński, Aleksander, 143–144, 143, 144, 235n30
Riepel, Joseph, 4, 23
Rink, John, 173–174, 194–195, 208

Rosen, Charles, 16, 222n1
Rossini, Gioachino, 139, 237n16
Rothstein, William, 31, 176, 224n11, 241n26
Rousseau, Jean-Jacques, 51, 56
Russell, Tilden, 5, 9, 17–18, 19, 23, 27, 89, 222n2, 226n2

Samson, Jim, 180, 196, 206, 219
Sand, George, 145, 159, 171
Schachter, Carl, 176
Schoenberg, Arnold, 225n26, 225n32
Schönherr, Max, 175, 187–192, 233n25
Schubert, Franz, 6, 239n11, 239n18, 240n25
Schumann, Robert, 145, 146, 163–164, 180, 190, 199, 238n4
Scott, Derek, 11, 111
sentence form, 200–201, 225n26. *See also* minuet
Solomon, Maynard, 228n18
Spohr, Louis, 6–7
Stadnicki, Edwin, 180
Stanhope, Philip Dormer, 3
Stefani, Józef, 140–141
Strauss, Johann, Sr., 13, 90, 97, 106, 139, 140, 141, 175, 178–181, 182, 188, 192, 195, 198, 204, 238n8; "Cotillons aus der Oper," op. 32, 117, 189; and the development of a vernacular musical language, 10–11, 180; "Josephstädter-Walzer," op. 23, 189; "Mittel gegen den Schlaf," op. 65, 191; as a popular musician, 113–114; rhythm, 190–191; showmanship, 182–183; treatment of the violin, 187. *See also* waltz (Chopin, Lanner, and Strauss, Sr.)
Sulzer, Johann Georg, 51
Sutton, Julia, 17, 19, 27
Świeszewski, Aleksander, 135–137, 135, 181, 193–194, 193
Szymanowska-Wołowska, Maria, 174, 235n24

Taubert, Gottfried, 223n6
Tomaszewski, Wojciech, 138, 235n21
Tomlinson, Kellom, 17, 18, 19–21, 22, 23, 24–25, 26–27, 59, 66–67, 223n6, 223n7, 223n9, 224n20
Trollope, Frances, 102–103, 104, 119, 181

Wagner, Richard, 118, 190, 238n7
waltz (Chopin, Lanner, and Strauss, Sr.): auxiliary progressions, 115, 123, 124, 144, 179, 186, 204–205, 211; cadential articulation, 114–115, 122, 178; choreography of (*valse à trois temps*), 93–95, 148; as compared to the minuet, 11–12; as concert music, 111, 127; dance-music relations, 106–127, 148–171; eroticism, 96–97, 231n16; feminine beauty, 115–119; gender, 94–95; hemiola, 116–117, 190–191; hypermeter in, 94, 109; metrical disruptions, 109–114; musical characteristics of codas, 111–114; one-bar anacruses, 109–111; origins, 91, 230n3; repetitive continuity, 99, 108–114; self-containment, 114–115; as a spectacle, 95–106, 113–114, 127–128; thematic design of, 119–120, 233n35; *valse mélancolique*, 155, 174–175, 238n4; variety, 119–127. *See also* under Chopin, Fryderyk; Lanner, Joseph; and Strauss, Johann, Sr.; Warsaw
Warsaw: ballet, 133; carnival season, 132–133; dancing masters, 133–134; music publishing, 134–137; Prussian occupation of, 138; social dancing in, 130–141; venues for dancing, 131; waltz, 138–141
Watteau, Antoine, 56–58, 57, 83
Weaver, John, 53
Weber, Carl Maria von: *Der Freischütz*, 148–149, 149, 150, 174
Wheelock, Gretchen, 9, 226n2
Wilson, Thomas, 12

Winckelmann, Johann, 227n9
Wodzińska, Józefa, 142
Wodzińska, Maria, 165
Wójcicki, Kazimierz W., 129, 138, 142
Woyciechowski, Tytus, 166–167, 168, 170
Wynne, Shirley, 76
Wysocki, Napoleon, 235n22

Yaraman, Sevin, 11, 148, 233n1, 233n23, 236n4, 236n8

Zamoyska, Countess Zofia, 141, 145
Zbikowski, Lawrence, 9–10, 107, 148, 232n20, 233n38
Zieliński, Jakub, 134
Zuckerkandl, Victor, 90, 106

ERIC McKEE is Associate Professor of Music Theory at Penn State University, where he teaches undergraduate and graduate courses in music theory. He received his doctorate from the University of Michigan. McKee has presented his research in England, Ireland, Germany, Poland, and Canada and has made numerous presentations at national conferences in the United States. He was a contributor to Halina Goldberg's *The Age of Chopin* (IUP, 2004), and his articles have appeared in such journals as *Music Theory Spectrum, Music Analysis, In Theory Only, College Music Symposium,* and *Theory and Practice.*

www.ingramcontent.com/pod-product-compliance
Lightning Source LLC
Chambersburg PA
CBHW060330100426
42812CB00003B/945